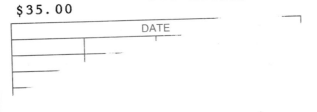

The Presidency of
GEORGE
BUSH

AMERICAN PRESIDENCY SERIES

George Washington, Forrest McDonald
John Adams, Ralph Adams Brown
Thomas Jefferson, Forrest McDonald
James Madison, Robert Allen Rutland
James Monroe, Noble E. Cunningham, Jr.
John Quincy Adams, Mary W. M. Hargreaves
Andrew Jackson, Donald B. Cole
Martin Van Buren, Major L. Wilson
William Henry Harrison & John Tyler, Norma Lois Peterson
James K. Polk, Paul H. Bergeron
Zachary Taylor & Millard Fillmore, Elbert B. Smith
Franklin Pierce, Larry Gara
James Buchanan, Elbert B. Smith
Abraham Lincoln, Phillip Shaw Paludan
Andrew Johnson, Albert Castel
Rutherford B. Hayes, Ari Hoogenboom
James A. Garfield & Chester A. Arthur, Justus D. Doenecke
Grover Cleveland, Richard E. Welch, Jr.
Benjamin Harrison, Homer B. Socolofsky & Allan B. Spetter
William McKinley, Lewis L. Gould
Theodore Roosevelt, Lewis L. Gould
William Howard Taft, Paolo E. Coletta
Woodrow Wilson, Kendrick A. Clements
Warren G. Harding, Eugene P. Trani & David L. Wilson
Calvin Coolidge, Robert H. Ferrell
Herbert C. Hoover, Martin L. Fausold
Franklin Delano Roosevelt, George T. McJimsey
Harry S. Truman, Donald R. McCoy
Dwight D. Eisenhower, Chester J. Pach, Jr., & Elmo Richardson
John F. Kennedy, James N. Giglio
Lyndon B. Johnson, Vaughn Davis Bornet
Richard Nixon, Melvin Small
Gerald R. Ford, John Robert Greene
James Earl Carter, Jr., Burton I. Kaufman
George Bush, John Robert Greene

The Presidency of

GEORGE BUSH

John Robert Greene

UNIVERSITY PRESS OF KANSAS

© 2000 by the University Press of Kansas
All rights reserved

Published by the University Press of Kansas (Lawrence, Kansas 66049), which was organized
by the Kansas Board of Regents and is operated and funded by Emporia State University,
Fort Hays State University, Kansas State University, Pittsburg State University, the University
of Kansas, and Wichita State University.

Library of Congress Cataloging-in-Publication Data

Greene, John Robert, 1955–
The presidency of George Bush / John Robert Greene.
p.   cm. — (American presidency series)
Includes bibliographical references (p.   ) and index.
ISBN 0-7006-0993-8 (alk. paper)
1. United States—Politics and government—1989–1993.   2. Bush,
George, 1924–   . I. Title. II. Series.
E881.G74   2000
973.928'092—dc21   99-35836

British Library Cataloguing in Publication Data is available.

Printed in the United States of America
10 9 8 7 6 5 4 3 2 1

The paper used in this publication meets the minimum requirements of the American National
Standard for Permanence of Paper for Printed Library Materials Z39.48-1984.

For Patty, T. J., Christopher, and Mary Rose
and for my parents, Peg and Jack Greene

CONTENTS

FOREWORD

The aim of the American Presidency Series is to present historians and the general public with interesting, scholarly assessments of the various presidential administrations. These interpretive surveys are intended to cover the broad ground between biographies, specialized monographs, and journalistic accounts. As such, each is a comprehensive work that draws upon original sources and pertinent secondary literature yet leaves room for the author's own analysis and interpretation.

Volumes in the series present the data essential to understanding the administration under consideration. Particularly, each book treats the then-current problems facing the United States and its people and how the president and his associates felt about, thought about, and worked to cope with these problems. Attention is given to how the office developed and operated during the president's tenure. Equally important is consideration of the vital relationships among the president, his staff, the executive officers, Congress, foreign representatives, the judiciary, state officials, the public, political parties, the press, and influential private citizens. The series is also concerned with how this unique American institution—the presidency—was viewed by the presidents, and with what results.

All this is set, insofar as possible, in the context not only of contemporary politics but also of economics, international relations, law, morals, public administration, religion, and thought. Such a broad approach is necessary to understanding, for a presidential administration is more than the elected and appointed officers composing it, since its work so often reflects the major problems, anxieties, and glories of the nation. In short, the authors in this series strive to recount and evaluate the record of each administration and to identify its distinctiveness and relationships to the past, its own time, and the future.

The General Editor

ACKNOWLEDGMENTS

A noted author once observed that acknowledgment pages in books had grown so lengthy that soon writers would be thanking anyone who had provided them with a paper clip. Perhaps. But writers understand that they succeed only because caring people looked past their often unreasonable demands, fits of impatience, and desire for perfection. I am grateful to everyone who passed on ideas, suggestions, and encouragement—and, in general, put up with me—over the ten years I took to research and write this book.

Bright young minds, refusing to accept a shoddy phrase or idea, blow a fresh breeze across the pages of a developing manuscript. I have profited more than I can repay from the ideas of my undergraduate students in history and government at Cazenovia College. Students in my various classes and seminars—particularly those on the Modern American Presidency—have heard pieces of this work. I have utilized with great profit the research essays of Jennifer Cross, Amber Dusenberry, and Debora Hall, and I am also grateful for the research help of Christine Caffrey, Esther Day, Wendy Frias, Kelly Hegedus, Jennifer Hull, and Erin Karasik. Particular thanks are due to Matthew Antonino, who has served as a valued critic, sounding board, and friend for the past four years.

All members of the faculty and staff at Cazenovia College consistently show patience and give their support to any colleague who is undertaking the development of a major project. Every day, I am grateful for their collegiality and encouragement. I am particularly grateful to President Adelaide Van Titus, Dean of the College Michael Fishbein, and Assistant

Dean Timothy McLaughlin. I am also grateful for the college's financial assistance, as I could not have completed the research for this book without help from the Cazenovia College Faculty Development Fund.

The George Bush Presidential Library, located on the campus of Texas A&M University in College Station, is the newest addition to the National Archives' Presidential Library System. Many of its treasures, as I have noted in the bibliographical essay, have yet to be opened for scholarly perusal. Nevertheless, its facility is state of the art, and its staff is first-rate, extending themselves to the researcher far beyond the call of duty. I am grateful to Library Director David Alsobrook and to Kate Dillon, Mary Finch, Warren Finch, John Laster, and Debbie Wheeler for their help and good humor. Many other archivists and librarians have helped me. Special thanks are due to Diane Barrie of the Ronald Reagan Library; Geir Gunderson, David Horrocks, and William McNitt of the Gerald R. Ford Presidential Library; Stanley Kozaczka of the Cazenovia College Library; and Carol Leadenham of the Hoover Institution on War, Revolution, and Peace.

Former president George Bush was gracious enough to take time out of his busy schedule to be interviewed for this book. I am also grateful to the many other members of his administration, and administration-watchers, who talked with me: James A. Baker III, David Bates, Phillip D. Brady, Douglas A. Brook, Andrew H. Card Jr., Richard B. Cheney, David F. Demarest, Edward Derwinski, Geraldine Ferraro, Barbara Hackman Franklin, C. Boyden Gray, Robert R. Green, Donald P. Gregg, Robert T. Hartmann, Dr. Daniel R. Heimbach, Ronald C. Kaufman, James R. Lilley, Frederic V. Malek, Edward N. Ney, Sean O'Keefe, Michael A. Poling, Rob Portman, Sig Rogich, Gen. Brent Scowcroft, Hugh Sidey, John Sununu, Carol Trimble, Chase Untermeyer, William Webster, and Clayton Yeutter. I also am thankful for the input of those individuals who preferred not to have their names listed here. Without breaking that confidentiality, I have used many of their ideas and insights to corroborate my own thoughts; their anonymity does not diminish the importance of their contribution to this book.

Since 1982, the Hofstra University Cultural Center, in conjunction with the Departments of History and Political Science of that institution, has put on a series of extraordinary conferences dealing with the modern American presidency. Scholars, administration alumni, and ofttimes the president himself get together for a series of valuable discussion sessions. The April 1997 conference on the Bush presidency was a real boon to this book. I am grateful to conference coordinators Natalie Datlof and Alexej Ugrinsky and to assistant to the coordinator Athelene A. Collins-Price for their labors.

I am fortunate to be able to publish my work with the University Press of Kansas—an author's house. Special thanks to my friend, director Fred M. Woodward, senior production editor Melinda Wirkus and production editor Rebecca Knight Giusti, marketing director Susan Schott, and copy editor Claire Sutton. All readers of the *American Presidency Series* owe a debt of gratitude to its general editors—the late Donald McCoy, the late Clifford S. Griffin, and Homer E. Socolofsky. Professor Socolofsky's reading of the manuscript was invaluable, as were the thoughtful comments offered by Prof. Robert Divine of the University of Texas.

When a writer talks to a class, the press, or a reviewer, the story of writing tends to become somewhat mythologized, as the project is portrayed in its most positive light. The author's family hears the truth—every day (in fact, they hear more of the truth on those days when a few good pages *don't* seem to get themselves written). It is to my wife and children that my work is always dedicated and to my parents, to whom this particular work is inscribed. But my immediate family hears the same grumbling (as well as stories of literary victories) as I write. I am grateful for their patience and for that of *their* families: Mark and Carrie Greene, Marsha and Ed Kernan, Bill and Dorothy Messer, Don and Jean Messer, Tom and Sonya Messer, Anne and Bob Reimann, and Doug and Joan Robertson.

I will forget more people than I thank, but among the many others who have given me their support are Cindy and Don Clark and family; Edward Galvin; Mary and Jack Hyla of the Four Seasons Resort in Old Forge (the place I got *hot* to write); the staff and faculty of the Jowonio School; Ken, Sherrie, and Julianna Kubiak; and Shirley Anne Warshaw.

1

★ ★ ★ ★ ★

THE LEGACIES
OF RONALD REAGAN

In November 1996, just before his political nemesis Bill Clinton won a resounding reelection victory, George Bush was the subject of one of cable television's most popular shows, the Arts and Entertainment Network's *Biography*. Yet after the program was over, one would hardly have known that Bush had ever been president. The first forty-five minutes of the hour-long show were dedicated to Bush's career before 1988, the year he was elected president. The last fifteen minutes offered such a platitudinal surface treatment of his presidency as to be almost useless—most notably, the Persian Gulf War was treated in less than two minutes. As for Bush's other policy decisions, they were simply not mentioned, except to say that he had "skillfully tied himself to the successes of the Reagan years."[1]

It has been the fate of George Bush to be compared to his larger-than-life predecessor. Indeed, most contemporary historians have concluded that Bush's presidency was little more than an attempt to continue the policies of Ronald Reagan—policies that are almost casually referred to in history textbooks as "revolutionary." The Reagan years did bequeath to Bush a nation that had recovered from the feebleness of the 1970s. One cornerstone of Reagan's legacy was a booming economy and a newfound pride in America's place in the world. But Reagan bequeathed a much more complex heritage to his vice president. The Bush presidency was not an interregnum, coasting on the economic successes of its predecessor. Rather, the heart of the Bush presidency lay in its attempts to deal with the economic instability and cultural anxiety that the Reagan years had also created. In so doing, Bush created a legacy for himself that was

1

just as complex as that of his predecessor, one that was far from a Reagan redux.

Americans rarely elect an ideologue as their president, instinctively fearing those who are truly convinced of the sanctity of their ideas. But in Ronald Reagan's case, America made a notable exception. Political scientist Walter Dean Burnham is correct when he maintained that Reagan was "the most ideological president, and the leader of the most ideological administration, in modern American history."[2] In 1980 Americans elected a president who for over three decades in public life had told them in no uncertain terms that he wanted to reverse not only the path taken by his party since the end of World War II but also many of the fundamental underpinnings of American society. Reagan's stated brand of political conservatism—a conservatism that was out of step with the mainstream of his party throughout the late 1960s and early 1970s—was simple and direct. He demanded a halt to three developments in American society since the 1960s: permissiveness in the nation's social conscience, the tax burden on ordinary Americans, and the weakening of America's place as the most powerful nation in the world. His was far more than a call for a return to a "simpler time"; Ronald Reagan wanted to begin anew.

As a result, Reagan did for conservatism what John F. Kennedy had done for liberalism—he co-opted it and energized it. As Kennedy had sparked a feeling of government service in young liberals, so too did Reagan spark the same feeling in young conservatives. Drawn to his engaging personality and his seeming rock-solid adherence to his stated principles, Americans accepted his message in near-record numbers. Believing in his message, they donated money in amounts heretofore unheard of. They also entered government in droves. Once there, these young conservative zealots, who called themselves the "true believers" (Edward Derwinski, a former congressman from Illinois who served in the Bush cabinet, called them "conservatives with a chip on their shoulder")[3] felt that they were participating in nothing less than a political, social, and economic revolution.

On the surface, there is evidence to support this assessment. During Reagan's presidency there was a marked reaction to the permissiveness of American society and a call for a return to what many conservatives began to refer to as "traditional values." Although Reagan hardly started this trend—it had been bubbling throughout the 1970s—he had long been one of its most vocal proponents. One key to Reagan's appeal in Middle America was his devotion to the past. He often spoke out in support of a return to what he termed "Christian values" in America. And people who shared his point of view believed that they could organize under his political banner. Fund-raisers such as Richard Viguerie proved that modern marketing tactics could be used to encourage Fundamentalist Christians, who had largely sat out politics since the 1950s, to participate in the process. The Moral Majority, founded by the Reverend Jerry Falwell, worked diligently to elect Christians to government positions, and their many successes were one of the major stories of the 1980s.

Reagan welcomed the support of Fundamentalist Christians and assiduously cultivated their votes. He pointed, with some amount of justification, to their political victories as evidence to support his claim that his administration had sparked a seismic change in America's social thinking. In a speech to the Conservative Political Action Conference, Reagan wistfully remembered that the move toward traditionalism had been one of the basic changes of his administration. He argued that before his election to the presidency, "The normal was portrayed as eccentric . . . the irreverent was celebrated. . . . [Liberals] celebrated their courage in taking on safe targets, and patted each other on the back for slinging stones at a confused Goliath who was too demoralized—and, really, too good—to fight back. But now, one simply senses it: the American people are no longer on the defensive."

In economics, Reagan also did as he promised and cut taxes. "Supply Side Economics," the mantra of Reagan conservatives, supported the belief that once personal taxes were cut, people could invest the savings. Then the government could collect enough taxes on investment income to balance the budget. There was certainly nothing new about Reaganomics—it was pure Hooverian individualism. Nevertheless, Reagan conservatives could point with pride to a series of tax cuts in the 1980s, most notably the Income Tax Act of 1981, which reduced federal rates by 10 percent over three years.

The foreign policy of the 1970s, to Reagan, had been replete with failures of American will. He spent the balance of his term trying to reverse the feeling that was best summarized in a question asked in a 1980 cover story for *Newsweek:* "Has America Lost Its Clout?" The defeat in Vietnam, détente with the Soviet Union and the People's Republic of China (PRC), an abandonment of nationalist causes in South America, and the inability either to prevent the taking of American hostages in Iran or to secure their release were proof for Reagan conservatives that America had been allowed to become a second-rate power.

By the end of his administration Reagan had reversed that trend. "Peace through strength" was the watchword of his administration, as Reagan presided over the greatest arms buildup in American history. His support of novel but flawed defense strategies like the Stealth bomber and the Strategic Defense Initiative ("Star Wars") made it clear that this was a president who had no qualms about spending the country back to world prominence.

This Reagan did, but a greater accomplishment was the change that he effected in the attitude of many Americans toward their country. An unfailing optimist, Reagan believed that once America was strong again, the entire nation would rally around the flag and achieve a unanimity of patriotism that had not been seen since World War II. Most Americans in the 1980s were passionately looking for a reason to abandon the pessimism of the 1960s and 1970s, and they embraced the mid-Victorian, flag-waving demeanor of their president with open arms. In a 6 April 1988 speech at the Center for Strategic and International Studies, Reagan could justifiably point to a change in the national attitude that had taken place under his watch, when he observed that "gone are the days when the United States was perceived as a rudderless superpower, a helpless hostage to world events. American leadership is back. Peace through strength is not a slogan, it's a fact of life—and we will not return to the days of hand-wringing, defeatism, decline, and despair."

The Reagan Revolution, then, was not just rhetoric, as many liberal observers have since claimed. There was a great deal of substance to its policies, and Republicans had much to crow about as they looked toward the 1990s. Yet, there was a correspondingly colder side to the Reagan years. In his seemingly sincere attempt to turn the clock back to a time when values were simpler and America's place in the world was strong and secure, Reagan unleashed a host of demons that plagued his successor.

The windfall of the Reagan tax cuts masked the fact that those cuts were responsible for the creation of a volatile and unstable economy. Reagan seems to have expected that the savings from his tax cuts would by itself be enough to stimulate the economy. Not so. He refused to offset his tax cuts with corresponding cuts in entitlement programs—indeed, federal outlays for Medicaid were exactly the same in 1987 as they had been in 1981, and in Social Security and Medicare, outlays had actually increased.[4] Those costs, combined with the enormous cost of the arms buildup, led to gaping deficits. Despite preaching a balanced budget (from his 1981 Inaugural Address: "You and I, as individuals can, by borrowing, live beyond our means, but only for a limited time. Why, then, should we think that collectively, as a nation, we're not bound by that same limitation?"), the federal debt tripled during Reagan's tenure to more than $2.7 trillion a year—the highest in American history. By 1988 the payment on the interest alone

4

was $140 billion a year. In the 1980 presidential primary, George Bush had predicted such a result when he branded Reagan's plan as "voodoo economics." Faced with a political dilemma, Reagan took the advice of several of his advisers and quietly approved "revenue enhancements" in 1982, 1983, and 1984—increased taxes on tobacco and alcohol, user fees on many federal services, and an increase in the Social Security payroll tax.[5]

As important as the deficit was the fact that because of Reaganomics, the gap between rich and poor in America was getting wider. Adherents of the theory that became popularized as trickle-down economics believed that the Reagan tax cuts would spur the economy to the point that excess monies would be able to trickle down to the poor and underprivileged. But for many people, this was a pipe dream; entertainer "Weird Al" Yankovic quipped that "the overprivileged were trickling down all over the underprivileged."[6] In his prescient analysis of the effect of Reaganomics on American society, *The Politics of Rich and Poor: Wealth and the American Electorate in the Reagan Aftermath,* Kevin Phillips noted that in 1988 the top half of 1 percent of the population of the United States had never been richer. In 1988 approximately 1.3 million Americans were millionaires; indeed,

President Ronald Reagan and Vice President George Bush. (Courtesy of the George Bush Presidential Library)

one source counted some 100,000 decamillionaires—people worth $10 million or more. By 1988 these Americans controlled 44 percent of the nation's income share—their highest percentage since 1949. However, the average family did not keep pace with the top income bracket. In fact, the median family income nosedived under Reagan, recovering in 1987 only to 1973 levels. The reason was simple enough: although wages were rising, so were prices. Only one-half of the nation's families were able to maintain their standard of living in the 1980s, and that was usually because both parents worked.[7]

Reagan's economic policies were criticized by liberals as succeeding at the expense of the poor and minorities. But in reality it was poor whites who were being hurt the most. In 1981 a total of 13 percent of Americans lived below the established poverty line; in 1986 it was 13.6 percent. In that time, the number of African Americans and Hispanics in that group had actually fallen, but the number of whites had risen.[8] Blue-collar whites felt the pinch long before Reagan left the White House. In the Rust Belt, unemployment was at 58 percent; throughout the country, farm incomes dropped to 1970 levels.[9] In January 1988, the week of Reagan's State of the Union Address, 72 percent of the people polled believed that rich Americans were better off than in 1981 and that the poor had lost ground.[10]

There was never any question that liberals would also denounce Reagan's foreign policy. It was a bit of an uphill battle for them, as they were flying in the face of a rampant patriotism that resulted from Reagan's flag-waving. However, in what became known as the Iran-Contra affair, liberal critics made their strongest case against the administration. With the much more than tacit approval of their president, White House aides had sold arms to Iran—a nation that only months before had been an American enemy. The purpose of the sales was to obtain the support of Iran in the release of American hostages held in Lebanon, although such releases never occurred. The sales were carried out in direct violation of American law, and the excess profits were secretly laundered through Israel and given to anti-Marxist freedom fighters in Nicaragua—the Contras. Administration critics saw these dealings as evidence of the continuation of a Nixonian "imperial presidency," with the chief executive reserving for himself the power to make foreign policy decisions despite laws intended to restrict his actions.

But Reaganites ignored the investigations and denouncements in the press that accompanied the Iran-Contra revelations. Instead, they took comfort in their belief that they had finally found a president who would take a tough stand toward the Soviet Union. In 1983, in a speech before the National Association of Evangelicals, Reagan denounced the Soviet Union as "the focus of evil in the modern world" and begged Americans not to "ignore the facts of history and the aggressive impulses of an evil empire." He professed that the days of communism were numbered (during a speech in Berlin: "Mr. Gorbachev, tear down this wall") and argued that victory in the cold war was an American birthright. Throughout his first term, Reagan generally pleased conservatives not only with his sabre-rattling but also by putting the force of the American military behind his words—most notably in Grenada and Libya. It seemed that the Nixon-Ford-Carter policy of accommodation toward communism—what had been called détente— had ended.

By the end of Reagan's second term, however, even his conservative supporters had begun to doubt his motives in foreign affairs. By 1986 the president shocked most observers by reaching out to Soviet president Mikhail Gorbachev, the father of glasnost (the encouragement of political debate) and perestroika (the stimulation of the Soviet economy by infusing doses of capitalism). By the time he left office in 1989, Reagan sounded like a moderate Republican seeking to reestablish détente. Perhaps this turnabout was caused, as some observers have suggested, by the influence of Nancy Reagan, concerned as she was about her husband's place in history. Perhaps it was as simple as the fact that Gorbachev and Reagan liked each other. James Baker, who served Reagan as both his chief of staff and his secretary of the treasury, has noted that "Gorbachev had an actor's gift to fill a stage with his presence. . . . Whenever we met, he exuded optimism, and in this regard, he reminded me time and time again of Ronald Reagan."[11] For whatever the reason, at their third summit in 1987 Reagan and Gorbachev signed a treaty limiting medium-range nuclear missiles (the Intermediate-Range Nuclear Forces Treaty), and Gorbachev agreed to withdraw Soviet troops from Afghanistan. To many conservatives, this relationship brought back memories of Nixon's visit to both the Soviet Union and China, and of Ford's wheat treaties with the Soviets, and it smacked of heresy.

Despite the turbulence of the Reagan years, the most startling observation about the state of America during the 1980s concerns those issues that did *not* worry it. Robert Teeter, a Republican pollster who served four presidents, reported that although Americans were generally alarmed by the excesses of the Reagan era, they were not about to support measures they saw as liberal Democratic alternatives. Indeed, Teeter's polls showed that the public was unmoved by any single issue.[12] Some observers even suggested that the Reagan administration was made of teflon—no criticisms stuck to it. This refusal by many Americans to challenge the administration on any of its policies—indeed, Reagan was reelected in 1984 by a near-record margin— is one of the most perplexing aspects of the history of the Reagan years.

In many ways, the explanation for this attitude—and a window into the state of the Union during the tenure of Ronald Reagan—is found in Jay McInerney's brilliant 1984 novel, *Bright Lights, Big City*. The main character, Jaimie Conway, is a fact-checker for a major magazine. Like many in his profession, he has aspirations of becoming a novelist. But he is a particularly shallow young man, dreaming of living a Hemingwayesque literary life at the same time that he is wallowing in the cocaine-laced lifestyle of the New York discotheque scene. Ultimately more concerned with dollars than dreams, Conway typifies the decade's young upwardly mobile urban professional—the Yuppie. In fact, McInerney implies that almost everyone in the 1980s had few qualms about shelving their dreams for a quick payday. Conway is surprised when he learns of the bitter disenchantment of Alex Hardy, the venerated—and drunken—former editor of his magazine. During a ten-martini lunch, Hardy, who knew all the greats of literature in the 1950s and 1960s, makes it clear to Conway that he has given up hope on the new generation of writers. Hardy voices his disenchantment rather gracefully: "The new writing will be about technology, the global economy, the electronic ebb and flow of wealth." The equally compelling 1987 movie based on the novel has Hardy putting it more crassly: "Money is poetry now . . . write about money."[13] The main character Gordon Gekko in another 1987 movie, *Wall Street*, echoes Hardy's sentiment when he proclaims that "greed, in all of its forms, is good."

The 1980s was an age of entepreneurism that makes the Roaring Twenties pale in comparison. Not the stock market crash of October 1987 nor evidence that the nation's savings and loan companies were beginning to melt down lowered the fever of many Americans to make a quick killing. Gross private domestic investment leaped from $402 billion in 1980 to an astounding $638 billion four years later.[14] This bull market fed a belief in academe that the study of business acumen was more worthwhile than the pursuit of humanistic learning. All over the country, college students abandoned the traditional liberal arts, the mainstay major of the 1960s and early 1970s, and instead gravitated toward programs that would earn them their MBA. It was not hard to understand why; financier Ivan Boesky spoke to the Business School at the University of California at Berkeley and encouraged the new graduates in their quest to accumulate as much wealth as possible. In 1985, one-third of the entire graduating class at Yale University tried to get jobs as financial analysts at First Boston Corporation.[15]

It was also an age of cultural voyeurism. If you couldn't grow wealthy from playing the market—as, we have already observed, most Americans couldn't—you could entertain yourself by watching *Lifestyles of the Rich and Famous*. It was an age of narcissistic indulgence. Billionaire entrepreneurs such as Donald Trump became pop icons; pop icon Madonna both reflected and refracted the times by proclaiming herself in song to be a "Material Girl." Indeed, the advent of the music video reflected the desire of many young Americans to sit back and watch rather than to use their imaginations while listening to a song on the radio.

Yet there were problems far more dangerous than America's cultural voyeurism, problems that quickly turned the 1980s into an age of anxiety. Recreational drug use had tripled since the 1970s, and by the 1980s cocaine had become the Yuppie drug of choice. Each year during the decade, one in six Americans ingested an illegal substance. By 1989 more than half the American population listed drugs as a grave threat to national security.[16] And by 1990 the Acquired Immune Deficiency Syndrome (AIDS) epidemic had claimed 200,000 victims. Reagan tried to ignore it; other conservatives insisted they had told us so (Pat Buchanan wrote, "The poor homosexuals. They have declared war on nature and now nature is exacting an awful retribution").[17] By decade's end, there were fights in high schools over whether or not to hand out condoms at a school dance. This was a scene that Reagan conservatives did not shy away from but one that nevertheless offered little pleasure or comfort. Because of AIDS, the morality of Reaganism had to confront the very real possibility that one could die from having sex.

As aptly put by Robert Shogan, Ronald Reagan "fell short of the expectations he had created."[18] It is unquestionable that the Reagan Revolution injured the nation's economic and social infrastructure. But that was difficult for Americans to see in 1988. Blinded by the culture of excess, few Americans worried about the deficit, AIDS, or the state of their family's values. Indeed, as Reagan ended his tenure in office, the vast majority of Americans clearly felt better about their destiny. Much of this glow was due to the calming effect of the man in charge. With his unmatched skill as a communicator, and with the simplicity of his message, Ronald Reagan was able to make most Americans think past the age of anxiety that his policies had created and concentrate instead on how good they felt about being Americans. He was, indeed, a tough act to follow.

2

"ONE SHOULD SERVE HIS COUNTRY"

Prescott Bush, an imposing man who could trace his lineage to Henry III of England, was raised in Columbus, Ohio, took his degree at Yale, and served in World War I. His wife, the former Dorothy Walker, was born in Kennebunkport, Maine, and attended private schools in St. Louis and Connecticut. When she met Bush, he was working for the Simmons Hardware Company in St. Louis. They were married in 1921 and moved to New York in 1924, where Bush soon became a partner in the investment firm of Brown Brothers, Harriman. Their second child, George Herbert Walker Bush, was born in Milton, Massachusetts, on 12 June 1924. He was named after his maternal grandfather and also inherited his nickname, "Poppy."

When he stepped into the national spotlight, much was made of George Bush's upbringing and background; he was charged by his political opponents with being out of touch with the masses (Texas governor Ann Richards quipped at the 1988 Democratic Convention: "George can't help it—he was born with a silver foot in his mouth"). But those many observers who dismissed Bush as a coddled member of the upper class did not take into account his rather disciplined upbringing. Both his mother and father were, to be sure, members of the genteel class—well educated, well pedigreed, well mannered, and well connected. They were also wealthy, but not so much so that they could claim membership in the leisure class who lived off their investment income. Prescott Bush did not have the money to engage in conspicuous consumption; even if he had, it would have been quite out of character for this staid New Englander to flaunt his wealth. The world in which the Bush children were raised, then, was one in which comfort was never an issue, but neither were the constant reminders that that comfort could not be taken for granted. Prescott refused to allow his children to loiter their way to adulthood; rather, he inculcated in them the same values of self-reliance and a mind-set of active service. George Bush's most favorable biographer, Fitzhugh Green, wryly noted that though the Bush family was comfortably insulated from the depression of the 1930s, Prescott "had to work hard to do so. Therefore, it was wrong to leave one's bicycle out in the rain."[1] Prescott Bush used his wealth as a safety net for his children. They were expected to go out, earn their own wealth, and do the same.

Akin to the value of hard work was that of public humility about their accomplishments. Boasting about good fortune, or flaunting their wealth or station, was expressly forbidden in the Bush household. One of his children later remembered with pride that Prescott Bush commuted to New York City from his Greenwich, Connecticut, home by train each day: "He'd *die* now with limos picking them up. He was a straphanger."[2] Bush's mother also inculcated in the children a sense of competitiveness. She was an outstanding tennis player and encouraged her children to excel in the game. Above all, both parents preached the sanctity of family ties. The nickname Poppy may have sounded both juvenile and preppy, but it emphasized Bush's direct link to his familial heritage.

Of course, with privilege came privileges. As the elected moderator of the Greenwich Town Meeting, Prescott Bush was, in the words of one observer, "taking care of the public schools his children would never attend."[3] Bush enrolled his sons in the Greenwich Country Day School; they lived at home until they completed the ninth grade, when they went away to prep school at Phillips Academy in Andover, Massachusetts—"Andover." The school's seal, which was designed by Paul Revere, proclaims the values that Dorothy Bush had already inculcated in her children—"Non Sibi" (not for self) and "Finis Origine Pendet" (the end depends upon the beginning).[4]

George was so attached to his elder brother, Prescott, that his parents allowed him to enter Andover one year early, so that the two boys might be together.[5] His time there was far from uneventful. In spring of his junior year, he contracted a serious infection in his right arm. He took the summer off and repeated a year. His brother Prescott believed that "that was the best thing that he ever did."[6] When he returned to Andover, his classmates were his own age. He became senior class president, president of Greeks, captain of the baseball and soccer teams, a member of the basketball team, and a participant in many other clubs and groups.[7] It was also during his senior year, while attending a Christmas dance at the Greenwich Country Club, that George met Barbara Pierce. She was attending

Ashley Hall, a girls' finishing school. Her father was the vice president of McCall's Publishing Company, and she could trace her family tree to Pres. Franklin Pierce.[8] She was sixteen; he was seventeen. Barbara later wrote that he was the first man that she ever kissed.[9]

Bush learned about the Japanese attack on Pearl Harbor while at Andover, walking near the chapel.[10] He later remembered that his reaction "was the same as every other American—'We gotta do something about this one.'"[11] Despite his father's wish for him to go to Yale, where he had already been accepted, Bush enlisted in the navy on 12 June 1942, his eighteenth birthday.[12] He was assigned to Chapel Hill, North Carolina, to undergo his preflight training. He then went to Minnesota to learn how to fly, and to Corpus Christi, Texas, to learn instrument flying and navigation. On 9 July 1943, he received his aviator's wings and was promoted to ensign.[13] Just nineteen, Bush was one of the youngest pilots in the navy. For almost one more year he traveled across the United States from base to base, practicing his carrier landings and learning to fly Grumman's three-man TBF torpedo bomber, nicknamed the Avenger. Late in 1943, a rather nonchalant Bush wrote his parents: "True, there is a danger to TB's which you know about, but I don't think we should consider that. Someone has to fly them."[14]

On 15 December 1943, Bush was assigned to the aircraft carrier *San Jacinto*, a part of the navy's Fifth Fleet. He saw plenty of action. During the June 1944 campaign in the Marianas, Bush was airborne for more than thirty-two hours, more than half of that time in strikes against Japanese who were dug in on the island of Saipan, where the marines were in the process of landing. During that battle, Bush and his crew were forced to ditch their plane in the ocean immediately after takeoff.[15] Later that summer, Bush flew air cover for the marine landings at Guam, Iwo Jima, and Chichi Jima.

On 2 September 1944, Bush and his crew were sent to bomb an enemy radio site at Chichi Jima. Bush remembered that "the minute we pushed over to dive, you could just feel the danger . . . some way about halfway down the run I was hit."[16] He later described the incident in a letter to his parents: "We got hit. . . . I told the boys in the back to get their parachutes on. . . . The cockpit was full of smoke and I was choking from it. . . . I felt certain that [the crew] had bailed out." (Both men were killed.) When Bush landed in the ocean, he realized that he had not hooked his life raft to his parachute; fortunately, the raft landed only a few yards from him.[17] A half-hour later, a sub in the area, the USS *Finback*, picked him up. Had the *Finback* not been there, the tides would have taken Bush to Chichi Jima, where he would have been captured; and corroborated stories of the treatment

Naval Ensign George H. W. Bush. (Courtesy of the George Bush Presidential Library)

of American prisoners on Iwo and Chichi Jima include incredible acts of barbarism, including cannibalism.[18]

Bush was by then eligible for leave. He used it to get married on 6 June 1945 (he reportedly mumbled to his new bride, "Enjoy it. It's the last time I'll ever dance in public").[19] Bush had also earned enough points for a discharge, but instead he opted to return to the Pacific (as he later remembered, "It was different then; 'we gotta go back and do our duty'").[20] However, the atomic bomb was dropped on Japan before he could be shipped back. Bush was discharged on 18 September 1945. He had flown 58 missions, accrued 1,228 hours of flying time, made 126 carrier landings, and earned the Distinguished Flying Cross.[21] Bush later said, "I had faced death, and God had spared me."[22]

When Bush enrolled at Yale University in fall 1945, he was part of the blitz on higher education that became known as the "GI Bulge." Many schools had been badly hurt by the drop in enrollment caused when young men left to fight in World War II, so they welcomed returning veterans, the vast majority of whom had their way paid by the GI bill, with open arms: Bush's class of some 8,000 freshmen was the largest entering class in Yale's history.[23] Colleges also made the effort to help veterans catch up for lost time with innovative—and abbreviated—programs. Bush enrolled in an accelerated program that allowed him to earn his B.A. in economics in only two years. He was also an outstanding baseball player, an excellent fielding first baseman whom major league scouts were observing.[24] Bush also advanced his contacts by being tapped for the Skull and Bones Club, a supersecret society whose members (one of whom had been his father) remained close for the rest of their lives, and by being elected to Phi Beta Kappa.

Given his background, as well as his experience in World War II, one should not be as surprised, as are many of Bush's biographers and political contemporaries, that he gravitated toward an adventurous rather than a "safe" career choice. It was, after all, in his blood: his great-great-grandfather, James Smith Bush, left his job as a storekeeper in the 1840s to move west to prospect for gold.[25] Having been weaned on self-sufficiency since his youth, Bush went his own way after his June 1948 graduation from Yale, going into an occupation that was loaded with the possibility of failure—the oil business. However, he did not go into the volatile trade without a safety net; his way was made much easier by his father's contacts. His father had been a member of the board of Dresser Industries and was a friend of the company's president, Neil Mallon. Mallon encouraged George to go into the oil business and agreed to take him on as the company's only trainee in 1948.

15

That year Bush moved to Odessa, on the Permian Basin in western Texas. He started at Ideco (International Derrick and Equipment Company) in a job that paid $375 a month and where he became a member of the United Steelworker's Union.[26] Dresser soon moved Bush to Pacific Pumps, one of its subsidiaries based in Huntington Park, California, where he worked as a salesman. But he soon wanted to become a part of the oil boom that was making the independent investors wealthy men; he wanted to "wildcat." In 1950, with a friend, John Overby, Bush formed an oil development company in Midland, Texas. Two years later, Overby and Bush merged their firm with one run by William and Hugh Liedke to form Zapata Petroleum, a name chosen for the Mexican revolutionary who recently had been played in the movies by Marlon Brando. By the end of 1954, Zapata assets included 8,100 acres of property and seventy-one active wells, which produced an average of 1,250 barrels a day. In 1959 Bush took over the presidency of a Zapata subsidiary, Zapata Offshore, and moved to Houston.

For a businessman of the 1950s, Bush was unusually devoted to his young family. Barbara developed into something of a frontier wife, quickly adapting to life in Texas. They soon had three children—George W. (born in 1946), Pauline Robinson (Robin, 1949), and John Ellis (Jeb, 1953). Soon after the birth of Jeb, tragedy struck; Robin was diagnosed with an advanced case of leukemia. The family's torture lasted seven months, as George and Barbara shuttled back and forth between Midland and New York's Sloan-Kettering Hospital, where the child received her treatment. Robin died in October 1953; for forty years Bush carried three good luck charms in his wallet—a ripped clipping of Barbara's engagement photo, a four-leafed clover, and a small gold medallion, on which was inscribed "For the Love of Robin."[27] Despite their tragedy, the Bush family continued to grow, with the addition of Neil (named after Neil Mallon, 1955), Marvin (named after Barbara's father, 1956), and Dorothy Walker (Doro, named after Barbara's mother, 1959).

Bush seems to have been bitten by the political bug after his father's 1952 election as U.S. senator from Connecticut, but he did not act on it until he moved to Houston. His way was a difficult one, however. The state was owned by the Democratic party, the vast majority of whom were ultra-conservatives. Bush also faced the problem of being branded as a carpet-bagger, an eastern liberal in oilman's clothing. To overcome these handicaps, Bush began to make his own political contacts, pulling close to him people who could help him overcome the carpetbagger image. Chief among them was James A. Baker III. As circumspect as Bush was gregarious, Baker's Texas pedigree was unquestioned. A classics major at Princeton and a University of Texas Law School graduate, he was an associate in Baker and Botts, the second oldest law firm in Texas. He was also a Democrat. But the bond between the two men went far beyond politics. Since Bush's early days as a Texas oilman, Baker had been his closest friend; Bush is godfather to one of Baker's daughters. When Baker's first wife died of cancer in 1970, the Bushes were there at the hospital. Bush was also close to Robert Mosbacher, of Houston's Mosbacher Energy Company. Tied to the Texas establishment, Mosbacher proved himself to be a fund-raiser without peer.

Bush's first shot at statewide office came in 1964, when he ran for the U.S. Senate seat then held by Democratic liberal Ralph Yarborough. Two years earlier, it looked as if Bush would be a shoo-in. The conservative bent of the state in 1962 gave the early lead in the 1964 presidential race to Republican reactionary Barry Goldwater over the sitting president, John F. Kennedy, whose policies had become obscenities for most Texans. Kennedy, then, could do little to help a Democratic senatorial candidate in the 1964 election. To make matters worse for the Democrats, Yarborough and John Connally, then the state's Democratic governor, were in open warfare, and the true leader of the state Democratic party, Vice Pres. Lyndon B. Johnson, was forced to sit out the feud in the name of party neutrality. Indeed, Kennedy went to Dallas on 22 November 1963 to try to patch up the feud between Connally and Yarborough and to try to make some inroads against Goldwater.

Kennedy's assassination completely changed the political landscape, both nationally and in Texas. Johnson was at the head of the national ticket in 1964, running with a more unified Democratic party and poised to destroy Goldwater's candidacy. This turnaround was the kiss of death for Bush. Along with almost every Republican challenger that fall, Bush was handily defeated, earning only 43 percent of the vote. He responded after learning of his defeat to Yarborough, "I guess I have a lot to learn about."[28]

In 1966, after selling his interest in Zapata, Bush tried for the congressional seat in Texas's Seventh District. Unlike his first foray into electoral politics, where he had been forced to court his party's Goldwater-dominated right wing in order to secure its nomination, Bush was able to run on a platform of moderate Republicanism, one that was closer to his own personal philosophy. Indeed, at several stops he made a point of saying that he was pro-choice on the abortion issue. The times also favored a moderate as an anti-Goldwater backlash permeated the party. Unopposed in the primary, Bush defeated his Democratic opponent with 56 percent of the vote.

Bush served two terms in Congress (he was reelected in 1968 without opposition) during a time of unprecedented conflict in the nation's history. The Republicans, in the minority in both houses of Congress, struggled to find a response to Johnson's policies that did not make them look like troglodytes. For his part, Bush supported the Vietnam War, a stand that said less about political philosophy (both support and opposition to the war cut across party lines) than it said about his feelings of duty. But Bush's moderate views on social issues placed him in the minority of his party, as he supported many portions of Johnson's Great Society programs. Bush caused a mild stir in Texas when he voted for the Johnson-supported Fair Housing Act of 1968. On 17 April he explained his vote to an audience of furious constituents in Houston: "One hundred out of 184 Republicans in the House voted for it. . . . I voted from conviction . . . not out of intimidation or fear, not stampeded by riots, but because of a feeling deep in my heart that this was the right thing for me to do."[29] Bush's refusal to paint the president as a demon—a task undertaken with gusto in 1968 by many other Republican congressmen—was greatly appreciated by Johnson, as was Bush's attendance at the president's farewell party in 1969 (Bush skipped a Nixon inaugural event to see the Johnson entourage off to Texas, telling a surprised Johnson aide, "Well, he's my president, and he is leaving town; and I didn't want him to leave this town without my being out here and paying my respects to him").[30]

Despite Bush's loyalty to Johnson, a desire to capture Texas in the fall election led Richard Nixon to publicly place Bush on the shortlist of vice-presidential candidates in 1968, even though the Nixon camp had already decided on Spiro Agnew as their running mate early that spring. Nevertheless, Bush's fealty was not lost on the Nixon White House. In the margins of a memorandum requesting an appointment for Bush with Nixon, Chief of Staff H. R. Haldeman scribbled, "We need more congressmen like Bush!"[31]

That constancy was prevailed upon in 1970, when Bush ran for the Senate a second time against Ralph Yarborough because Nixon asked him to. Bush had every reason to feel confident of victory. Yarborough's liberalism had long since begun to grate on Texans, and Bush had even reaped the rewards of his past loyalties and received the tacit support of Lyndon Johnson.[32] But Yarborough was unexpectedly defeated in the Democratic primary by Lloyd Bentsen, a more conservative Democrat who had the support of the popular John Connally. Despite the fact that Nixon himself campaigned in Texas for him, Bush lost the general election, winning only 46 percent of the vote. He was devastated by the loss. After the results were announced, he told Mosbacher, "I feel like General Custer."[33]

Nixon had promised Bush a good appointment if he lost in Texas, and on 11 December 1970 Bush was named as ambassador to the United Nations. Not surprisingly, given his complete lack of experience in foreign policy, his Senate confirmation hearings were tough. But the administration never wavered in its support for the nomination. The reason was simple enough— as Nixon adviser Charles Colson noted in a July 1971 memo, Bush "takes our line beautifully."[34] This assessment remained true of the ambassador even when he was double-crossed by the administration over the issue of the expulsion of Taiwan from the UN and the entrance of the communist People's Republic of China (PRC). As the Security Council debated the measure, Nixon instructed Bush to "hold the line" against Taiwan's expulsion. This Bush did, giving a stirring pro-Taiwan speech the night before the vote. However, Nixon had not told Bush that the administration was actually courting the PRC and covertly campaigning for that nation's acceptance into the UN at the expense of Taiwan. Taiwan was finally expelled by a 75-to-35 vote—the outcome that the administration wanted, despite Henry Kissinger's statement to Bush that he was "disappointed." When in July 1971 the administration announced its rapprochement with the PRC, to include a trip by Nixon to that ancient land, Bush was furious over how he had been used; but as usual, he kept his own counsel.[35]

Bush's career path was changed once again on 17 June 1972. On that evening, five burglars were arrested after breaking into the headquarters of the Democratic National Committee (DNC) at Washington's Watergate Hotel. The botched operation—an attempt to fix defective telephone taps that had earlier been placed in the offices of DNC chairman Larry O'Brien— turned out to be only the final chapter in a five-year story of abuse of power by the Nixon administration. As the press, prosecutors, and congressional investigators began to unravel the story, Nixon came to believe that he needed a steadier hand leading his defense from within the Republican party. Kansas senator Bob Dole was serving as the head of the Republican National Committee (RNC) at the time of the break-in, but his well-known penchant for angry outbursts promised to make an already volatile situation even more troublesome for the White House. After his 1972 reelection, Nixon offered the chairmanship to Bush.[36]

Until the final weeks of the Nixon administration, Bush was a tireless defender of the president. However, when the final batch of tapes was released, tapes that clearly showed Nixon to be guilty of an obstruction of justice, Bush finally backed off. He turned down a demand by Nixon aide John McLaughlin for more mailing lists from the RNC so that the White House might organize some last-minute support.[37] On 7 August, during Nixon's last cabinet meeting, the president inexplicably attempted to shift the conversation to the economy. Several of those present, including Bush,

19

tried to shift the talk back to the possibility of impeachment, but Nixon would hear none of it. The following day, Bush sent Nixon a letter, telling him that his base of support in the Republican party had vanished and that he should resign. The next day, Nixon did so.[38]

Bush's calm demeanor during the Watergate crisis, as well as his friendship with the new president, Gerald Ford, almost won him the vice presidency. According to the Twenty-Fifth Amendment, Ford was required to nominate for congressional approval a person to serve as vice president. Bush was asked to submit names from Republican state chairmen, and House and Senate leaders were requested to canvass their membership. The tally from the combined polls showed Bush with 255 votes, followed by former New York governor Nelson Rockefeller with 181. But it was soon learned that Bush's 1970 senatorial campaign had received some $100,000 in illegal contributions from a Nixon White House slush fund (the Townhouse Operation). Ford went instead with Rockefeller and offered Bush the ambassadorships to Britain or France; Bush asked instead for China, and he received the post.[39]

Bush spent an uneventful year as the American envoy to the PRC (the United States not yet having full diplomatic relations with that nation, he did not have ambassadorial rank). The closest he came to having an active role in foreign policy was his encouraging the leadership of the PRC to exert pressure on the Khmer Rouge captors of the crew of the merchant vessel *Mayaguez*. A Government Accounting Office report following that crisis concluded that pressure from the PRC may well have led to the eventual release of the crew.[40] Nevertheless, after Bush had served for only one year, a White House aide wrote, "It's my impression and partial understanding that George Bush has probably had enough of egg rolls and Peking by now (and he's probably gotten over his lost V.P. opportunity). He's one hell of a presidential surrogate. . . . Don't you think he would make an outstanding candidate for secretary of commerce or a similar post sometime during the next six months?"[41]

Certainly Bush had proven his abilities as a "surrogate" while at the RNC, and one historian suggests that Ford considered Bush for his secretary of commerce, to replace the ailing Rogers Morton.[42] If he did so, the idea was short-lived. Bush's desire to come home coincided with a political problem that Ford needed to erase before the upcoming presidential election. Early in 1975, allegations against the Central Intelligence Agency (CIA) had led to a series of investigations. The resulting reports made it clear that the CIA had been involved in domestic abuses that went far beyond the mandate of its charter. The administration was looking to clean house at the agency, and Bush's name was floated to Ford as a possible replacement for Director of Central Intelligence (DCI) William Colby.

At the RNC, Bush had already proven his ability to rein in a wildcat organization. Still, his political ambitions were well known. Certain to be raked over the coals during the congressional confirmation process as a purely political appointment, he was hardly everyone's first choice. On a list provided the president of fifteen "candidates worthy of consideration" by Chief of Staff Donald Rumsfeld, Bush's name indeed made the A list. The pros Rumsfeld listed in favor of his nomination were "experience in government and diplomacy, generally familiar with components of the intelligence community and their missions; [and] high integrity and proven adaptability." But the one con almost cost Bush the appointment: "RNC post lends undesirable political cast."[43] He was ultimately favored by only three of eight Ford advisers.[44] Ford's first choice was Washington lawyer Edward Bennett Williams (whose name was on Rumsfeld's sixty-four-name B list of possible appointments). But Williams refused the offer, and the president turned to Bush.[45] Kissinger cabled him on 1 November 1975, offering him the position. Bush's response, cabled the next day, is a fascinating and candid document, serving not only to reveal how shocked he was to receive the offer but also to show in microcosm his sense of duty to the president:

> Your message came as a total and complete shock. . . . Here are my heartfelt views. . . . I do not have politics out of my system entirely and I see this as the total end of any political future. . . . I sure wish I had time to think and sort things out. Henry, you did not know my father. The President did. My Dad inculcated into his sons a set of values that have served me well in my own short public life. One of these values quite simply is that one should serve his country and his President. And so if this is what the President wants me to do the answer is a firm "Yes." In all candor I would not have selected this controversial position if the decision had been mine, but I serve at the pleasure of our President and I do not believe in complicating his already enormously difficult job.

Never one to gush, in public or in private, Kissinger responded quickly: "The president was deeply moved—as was I—by your message. He is deeply appreciative of the nobility of your decision. . . . You are indeed a fine man."[46]

Yet the nomination was not a cinch. After a discussion with Mike Mansfield (D-MT), Ford scribbled a note to himself: "Geo[rge] Bush—for him, but he must say no to politics."[47] In order to get Bush through the confirmation process, on 18 December 1975 Ford wrote John Stennis (D-MS) that if Bush was confirmed by the Senate, "I will not consider him as my vice-presidential running mate" in 1976, a promise that Bush reiterated during his committee testimony.[48] It was this promise that won

Bush the approval of the Armed Services Committee as well as of the full Senate.

Bush performed admirably at the CIA. Six months into his new job, he outlined his successes in a memo to Ford. He noted that he had made thirty official and thirty-three unofficial appearances on Capitol Hill, had had thirty-three meetings with his station chiefs, had appeared sixteen times before groups at Langley, and had made twenty-one visits to intelligence community installations and contractor sites. According to Bush, "Morale at CIA is improving. . . . our recruitment is up. Our people are willing to serve abroad and take the risks involved." Bush's view—"things are moving in the right direction"—was shared by virtually every observer of the agency during his tenure.[49]

Nonetheless, when Jimmy Carter was elected in 1976, Bush became the first DCI in the history of the agency to be dismissed by an incoming president-elect. Bush was particularly disappointed by Carter's decision; he felt that he should be allowed to stay on at the CIA to demonstrate that the administration saw intelligence gathering as a bipartisan effort. Nevertheless, Bush found himself out of government for the first time since 1966. But thanks largely to the contacts of Baker and Mosbacher, he was quickly embraced by corporate America, although he had never been a part of it. He joined the executive committee of the First International Bank in Houston and sat on the boards of several other banks.[50] Yet this interim was never more than a holding pattern for 1980. In 1978, two Political Action Committees were created to help him raise money for a presidential run.[51] On 1 May 1979, Bush announced that he was a candidate for the Republican nomination for the presidency.

While Ronald Reagan was co-opting the conservative wing of the Republican party, Bush courted the moderates. In the Iowa caucuses, Bush's appeal to that wing, as well as an early start in the state that took the better-organized Reagan campaign by surprise, allowed him to edge out Reagan by 2,182 votes.[52] However, Bush himself sowed the seeds for future trouble when he jubilantly announced, "I've got the momentum. . . . I'm on my way." When a reporter pressed for a more concrete statement of the candidate's beliefs, Bush replied, "I'm just going to keep going. I've got Big Mo."[53] "Big Mo" sounded childish; instead of gaining more momentum from the victory, the Bush campaign was forced to respond to charges that their candidate was a juvenile preppy—a criticism that became known as the "wimp factor." It was a powerful weapon for Bush's opponents in conservative New Hampshire, a state where Bush was already running seventeen points behind Reagan.[54] The *Manchester Union-Leader*, the state's reactionary paper, proclaimed that Bush was no more than a "spoon-fed little rich kid."[55]

Any hopes for a Bush comeback on the shoulders of "Big Mo" were dashed during a debate in Manchester. Bush had agreed to a one-on-one debate with Reagan, but when the sponsor backed out, the better-financed Reagan campaign agreed to pick up the tab. As a condition of his financial largesse, however, Reagan demanded that the other four Republican candidates—Phil Crane, Howard Baker, John Anderson, and John Connally—be allowed to participate. The Bush campaign saw the trap; Reagan had more to gain if five candidates ganged up on Bush. With Reagan footing the bill for the debate, Bush had no choice in the matter. Yet instead of facing the inevitable, Bush dug in and continued to voice his opposition to a panel debate (he told a supporter, "I've worked too hard for this and they're not going to take it away from me").[56] Always quick to sense a dramatic moment, the night of the debate Reagan marched into the hall, followed by the other contenders. Rather than standing his ground, Bush sat meekly on stage, looking as if he had been hit by a steamroller—which, indeed, he had. When the moderator, a Bush supporter, tried to call attention to the fact that Reagan had changed the rules on Bush, a sanctimonious Reagan declared, "I paid for that microphone, Mr. Green."* Reagan swept New Hampshire, 49 percent to 23 percent for Bush.[57] From that point on, nothing, not even Bush's attempt in Pennsylvania to brand Reagan's fiscal policy as "voodoo economics," could save the campaign. It was out of money, and Baker told Bush that if he stayed in the race, he would only further anger an already piqued Reagan, thus losing all hope of getting the vice-presidential nod.[58] Bush withdrew from the race on Memorial Day.

The polls clearly showed that the conservative Reagan would have to balance his ticket with a moderate as his running mate. But because of the Manchester debate and the charge of voodoo economics, Reagan's advisers, particularly his wife Nancy, were adamantly against his choosing George Bush (Ed Rollins, a Republican political operative who worked for Reagan, remembered that the First Lady privately called Bush "Whiny" and made fun of his speaking style to friends).[59] Their moderate of choice was Gerald Ford, and Reagan quickly became entranced with the thought of a "dream ticket"—it would be the first time that a former president ran for the vice presidency. Ford was clearly in favor of the idea, but he publicly communicated his eagerness to CBS's Walter Cronkite in a televised interview. Furious with Ford for destroying the surprise announcement he had planned for the convention, Reagan abruptly rescinded his offer to Ford and called Bush.

*The moderator's name was actually Jon Breen.

Chase Untermeyer, a close friend of Bush who was then serving in the Texas legislature, wryly observed that Bush was chosen by Reagan because he was "the most attractive surviving moderate."[60] But Nancy Reagan was livid, and many of Reagan's advisers grumbled that Bush would hurt the ticket in the conservative Midwest. Bush, however, already showing the loyalty to Reagan that would mark his vice presidency, repressed his moderate stand on abortion and agreed to support the ticket's pro-life stand.[61] He campaigned doggedly, and the ticket swept to victory against Carter that fall.

Bush's major task as vice president was to be the administration's front man on the road. Between 1981 and 1989, Bush put in 1.3 million miles of travel, visiting the fifty states and sixty-five different countries. In 1982 he met Deng Xiaoping; in 1983 he visited the bombed marine barracks in Lebanon; at the 1984 funeral of Soviet premier Yuri Andropov, he first met Mikhail Gorbachev. But Bush had to overcome being seen as an intruder—and even as a possible moderate challenger if the Reagan Revolution went awry—by both the First Lady and by most of the president's staff. This he never fully did, but he was able to accomplish the one goal necessary for a successful vice presidency: by all accounts, he and the president got along well.[62] As Bush later remembered, "There was never a hint of negative feelings left over from our fight for the presidential nomination because Reagan's instinct, I learned, is to think the best of the people he works with. . . . We would run and serve together as a team."[63] At regular Thursday luncheons, which had been arranged by new Chief of Staff James Baker, Bush and Reagan eschewed a formal agenda and simply chatted for an hour.[64]

The close relationship between the two men was cemented after the 3 March 1981 assassination attempt against Reagan. At the time of the attack, Bush was flying in Air Force Two, returning from a trip to Texas. On learning of the attempt on Reagan's life, Bush immediately began jotting down his thoughts on the first piece of paper he could find, an Air Force Two welcoming brochure: "Enormity of it comes upon me twenty minutes out of Austin. Pray—literally—that RR recovers. Element of *friend* not just in C[ommander] in C[hief] president. Decent, warm, and kind."[65] An obviously overwrought Alexander Haig, then secretary of state, had proclaimed to the nation that he was "in charge"—an unfortunate misrepresentation of the constitutional line of succession as well as a statement of just how frenzied the situation was in the White House in the hours after the attack. When Bush arrived, he put things aright with his equilibrium and sense of purpose. The Secret Service wanted him to return directly to the White House, but the vice president refused, saying that "only the president lands on the South Lawn."[66] He also refused to take the president's seat at the cabinet table in the days after the near-tragedy. One Reagan operative paid Bush the ultimate compliment: "George Bush is too much of a gentleman to be reminded how to behave at a time like that."[67]

Bush's influence in the foreign affairs of the first Reagan term also seems to have been substantial. C. Boyden Gray, then serving as Bush's personal counsel, believes that Bush was "really the de facto national security adviser . . . until [George] Shultz came in and settled things down."[68] This observation is borne out by events. Reagan appointed Bush to conduct meetings of the National Security Council (NSC) when he was not present and put the vice president in charge of the NSC's Planning Group. This move angered Haig and may have played a part in his resignation early in Reagan's first term and his replacement with George Shultz. Bush may also have helped to initiate the administration's tilt toward Iraq in the Iran-Iraq war.[69] Bush was personally responsible for reversing the view of several European leaders on the deployment of U.S. Pershing missiles in Europe, particularly Margaret Thatcher's and Helmut Kohl's—two leaders who would become especially important in the subsequent Bush administration.[70] Bush's private discussions with Deng Xiaoping also helped the administration win an agreement with the PRC that governed arms sales to Taiwan.[71]

Bush was put in charge of the administration's Task Force on Regulatory Relief, a role that was completely compatible with his belief, shared by moderate and conservative Republicans alike, that government had become too intrusive in the lives of businessmen. Moreover, it gave Bush the opportunity to win over some of the same conservative economists who had castigated him for his "voodoo economics" remark.[72] Gray, himself a specialist in regulatory legislation, served as Bush's assistant on this task force, which recommended that hundreds of federal regulations be scrapped or changed.[73]

In the 1984 reelection campaign, once again Bush was placed in a situation where he had to debate his opponent; once again, this spelled trouble. Bush could hardly refuse to debate Geraldine Ferraro. The Democratic congresswoman from New York was the first woman to run on the national ticket of one of the two major parties; and given her superstardom, Bush could not give her a free pass. During the debate, however, he was not only condescending to Ferraro, he was downright rude (Ferraro later remembered that Bush "had to prove himself").[74] After the debate, he chortled that "we kicked a little ass tonight."[75] Not surprisingly, the press was highly critical of Bush for the rest of the campaign.

As the Iran-Contra scandal dominated the final two years of the Reagan presidency, so too did it threaten to hurt Bush's chances to win the presidency for himself in 1988. It seems well established that Bush was in the room when Reagan approved the arms-for-hostages deal. When the discussions turned toward the proposal for funneling the profits from the deal to the Nicaraguan Contras—a clear violation of the law—Bush's role becomes more difficult to assess. He was absent from many of the key meetings where the covert aid was discussed but present at others. Yet most observers agree that at those meetings, Bush rarely said anything, a circumstance that allowed him to claim that he was "out of the loop" on Iran-Contra.

Bush's performance concerning Iran-Contra was totally in character with how he viewed his vice presidency. Loyalty was his by-word. Even if he had disagreed about an issue, it was totally out of character for him to speak up in opposition to the president at a meeting with others present. Having a weekly meeting with Reagan and being present at most of the meetings where the covert aid was discussed unquestionably put the vice president *in* the loop. And despite his rather consistent denials, it is difficult to believe that Bush knew nothing about the supplying of arms to the Contras. One of the runners of the arms, Felix Rodriguez, was a Bush acquaintance from the CIA days; and during a meeting with Bush, Rodriguez briefed him, according to the agenda, "on the status of the war in El Salvador and resupply of the Contras."[76] But since Bush gave Reagan the benefit of his counsel only in private—and at present there are no tapes or notes of those meetings—we cannot yet be sure, to paraphrase Howard Baker in 1973, "what the vice president knew and when he knew it."

On 13 October 1987, at Houston's Hyatt Regency Hotel, George Bush announced his second candidacy for the presidency. When he said that his campaign would not travel in "radical new directions" but would give "steady, experienced leadership," Bush sounded for all purposes as if he would run his campaign as a defense of Reaganism. The presidential campaign of 1988 had many facets—but that was not one of them.

3

★ ★ ★ ★ ★

"JUGULAR POLITICS"

It was clear by 1986 that the Iran-Contra revelations had cost Bush heavily. As the presidential-election season kicked into high gear, Bush was trailing his leading Democratic rival, former Colorado senator Gary Hart, in virtually every poll. Smelling blood, challengers from within the Republican party jumped in. One exploratory candidacy was brief: Lee Iacocca, chairman of Chrysler Motors and one of the business icons of the early Reagan years, let it be known that he was interested in the nomination. However, when he was fired as head of the advisory commission on the restoration of the Statue of Liberty and Ellis Island (a move that Iacocca attributed to Bush), he stalked from the arena, grumbling that he would never enter politics again and that the people in Washington were "schizos."[1] Before 1987, former Delaware governor Pierre S. (Pete) DuPont, former Nixon and Ford staffer and Reagan's secretary of state Alexander Haig, former secretary of defense Donald Rumsfeld, and Reagan chief of staff and former senator Howard Baker had made trips to Iowa and New Hampshire. Yet none of these men, accomplished politicians but neophytes in the presidential arena, was considered strong enough to go the distance.

Bush had three serious opponents for the nomination, however. Two came from Congress. Although never a man of strong ideological convictions, Kansas senator Bob Dole nevertheless could bask in the reflected glory of the Reagan Revolution—as majority leader, it was he who had shepherded most of its measures through Congress. Many Republicans worried about Dole's "dark side"—grouchy and sarcastic on a good day, few could forget his blaming World War II on the Democratic party when campaigning as Gerald Ford's running mate in 1976—but he had a strong base in the Midwest. If he could win the Iowa caucuses in January, and if that victory brought more donations to his campaign, he could pose a threat to Bush in conservative New Hampshire. However, many disillusioned movement conservatives, rightfully sensing that neither Dole nor Bush was one of their own, turned to New York congressman Jack Kemp, an indefatigable speaker and party fund-raiser with indisputable conservative credentials.

Throughout 1986 Dole hammered at Iran-Contra, and Kemp hammered at the economy. But a more gut-level message, sent by the Reverend Pat Robertson, appealed to the right wing of the party. Both an originator and a beneficiary of televangelism in the 1980s, Robertson's *700 Club* was one of the most watched shows on cable television. In a party where 20 percent of its membership listed themselves as born-again Christians, Robertson had a natural constituency, one that an NBC reporter assessed as "not wide, but deep," and one that had proven willing to donate heavily for its causes.[2] Throughout 1986 Robertson went around the country, telling audiences that he was waiting for his "call" to the nomination. His strong showing in the Michigan selection choice in late May 1986 was treated as a shocking upset by much of the press. The early success of Robertson's candidacy revealed that there was a morally identifiable constituency in the Republican party that could not be counted upon to support the vice president.

At best, Bush faced a grueling primary campaign, and party insiders remembered that he had not survived the process in 1980. Members of Reagan's staff, who had never completely trusted Bush, leaked that if Bush imploded early in the primary scene, they would support Reagan's friend Nevada senator Paul Laxalt over the vice president.[3] There was even some talk in summer 1986 that made the papers about a plan afoot to amend the Constitution so that Reagan could run for a third term. It was clear that Bush needed help.

Harvey LeRoy Atwater would provide that help. Born in 1951 in Atlanta, Atwater was a born clown, ladies' man, and hell-raiser. Always looking for the spotlight (quipping to a reporter that "I never really became an adult. . . . I made my own [rules] up"),[4] he naturally gravitated to politics, serving as an intern in the office of Sen. Strom Thurmond (R-SC) before he set out to become a political kingmaker. Between 1974 and 1978, Atwater had worked in or directed twenty-eight winning campaigns; in 1980 he ran Reagan's winning primary and general election operation in South Carolina. Thurmond recommended him for a low-level job in the White House Office of Political Affairs; and from that vantage point, Atwater's star shot into the political heavens. Indefatigable, and an incredible organizer and fund-raiser, Atwater was honored in 1982 by the Jaycees as one of the nation's Ten Outstanding Young Men (one of the other ten was the freshman senator from Indiana, Dan Quayle).[5]

Atwater's biographer, John Brady, quips that the pairing of Atwater and Bush was the "odd coupling." On its surface, this seemed to be an understatement. The two men met in 1973, and their relationship survived even the bitter primary campaign of 1980 when Atwater had cast his lot with the other side. For Bush, whose family and staff never fully trusted Atwater's loyalty or accepted his compulsive womanizing, he was a curiosity—the political genius as prodigal son. But he was also a Reaganite and a southerner, and Bush needed as many of both on his team as he could get. More important, Bush needed a pit bull, someone who could help him bury the wimp factor and force his opponents to be on the defensive. In 1987 Bush wrote that "jugular politics—going for the opposition's throat—wasn't my style."[6] This was true enough: moments such as Bush's gloating after his debate with Geraldine Ferraro were rare. But negative politics was Atwater's style, and Jim Baker, who had been named Bush's campaign manager, was wise enough to allow Atwater room to create. Recognizing that after the 1980 experience he needed to attack to win, Bush placed his primary campaign into Atwater's hands.

In Iowa, Dole had played his midwestern populist credentials to the hilt, even to the point of refusing Secret Service protection so as to make Bush, who would arrive in a caravan befitting the vice presidency, look even more elitist. Indeed, Atwater was told that Bush might place third, behind Dole and Robertson.[7] To Atwater, the problem was obvious: it was the wimp factor. Bush was perceived by the large majority of Iowans to be an effete eastern snob who didn't have what it took to run a bruising thirteen-month campaign. To make matters worse, the vast majority of Iowans professed themselves to be disgusted with Iran-Contra and were poised to take out their wrath on the vice president.

On 25 January 1988, only a few days before the Iowa caucuses, an opportunity presented itself to gain some ground. Bush had agreed to do a live satellite interview with CBS News anchor Dan Rather. Roger Ailes, a media consultant who had started as a prop boy in Cleveland, moved up to producer of the *Mike Douglas Show*, and coordinated the media campaign for Richard Nixon's successful 1968 campaign, had been recruited by Atwater the previous fall. As senior director of marketing for the Bush campaign, Ailes was put in charge of getting Bush ready for Rather. For Ailes and Atwater, it was simple—Bush had to see Rather as the enemy and be prepared to take the offensive as quickly as possible. This was drilled into Bush in the pre-interview preparation, and by all accounts he went into the interview ill-tempered and ready to pounce. When Rather opened with a taped piece emphasizing Iran-Contra, Bush immediately charged Rather with changing the ground rules for their interview. What followed has gone down in political lore:

> RATHER: I don't want to be argumentative, Mr. Vice President.
> BUSH: You do, Dan.
> RATHER: No—no sir, I don't.
> BUSH: This is not a great night because I want to talk about why I want to be president, why those 41 percent of the people are supporting me. And I don't think it's fair—
> RATHER: Mr. Vice President, these questions are designed—
> BUSH: . . . to judge a whole career, it's not fair to judge my whole career by a rehash on Iran. How would you like it if I judged your career by those seven minutes when you walked off the set in New York?[8]

Bush's reference to the night that Rather, in a fit of pique because a U.S. Open Tennis match had delayed the start of his newscast, had stalked off the set, leaving seven minutes of dead air, was seen by many viewers to be in poor taste. But Atwater loved it. Bush had been tough—certainly no wimp—and he had been able to avoid talking about Iran-Contra. Atwater later claimed that the Rather interview "was the most important event of the primary campaign."[9] It certainly lifted the gloom that had been hanging over both Bush and his campaign. It was, however, too little too late for any one event to help Bush in Iowa. The magnitude of his defeat there—Bush not only lost to Dole, but as predicted, he came in third behind Robertson, winning 17,000 fewer votes than he had won in 1980—astounded most observers.[10]

Had it not been for the steadying hand of New Hampshire governor John Sununu, it is likely that Bush would have lost in that state as well, thus effectively ending his candidacy. Sununu remembered that Atwater had come to him as early as 1986, and the fire-breathing governor, with the help of Andrew Card, formerly Reagan's liaison to local governments and then the Bush campaign manager in New Hampshire, had helped Atwater put together a strategy for that state.[11] It yanked the Bush campaign on the offensive. Ailes and Sig Rogich, the campaign's director of advertising, created a series of one-half-hour shows, "Ask George Bush," one of which implied that Dole would raise taxes, a charge Dole flatly denied.[12] Ignoring Dole's denials, Ailes and his wife created an ad that showed Dole as a two-faced "Senator Straddle"; the ad accused Dole of taking both sides on Pentagon spending as well as secretly favoring a tax increase.[13] Sununu saw to it that the ads were carried by both local and Boston stations. Helped by the fact that the Dole campaign was more poorly financed and organized in the Granite State than it had been in Iowa, on 16 February, Bush won 38 percent of the vote to Dole's 28 percent (Kemp won 13 percent, DuPont 10, and Robertson 9). The evening of the primary, after Bush had been declared the victor, NBC's Tom Brokaw interviewed both Bush and Dole. Appearing on the screen together, they answered a few pro forma questions. Then both candidates were asked if they had anything to say to the other. Bush was gracious in his praise of Dole; when it was his turn, a sullen, exhausted Dole looked into the camera and growled, "Yeah. Tell him to quit lying about my record."

It was not a good time for Dole's famous temper to show itself. The first Super Tuesday, when seventeen states—fourteen of them southern and border states—would attempt to gain more influence in the nominating process than they could get by holding their primaries alone, was to be 8 March. Bush had long been ready for Super Tuesday. Since 1984 he had been courting the conservative vote, so important to success in the South. He had done so with no particular subtlety; his open fawning upon leaders like televangelist Jerry Falwell, who eventually gave Bush his support, led conservative columnist George Will to call Bush a "lapdog." Yet everyone in the Bush camp remembered that he hated doing this. His moderate tendencies led him to disagree with southern conservatives on virtually every issue, and he was repulsed by the recent revelations of sex and financial scandal in the big televangelist empires. But as one observer told two *Time* correspondents, "It had the effect of putting enough deposits in those accounts so that we didn't have to worry about them anymore."[14] Bush did not completely abandon his moderate stance, however, as he refused to support the drive for a protectionist tariff that was popular in the South.[15]

Just as important was the money that Bush had been pouring into the South, creating what Atwater aptly called a "firewall," designed to pick Bush up from the expected loss in Iowa and what had once been a probable loss in New Hampshire. Bush was able to buy block advertising; some of the most effective were Rogich-produced spots in South Carolina that featured Barry Goldwater in support of Bush.[16] Three days before Super Tuesday, in Atwater's home state of South Carolina, Bush won half the vote. On Super Tuesday, he swept every state but Washington.

The New Hampshire comeback and the firewall strategy in the South, both based on attack tactics, had won Bush the nomination. It did not take much longer for a philosophical Kemp, a buoyant Robertson, and an embittered Dole to drop out of the race. Yet Bush continued to be hampered by problems from within the Reagan administration. The president had vetoed a Civil Rights bill; Attorney General Edwin Meese was linked to a scandal revolving around defense contracts; charges had been levied against former Reagan aide-turned-lobbyist Michael Deaver that he had been improperly profiting from his White House connections; and the press was harping on revelations that First Lady Nancy Reagan consulted an astrologer about political and social decisions. Moreover, the congressional and presidential investigations into Iran-Contra were satisfying no one with their nondescript findings and recommendations. These predicaments chipped away at the popularity of the Republican party in general, and of Bush in particular. At the Democratic convention held in Atlanta in mid-July, Edward Kennedy (D-MA) harassed Bush with a litany of charges, followed by a chorus of "Where was George?" hooted by the delegates. When that convention ended, its nominee, Massachusetts governor Michael Dukakis, led Bush by as many as seventeen points.

In retrospect, the two strongest hopes for the Democratic party in 1988 were the two men who refused to run. In 1985 Edward Kennedy told the *Washington Post* that he was "personally convinced that [I] can gain the Democratic nomination"; one month later, he took himself out of the race.[17] New York governor Mario Cuomo then began a year-long flirtation with a candidacy, refusing to say whether or not he was running. But his coyness tried the patience of both his party and the nation (*Washington Post* reporter David Broder spoke for many when he wrote that "the Democrats . . . will not waste their time trying to decipher an enigma").[18] On 19 February 1987, at the end of a New York City radio talk show, Cuomo announced that he was not running.

With Kennedy and Cuomo out of the race, the road to the Democratic nomination was littered with lesser political lights, all of whom had trouble raising funds and many of whom watched their campaigns self-destruct. Former Colorado senator Gary Hart, who had nearly bested Walter Mondale for the presidential nomination four years before, was in the race for only a few weeks in April 1987, until it was revealed that he was involved in a questionable relationship with a young model. Hart angrily suspended his campaign, blaming the media for intruding in his personal life. Senator Joseph Biden of Delaware watched his candidacy implode when it was revealed that he had publicly misrepresented his law school grades and that he had been regularly quoting a British Labour leader in his speeches without proper attribution. None of the other candidates—Cong. Patricia Schroeder of Colorado, former governor of Arizona Bruce Babbitt, Missouri congressman Richard Gephardt, and Senators Paul Simon of Illinois and Albert Gore Jr. of Tennessee had any depth of support (collectively numbering seven candidates at one point in the early campaign, the press derisively called the field the "Seven Dwarves"). Only the Reverend Jesse

Jackson stuck out the campaign all the way through to the convention. He scored several impressive early victories—at the end of the race, he had won a majority of the total popular vote in the Democratic primaries. But a key loss in New York, where memories of his 1984 labeling of New York City as "Hymietown" still ran deep, helped to scuttle his campaign.

The eventual Democratic nominee, Gov. Michael Dukakis of Massachusetts, had a life experience and a personality that were the exact opposite of that of George Bush. His father had immigrated to the United States at age sixteen; by age twenty-eight he had become the first Greek immigrant to graduate from Harvard Medical School. His mother came to the United States from Greece at age nine; she became the first Greek immigrant to graduate Phi Beta Kappa from Bates College. Michael, the second of two boys, excelled at sports and academics (his yearbook picture was labeled "Chief Big Brain in the Face"). After graduating Phi Beta Kappa from Swarthmore in 1955, then spending two years in the army as a clerk-typist, Dukakis graduated from Harvard Law School in 1960. But law was never his passion. In 1962 he won the first of four terms in the Massachusetts legislature, where he earned a reputation as a maverick, supporting rules reform and fronting an organization that one close observer labeled a "throw the bums out organization."[19] After an unsuccessful run for attorney general, he was elected governor in 1974. Four years later, after taking his challenger too lightly, Dukakis was defeated for renomination in the Democratic primary. Stunned, he spent the next four years planning his comeback; he recaptured the statehouse in 1982.

During the next two terms, Dukakis was generally given credit for turning his state around from the recession of the early Reagan years. Trumpeted as the "Massachusetts Miracle," Dukakis was whisked into contention for the Democratic nomination for the presidency, where a well-planned campaign, virtually devoid of reference to divisive issues, allowed him to emerge at the end of the primary process as the only candidate left standing. His personality—distant and intense, with an air of superiority (Andrew Card, who knew Dukakis from his days in Massachusetts politics, remembered that the governor often acted as if "'people should do what I want because I'm smart'")—promised to contrast unfavorably to that of the more garrulous Bush.[20] But Dukakis was the beneficiary of the troubles at the end of the Reagan presidency, and he carried a sizable lead over George Bush into the Democratic convention.

As it had in the primary season, the Bush campaign went on the attack against Dukakis, even before Bush had been nominated. Sig Rogich went to Atwater with the idea for a series of ads to run in between the two national conventions that would castigate the Democrats but name no specific candidate. As such, the ads could be paid for by the Republican National Committee from their "soft money" funds, an expenditure that did not have to be debited to the Bush campaign. Atwater approved the idea, and Robert Mosbacher raised some $6 million to fund the ads. They referred viewers back seven years, reminding them of how things had been before Ronald Reagan and asking, "Why go back seven years?" The ads were a huge success, helping to bring Bush some nine points closer to Dukakis before the opening of the Republican convention in New Orleans.[21]

The second decision designed to help close the gap with Dukakis became much more problematic. The Friday before the Republican convention opened, Bush met with his senior staff to discuss the vice-presidential selection. The result of that meeting was the development of a shortlist that included Bob Dole and his wife Elizabeth, who had served in the Reagan cabinet; Jack Kemp; and Senators Pete Domenici of New Mexico, John Danforth of Missouri, Alan Simpson of Wyoming, and Dan Quayle of Indiana. Despite the virulent opposition of Jim Baker, Quayle was first on the list of Craig Fuller, Bush's chief of staff, and of Roger Ailes, who had worked on Quayle's 1986 reelection campaign to the Senate. He was a bit lower on others (Atwater wanted Libby Dole) but the general consensus was that Quayle would be a strong choice.

For many observers, the vice-presidential choice was the first opportunity to notice an important Bush trait—that of letting virtually no one in on important decisions until the last minute. In his study of military decision making in the Bush presidency, Bob Woodward explained this trait as being that "of an intelligence agent," noting that Bush would "'compartment' information, dividing it into pieces so that only he himself knew the whole."[22] On the day that Bush flew to the convention, he told several of his aides that he had made up his mind, but he would not tell them whom he had chosen. On his arrival in New Orleans, he met Reagan at the airport and whispered his choice to him.[23]

James Danforth Quayle, the junior senator from Indiana, had graduated from DePauw University in 1969, and he joined the National Guard rather than risk being drafted, according to him because he wanted to immediately go into the law. He graduated from the law school of Indiana University at Indianapolis, but he never practiced. Instead, he went to work as the associate publisher of the *Huntington Herald-Press,* a local newspaper owned by his father. It took only a year for Quayle to abandon journalism and enter politics. In 1976 he was elected to the first of two terms in the House, where he was the second youngest member. In 1980 Quayle rode Reagan's coat-tails to a Senate seat, defeating eighteen-year incumbent Birch Bayh.[24]

Quayle did not find his way onto Bush's shortlist by accident. Nor was his final choice as Bush's running mate a hasty, overnight choice by a harried presidential candidate. As reported by Bob Woodward and David Broder, who interviewed both Quayle and his wife, Marilyn, for a 1992 series of articles in the *Washington Post*, the Quayles had launched "an unofficial, sub rosa campaign to become Bush's choice" immediately after the New Hampshire primary. Quayle lobbied to be chosen as the convention's keynote speaker so that he could prove himself on national television. He also pushed for more visibility in the Senate, backing off from issues that were near and dear to the Reagan conservatives, so that he could get closer to the Bush campaign.[25]

As Bush pondered his shortlist, Quayle's negatives were notable. His attendance record as both congressman and senator was well below average, and his one major piece of sponsored legislation, the Job Training Partnership Act of 1982, probably would not have passed had it not been cosponsored by Edward Kennedy. He had also had a brush with scandal, appearing at a Florida golf resort in 1980 at the same time as did Paula Parkinson, a former lobbyist who had posed nude for *Playboy* (Quayle said that he had played a round of golf, then left the day after she arrived).[26] Moreover, his choice was certain to upset Richard Lugar, the senior senator from Indiana, who had entertained the possibility of running for president in 1988, and who, his staff believed, wanted the vice-presidential nod.[27]

In other ways, however, Quayle was the perfect choice. Although his father was a far-right conservative and a member of the John Birch Society, Quayle was no ideologue. Indeed, he viewed his conservatism in the same moderate tones as did George Bush. In 1980 Quayle was quoted as arguing that "conservatives have very different ideas than the New Right where we ought to go. Some of the New Right people really want to turn the clock back . . . on affirmative action and all the civil rights gains. . . . We won't let them."[28] Like Bush, Quayle had a deep loathing for government bureaucracy. He also had shown the type of political loyalty that so impressed Bush; he had voted against his party an average of only 10 percent of the time in all his years in Congress.[29]

Indeed, what has been completely missed by virtually every observer is that the choice of Dan Quayle as George Bush's running mate was an inspired one. He complemented Bush in every way and brought to the ticket many strengths that Bush lacked. His youth would play well in the eighteen-to-twenty-nine-year-old voting bracket so coveted by Bush. His family values would appeal to the movement conservatives and the Robertson right; even the Parkinson flap could not stop Broder and Woodward from concluding that "family comes first for the Quayles, not just rhetorically in the speeches they both give, but in the ordering of their daily lives."[30] He tested well as a potential candidate between the Rockies and the Mississippi, a part of the country that still distrusted George Bush as an elitist yuppie. And although he was not an accomplished speaker, Quayle possessed an energy behind the podium that Bush often lacked.

Yet Bush biographer Herbert S. Parmet quotes Bush's diary entry on the subject: "[Quayle] was my decision and I blew it, but I'm not about to say that I blew it!"[31] Bush was rarely introspective about such matters, and it is surprising to find out that he was so about his choice for the vice presidency. Nevertheless, Bush did not "blow" the choice. The choice was a home run; what *followed* Bush's decision was a series of disasters. The first problem lay in Bush's handling of the announcement. He held his cards close to his vest for too long, and his staff was completely unprepared to deal with the inevitable press questions surrounding the appointment. One member of Jim Baker's staff was so caught off guard that he had to race to find biographies of Quayle in *Congressional Quarterly* and the *Almanac of American Politics*.[32] This measure of surprise kept Bush's staff from planning for possible damage control when the press began to delve into Quayle's background. As a result, when the press ran with the stories on the National Guard, Paula Parkinson, and a rumor that his father had bought Quayle's way into law school, the Bush campaign learned about these problems at virtually the same time as the public.

The second problem turned out to be Quayle himself. When Bush introduced his choice to the public, Quayle turned to an obviously stunned Bush, jabbed at the vice president, and with a wide grin shouted, "Go get 'em!" It looked sophomoric, and the press pounced on the young man with obvious glee. During the invocation on the last day of the convention, just before Quayle was confirmed by the delegates, the speaker intoned, "How can we thank thee for this electrifying young Giant from Indiana?" The television cameras caught several of the delegates repressing a snicker. But an even bigger problem was that Quayle had become an overnight laughingstock on the late-night talk shows (Johnny Carson one-lined: "Do you get the feeling that Dan Quayle's golf bag doesn't have a full set of irons?"). Literally overnight, Quayle had gone from young Republican-conservative superstar to being the campaign's new "wimp." For several weeks, he became what no presidential candidate wants their running mate to become—*the* story. Then he disappeared from sight, as the Bush campaign took over his schedule, sending him to parts of the country where he could do little damage.

Thanks to the flap over Quayle, Bush's acceptance speech to the convention took on a whole new meaning. Democrats were already beginning to charge that Bush's choice for his running mate said less about Quayle than it did about Bush's penchant for secret decision making. They also claimed that Quayle's flaws would put the country in danger if something should happen to President Bush. More so than ever, it was imperative that George Bush look and sound presidential when he faced his party for the first time as its nominee.

The speech, as crafted by Peggy Noonan, was up to the task. Noonan, who had recently left a position as a speechwriter for Reagan to raise a family, had reluctantly agreed to join the Bush campaign. In her witty memoir of the period, Noonan takes her readers through her decisions on some of the speech's most memorable phrases, delivered by Bush with an energy and air of certainty that surprised even his closest supporters. Bush called for a "kinder, gentler nation" based on individual acts of volunteerism (Noonan remembered that the phrase came to her after reading a note from Bush where he described his motivation in politics: "I know what drives me . . . everyone matters"). Those volunteers would become "a thousand points of light." (Noonan: "Why stars for communities? I don't know, it was right.")

But the most memorable line of the speech, delivered with theatrical pauses that would have made Reagan proud, brought the convention to its feet: "The Congress will push me to raise taxes, and I'll say no, and they'll push, and I'll say no, and they'll push again. And all I can say to them is: read my lips. No new taxes." According to later published reports, Richard Darman crossed that line out of an early draft of the speech, pronouncing it "stupid and irresponsible." Angling for a position in the administration, perhaps at the Office of Management and Budget (OMB), Darman panicked at the thought of being backed into a corner on taxes. But Ailes and Noonan were adamant; the phrase offered *the* sound bite of the speech, a line that Noonan later defended as "definite. It's not subject to misinterpretation. It means, I mean this." In the short run, Ailes's and Noonan's instinct was correct. Immediately following the speech, Mosbacher found Noonan in the pandemonium of the convention hall and yelled, "Out of the park! Out of the damned ball park!"[33] He was right. Despite what it later cost Bush when he proved incapable of keeping his promise, it was the best speech of his political career. And he had cut Dukakis's lead in half.

Lee Atwater's strategy for that fall was to paint Dukakis as a stark raving liberal by highlighting his stand on specific, red-meat issues that would resonate with the core of voters who had long supported Ronald Reagan.

The Bush campaign attacked Dukakis as a "card carrying member" of the American Civil Liberties Union (ACLU), a charge that was true enough, but in the hands of Atwater and Ailes, it sounded just short of criminal. Yet Dukakis was not merely castigated as a liberal; the Atwater-led assault portrayed him as a man whose very patriotism was open to debate. As part of this strategy, Bush co-opted the American flag as a virtual symbol of his campaign. In 1977 Dukakis had vetoed a bill passed by the Massachusetts state legislature that would have required teachers to lead their class in the Pledge of Allegiance. With a flag in his lapel, Bush hammered at this point and drew wild responses from crowds throughout he country, as he asked, "What is it about the Pledge of Allegiance that upsets him so?"[34] Dukakis was also assailed by Bush for failing to keep taxes down in his own state of "Taxachusetts."

Bush as attack dog was news in its own right. After having depicted Bush in his Pulitzer Prize–winning comic strip "Doonesbury" as "having put his manhood in a blind trust," Garry Trudeau created "Skippy"— Bush's evil twin who emerged on the campaign trail. If Bush did not revel in such a campaign, as some of his advisers have later claimed, he was nonetheless very good at it. He seemed both natural and comfortable in campaign situations, as when he invaded Dukakis's home state and rode around Boston Harbor in a skiff while delivering a mocking litany on the governor's unwillingness to clean up the sludge (Bush snidely claimed that Dukakis would probably get his naval advice from the rubber ducky in his bathtub).[35] In a very real sense, as observed by John Brady, the Bush campaign created a negative "record" for Dukakis and forced him to defend it, as would an incumbent, running for reelection.[36] Many of Dukakis's ads pushed the theme, "He'll do for America what he did for Massachusetts." Bush ads replied, "We can't afford that risk."

The 1988 campaign thus became one of symbols rather than issues. And the most memorable symbol was that of a convicted murderer. Though many states had programs to allow their prisoners time away from their incarceration to reward good behavior, only Massachusetts extended that privilege to men and women who were serving life sentences for murder.[37] While on a furlough from a Massachusetts prison in 1987, convicted murderer Willie Horton made his way to Maryland, broke into a home, pistol-whipped the owner, cut him twenty-two times across the midsection, and then raped his wife. In February 1988, Dukakis announced that he would no longer oppose—as he had done in the past—a ban on the furlough program for convicted killers. James Pinkerton, Bush's director of opposition research, came across the issue and passed it along to Andrew Card, then the Bush campaign manager in New Hampshire. Card, who knew the victim's family, recalled that he researched the issue and passed it on to

Atwater. From that point, Card remembered that the furlough issue became "very attractive."[38] Reportedly, Atwater became fond of saying that "if I can make Willie Horton a household name, we'll win the election."[39]

Both things happened. Although the Bush campaign never technically produced an advertisement that showed Willie Horton (that was done by the National Security Political Action Committee, and the ads were pulled from the air after a short period of time; Card remembered that "we didn't even want them to run it"),[40] the team did create an ad that became a classic of attack advertising. Titled "Revolving Door," the ad showed prisoners (who were actually members of the Young Republican Group at Brigham Young University, acting in real prison uniforms loaned them by the state prison in Utah, where the ad was shot) walking through a turnstile as they moved in and out of prison.[41] The copy was devastating:

> As governor, Michael Dukakis vetoed mandatory sentences for drug dealers. He vetoed the death penalty. His revolving-door prison policy gave weekend furloughs to first-degree murderers not eligible for parole. While out, many committed other crimes like kidnapping and rape. And many are still at large. Now Michael Dukakis says he wants to do for America what he's done for Massachusetts. America can't afford that risk.[42]

Bush himself referred to Willie Horton by name more than once in his speeches and alluded to him in many more. For example, on 2 September, in New Jersey, he said, "We need a president who believes in family values, like saying the Pledge of Allegiance. . . . We need a president who is not going to offer some kind of program to furlough a murderer so he can go out and rape and pillage again. We need a president who will support our law enforcement community in going after these drug traffickers. . . . I am that man."[43]

While the Bush juggernaut of 1988 was one of the most effective campaigns in modern memory, it is also true, as Atwater later quipped, "We couldn't have done it without them."[44] Dukakis and his campaign were clearly caught off guard by the effectiveness of the venom coming from the Bush camp. Early in the campaign, Dukakis made the same mistake he had made in his gubernatorial campaign of 1978: he took his opponent for granted. Reminiscent of the 1948 campaign of Thomas Dewey, which had as its basic assumption that the brash Harry Truman was unelectable, the Dukakis campaign was haughty and overconfident, refusing to counterattack. Dukakis seemed to be waiting for Bush to self-destruct or to tire of his attack campaign. To the governor's surprise, neither happened. His own feeble attempts to create a favorable image of himself usually backfired, as was the case during a visit to a General Dynamics plant in Michigan, when he took a ride in an M-1 tank. Wearing a helmet that made him look like the cartoon character Snoopy, Dukakis appeared absolutely foolish— a point noted by the attendant press corps, which could not contain its laughter.[45] The Bush campaign pounced quickly on the gaffe. Rogich, who remembers first seeing in his hotel room the footage of Dukakis's ride, quickly realized that it would make a good ad. However, it was difficult to get the footage, protected as it was by the networks. Rogich was finally able to buy it from an ABC archive, and he used it as the background of an ad that highlighted a list of the defense initiatives that Dukakis opposed: "And now he wants to be our commander-in-chief. . . . America can't afford that risk".[46]

Perhaps the most devastating moment in the Dukakis campaign came during the second presidential debate, held at the Pauley Pavilion on the campus of the University of California at Los Angeles on 13 October. Bush had shown in previous campaigns that he was a weak debater. In 1988 this weakness did not matter. The moderator of the debate, CNN's Bernard Shaw, had the first question, which went to Dukakis: "Governor, if Kitty Dukakis were raped and murdered, would you favor an irrevocable death penalty for the murderer?" The question, which had been born of the furlough issue, and which was at best on the ethical borderline, was made to order for Bush. Either Dukakis would say no, thus showing him once again to be soft on crime, or he would say yes, thus opening himself up to charges of flip-flopping on the issue. In the end, few people remembered what Dukakis said, but everyone remembered how he said it— matter-of-factly, with no passion or outrage in his voice, as if he was merely producing a pat answer from his briefing book. John Tower, former Texas senator then serving as a member of the Bush campaign's spin team, remembered going into the pressroom following the debate and telling them "what the reporters themselves had been thinking: whatever Michael Dukakis's qualifications for the job might have been, his coldness and detachment were appalling."[47] The Bush campaign had not only succeeded in burying the wimp factor for Bush, but Dukakis had been painted as one.

The nastiness of the campaign had grasped the attention of the American people, but it did not propel them to the polls; the turnout on 8 November 1988 was the lowest since 1924. Although the results were hardly of landslide proportions, Bush's victory was convincing. He won 54 percent of the popular vote and 426 electoral votes to Dukakis's 112.[48] Bush swept the South, Midwest, and Southwest; Dukakis won only ten scattered states and the District of Columbia.

George Bush and Michael Dukakis, second presidential debate, 13 October 1988, Pauley Pavilion, UCLA. (Courtesy of the George Bush Presidential Library)

One month before the election, *Reader's Digest* held separate interviews with both Bush and Dukakis, ultimately asking, "In the final analysis, what is going to decide this election?" Bush replied, "The economy and foreign affairs—it has ever been thus." Dukakis replied "strength and values."[49] Both men were wrong, as Dukakis admitted in a later interview: "Look, there's no question that the negative campaigning hurt us. . . . I think that one of the lessons of the campaign is you have to . . . respond quickly."[50] Dukakis's self-flagellation has some merit; his campaign was poorly run. The press also bore some responsibility. A prescient study of the campaign by William Boot concluded that the press turned away from tough scrutiny of the conduct of the candidates and was satisfied instead with airing the sound bites that the campaigns provided—and the Bush campaign provided better sound bites (in the words of one ABC reporter: "George Bush wanted some free advertising. We gave it to him").[51] But the major reason for Bush's victory was the ability of his handlers to understand that a new form of political campaigning—one based on quickly identifiable symbols and sound bites—was the way to get to an electorate that had stopped reading and started watching music videos on television. Dukakis clung to the old style of politics and paid the price. The most incisive assessment of how Bush won came from Gerald Boyd of the *New York Times*, who observed that Bush "pick[ed] the right fights and [got] the right opponent."[52]

Despite Bush's election, a closer look at the 1988 electoral results bode ill for the future of the Republican party. Bush's victory was hardly a mandate. For the first time in twenty-eight years, the Democrats gained seats in both houses of Congress while losing the presidency. Indeed, the Democrats controlled both houses: in the Senate they outnumbered the Republicans 55 to 45; in the House, 262 to 173. The phrase "divided government" was now in every observer's political lexicon. Equally important was the fact that Bush had not won his victory as emphatically as had Ronald Reagan in 1984. Bush had received 5.4 million fewer Republican votes than had Reagan in 1984, lost 500 counties that Reagan had won, and received less support from Independents and "Reagan Democrats." Indeed, in virtually every category of voter, Bush's share of the vote had dropped from that won by Reagan.[53]

More important was the extent—quite aside from the fact, as George Will observed, that the Bush campaign had been "unattractive but effective,"[54]—to which many of the same voters who had voted for Bush were beginning to grumble about the state of American political campaigns. In his prescient 1996 study, *The Governing Crisis: Media, Money and Marketing in American Elections*, W. Lance Bennett has argued that the 1988 election began a political era "in which electoral choices are of little consequence. . . . The best hopes for creative leadership are effectively screened out by political and economic forces that are only dimly understood. . . . Our national politics have created a system in which the worst tendencies of the political culture . . . have been elevated to the norm in elections.[55]

Indeed, the public was voting in record smaller numbers, and they grumbled while doing so, not finding any of the candidates to be up to their standards. Fewer than 10 percent of those who voted thought that the candidates adequately addressed their concerns; by election day, two-thirds of those who voted wished that two different candidates had been running.[56] Only 43 percent of those who voted on election day had a favorable opinion of Bush; 32 percent liked Dukakis, and the remainder either did not have a preference or disliked both candidates.[57] Although it was two years from its appearance, the groundswell for Ross Perot had its seed planted in the negative campaign of 1988.

4

★ ★ ★ ★ ★

"THE UNTOUCHABLES"

Within twelve hours of his election, Bush announced that he would nominate James Baker as his secretary of state. The choice, as Bush remembered in his memoirs, "was what we call in golf a 'gimmie.'"[1] Bush's closest friend, Baker had run Bush's campaign for the Senate in 1970 and had served as his campaign manager in the 1980 and 1988 presidential campaigns. Moreover, his service as Reagan's chief of staff and secretary of the treasury served as a bridge to the party's conservative wing. Baker later characterized their bond as a "big brother–little brother relationship"; to the president-elect he was "Jimmy," a man who could be turned to for personal as well as political aid (Baker reportedly called his friend "Bushie" in private).[2]

Bush's choices for his transition team, announced the same day as Baker's appointment, also contained no surprises. Craig Fuller, Bush's chief of staff as vice president, and Robert Teeter, a Republican pollster who had served Nixon, Ford, Reagan, and Bush, were chosen cochairmen. Joining them on the transition team were two Bush aides who were reprising their roles from the campaign: C. Boyden Gray as the transition's general counsel and Sheila Tate as press secretary (Tate was soon replaced by Marlin Fitzwater, who had served since January 1987 as Reagan's press secretary). Chase Untermeyer, a Bush family intimate, was named personnel director. The team would oversee an operation with 125 paid staff members, which would be covered by $3.5 million of congressionally appropriated funds. Their task was to recommend appointments to the president and then to clear them through the vetting process. Not a formal member of the transition team, but seminal to the process nevertheless, was Bush's eldest son, George W. Bush. He chaired an internal group, which included Baker aide Margaret Tutweiler, Untermeyer, and Atwater. Dubbed "the Scrub Team" by insiders, it was responsible for "scrubbing" all potential appointments to make sure that their loyalties were to Bush and not to Reagan.[3]

It was the influence of the Scrub Team that led Bush to choose neither Fuller nor Teeter to be his White House chief of staff. Teeter's lack of administrative skills was well known. Fuller, however, had been with Bush since the vice-presidential days. He was also Baker's candidate for the job.[4] But Fuller had long been suspected of leaking to *Washington Post* reporter David Hoffman, a sin Bush could not forgive.[5] Moreover, as Untermeyer later recalled, Fuller had "run quite afoul of George W. Bush" by being "insufficiently attentive" to the family and friends around the vice president, pushing them aside in an effort to get ahead. Untermeyer remembered that George W. Bush started the "drumbeat" that ended in Fuller's being passed over for chief of staff.[6]

If loyalty cost Fuller the job, it played a major role in winning it for John Sununu. Bush's political debt to him was immense. In his victory speech in November 1988, an exultant Bush had shouted "Thank you, New Hampshire!" He had not forgotten that primary victory, in which Sununu played a pivotal role, turning his electoral fortunes around. But Sununu also had other strengths for the position. He came with government experience that neither Fuller nor Teeter could match. He had served as a New Hampshire state representative from 1973 to 1974 and as governor of that state from 1983 to 1988, leading Bush to quip that "you want someone who's run for sheriff" as chief of staff.[7] Sununu also appealed to conservatives, who approved of his anti-Soviet leanings.[8] His appointment may well have solved another problem for Bush: adding a strong presence at chief of staff would help to blunt fears that Baker was going to dominate Bush, much like a "deputy president."[9]

But most important was the fact that Sununu filled a gap in Bush's managerial style. Teeter's experience was as a pollster; Fuller, as one reporter put it, "preferred a low-key devotion to process rather than the rough and tumble of political combat."[10] Neither was the best choice to rein in an often rollicking White House staff. Sununu, on the other hand, had the reputation for being the type of manager who would complement Bush's often paternalistic approach to his subordinates. Andrew Card, who became Sununu's deputy, remembered that the governor's appointment would "give George Bush something that he needed in the White House— a little bit of bite . . . and John Sununu has a lot of bite."[11] Tough, blunt to a fault, Sununu provided the nasty edge to Bush's "kinder, gentler" persona. In a 1997 interview, Sununu observed that "the president was smart enough to complement his style"; he was much more blunt with the press in 1989, telling the *New York Times*, "I don't know what they expect me to do. I don't have a reputation for assault and battery. What do they think I will do to the system, break it?"[12]

The transition itself should have been an easy one. After all, the Republicans had kept their hold on the executive office, and, on the surface at least, staffing decisions seemed to be few. But Bush had two tasks that he felt had to be accomplished before the beginning of the new administration. The first was to bind the wounds of the campaign by showing the American people a "kinder, gentler" George Bush. This effort began immediately, with a campaign of kindness toward the press. After a Reagan presidency that had angered journalists with its deception and lack of access, the press was pleased to see the president-elect inviting reporters for a background interview, or—the plum prize—an invitation to join Bush on his morning jog. During the three months of the transition, Bush gave more press conferences than had Reagan over the past two-and-one-half years.[13] He also met with members of the political opposition, who proclaimed to the press a new warmth of relations that had long been absent (after a meeting with Bush, Jesse Jackson exclaimed, "Reagan had a closed door policy for eight years. You couldn't get an audience with him").[14] In the immediate run, it worked. Bush received generally high marks from the press, like the *Washington Post*, which described his style as "unscripted . . . a more free-wheeling, self-confident style than the choreographed Reagan."[15] There was talk of an end to the Imperial Presidency; the bile of the recent campaign seemed forgotten.

Bush also wanted to make it clear that he did not intend to operate in the shadow of a Reagan presidency. This desire was never hidden from the public view, but most observers dismissed Bush's promise to choose a "brand new team" as necessary postelection rhetoric. A joke was making the rounds in Washington at the time that even with the advent of a new administration, no one was going to have to change their Rolodexes. Certainly it seemed probable that, because the Republican party had retained the executive branch, there would be few startling changes and that, as under Reagan, conservative groups could continue to expect their share of the spoils.

The observers were soon proven wrong. The word came down that all Reagan holdovers had to be out of their offices by 20 January—no exceptions.[16] If they did not leave, there were reports that Reaganites would be threatened with having their taxes audited.[17] Bush also made it clear that his style of governing was different from his predecessor's. He announced to the press that he was going to be a "shake me, wake me kind of president" and volunteered that he was going to "personally read" the morning intelligence report.[18] He also announced that all his appointments would be completely screened for ethical and financial irregularities and that he would institute a code of conduct for his administration. Far from the "friendly takeover" that many members of the press, and, later, one influential scholarly book viewed it to be, Bush sounded as if he were taking the office away from a president of the other party.[19]

The composition of the cabinet, on its surface, seemed to contradict this observation. Indeed, it looked like Reagan redux. Seven Reagan cabinet members were asked to continue in the Bush administration, either being retained in their old department or reassigned. Baker's move from Treasury to State was a sign to most observers that foreign policy would dominate the new administration.[20] Bush also kept his friend Nicholas Brady at Treasury and retained Lauren Cavasos at Education and Richard Thornburgh as attorney general. Two other former Reagan cabinet members were given new assignments under Bush: Elizabeth Dole, who had been secretary of transportation from 1983 to 1987, was made secretary of labor, and Clayton Yeutter was moved from U.S. trade representative (USTR) to Agriculture. The Thornburgh appointment can be seen also as a paean to the party's conservatives, as was the appointment of New York congressman Jack Kemp at Housing and Urban Development.

Bush's sense of loyalty led to other cabinet appointments. He paid back two enormous political debts by naming John Tower as secretary of defense and Robert Mosbacher to Commerce. He also paid back governor of Illinois James Thompson, who had made an early withdrawal from the 1988 presidential race, by naming Samuel Skinner, the former chairman of the Northern Illinois Regional Transportation Authority and the chairman of the Bush campaign in Illinois, to Transportation. Edward Derwinski, also of Illinois, was no crony of Thompson, but he had had a long relationship with Bush, serving with him in the House and by his side again in 1971 as a delegate to the General Assembly of the United Nations. He was named secretary of veterans' affairs. Minorities and ethnic Americans got four slots—Cavasos was the first Hispanic to have been named to the cabinet; Derwinski was the first Polish American to be named to a Republican cabinet in the nation's history. African-American Louis Sullivan, president of Morehouse College of Medicine, was named secretary of health and human services, and Manuel Lujan, a former congressman from New Mexico and a Hispanic American, was named to Interior. The second woman appointed to the cabinet was Carla Hills as USTR; she had been secretary of labor under Ford. Retired admiral James D. Watkins, a former nuclear submarine commander, rounded out the cabinet as secretary of energy.

Yet those who judge (or judged) the Bush administration by the makeup of its cabinet know little about its relative power in the modern presidency. In short, it has none. Richard Nixon began the practice of centering policy decisions at the White House, leaving the departments with little power, save whatever advisory role the president deigned to assign specific cabinet members. Nixon's successors had kept that paradigm intact. With the exception of Baker at State, and often Thornburgh at Justice, Bush had absolutely no intentions of dispersing power back to the departments. Bush kept the two cabinet councils that had been formed under Reagan—the Domestic Policy Council and the Economic Policy Council—but little policy

The first Bush cabinet, 1989. *Back row, left to right:* Lauren Cavasos, Clayton Yeutter, Louis Sullivan, Richard Darman, Samuel Skinner, Adm. James D. Watkins, Carla Hills, Robert Mosbacher, Jack Kemp, and Edward Derwinski. *Front row, left to right:* Elizabeth Dole, John Tower, James Baker, Bush, Dan Quayle, Nicholas Brady, Richard Thornburgh, and Manuel Lujan. (Courtesy of the George Bush Presidential Library)

flowed from them. As the administration carried on, cabinet meetings became more infrequent. Though he made it clear to his staff that any member of his cabinet could see him at any time, Bush reserved the policy-making role for his White House staff.[21]

On that level, Bush wanted to clean house, as the appointment of the two members of his staff most responsible for policy decisions bears out. Richard Darman had been a presidential assistant and deputy secretary of the treasury under Reagan, but he had infuriated Reagan conservatives by his behind-the-scenes engineering of the administration's retreat from the 1981 tax cut. Thus his appointment as Bush's director of the Office of Management and Budget sent up flares to the press, signaling that Bush was not truly wedded to his "no new taxes" pledge. That assessment was correct, and Darman's role in effecting the reversal in Bush's declaration was substantial. But the forty-three-year-old Darman was never an intimate of Bush; indeed, speculation had it that the two men did not really like each other. Perhaps this was because of Darman's consistent self-promotion in the press; perhaps it was because of his corrosive personality. Darman himself remembered that he hoped that Sununu's reputation for irritating people would become "less notable. Unfortunately, it didn't. Soon, we were *both* said to be arrogant and abrasive."[22]

The choice of Brent Scowcroft as national security adviser was indicative of an even greater split with the Reagan conservatives on policy. The son of a Utah grocer, the sixty-three-year-old retired air force general and Russian history professor at West Point had served in the U.S. Embassy in Belgrade, as an NSC aide under Nixon, and as Ford's national security adviser. Scowcroft had been a consistent critic of Reagan's foreign policy. He had supported neither the "evil empire" stance nor the race at the end of the Reagan administration to achieve détente with Mikhail Gorbachev. He had also publicly differed from the administration on arms control.[23] He continually warned of the "clever bear syndrome"—the penchant of the Soviet Union to lull the Americans to sleep while maintaining their imperialist aspirations.[24] At the press conference announcing his appointment to the NSC, Scowcroft was clear: "I want to have a new look. We're going to formulate *our* policies."[25]

Scowcroft's appointment also sent a political signal, as Bush remembered it, that "the NSC's function was to be critical in the decision-making process."[26] A key initial step was the issuance of a National Security Directive (NSD-1) on the day of Bush's inauguration. This order restructured the NSC by creating two subcommittees of that statutory body. The Principals Committee, designed to review national security policy, included the members of the NSC plus the chief of staff; as a result, Sununu had a much greater impact on, and input into, foreign and security policy than any of his predecessors. The second one, the Deputies Committee, consisted of the deputies of each of the principal members of the NSC and was charged with the development of policy options. Robert Gates, Scowcroft's deputy, quickly became the first among equals on this committee.[27]

Had there not been a Democratic majority in both houses of Congress, which would have to confirm Bush's major appointments, the transition from the Reagan administration to the Bush administration might have gone off without major incident. As it was, only two of Bush's early appointments met with any significant opposition on Capitol Hill. Louis Sullivan was criticized for his pro-choice stance, but that condemnation was muted by the time of his hearings, largely because no one in Congress had the stomach to turn down Bush's only African-American nominee. But the Democrats were champing at the bit for a chance to exact their pound of flesh for the rancor of the campaign. In that climate, allowing the name of John Tower to be placed in nomination for any position, much less that of secretary of defense, was like dangling a red flag in front of a bull.

Born in 1926, John Tower left Southwestern University in June 1943, joined the navy, and served during World War II on a landing craft in the Pacific. After the war, he taught political science, sold insurance, and was a radio announcer. He was persuaded to run against Lyndon Johnson for the Senate in 1960, the same year that Johnson concurrently ran for the vice presidency. Tower lost that election, but the following year, after Vice President Johnson was forced to give up his Senate seat, Tower ran again and won. His victory put life back into a Texas Republican party, which to that point had been moribund. It also encouraged young Republicans like George Bush to run for office.

Bush soon found himself in Tower's debt. In 1970, when Bush was running for the Senate, Tower was the chairman of the Republican Senate Campaign Committee. He gave Bush monies that amounted to nearly twice as much as that given to any other senatorial candidate.[28] Tower supported Bush in each of his congressional races and stuck with him during the 1980 presidential primaries. As chairman of the Presidential Commission charged to investigate the Iran-Contra affair, he later wrote in his memoirs that "the working assumption was—and indeed had to be if we were going to conduct an honorable, credible inquiry—that George Bush was directly involved. That assumption was *never* borne out by our investigation."[29] After the report was released, Atwater recruited Tower, who had introduced Bush at the 1987 Houston rally where he announced his candidacy for the presidency, as a surrogate campaigner. Tireless on the stump, Tower's presence gave credence to the campaign's claim that Bush was innocent of any wrongdoing in the scandal. He also accompanied Quayle on several legs of the campaign, making sure that there were no more major flare-ups. Clearly, Tower was a man who had to be rewarded.

However, several members of the Bush team objected to Tower's being named to Defense. Their reasons were legion. Rumors of Tower's womanizing and excessive drinking had floated around Washington for more than two decades. Only days after the election, a story surfaced in the *Atlanta Constitution* claiming that his second marriage had ended because of "marital misconduct," a charge that was soon carried on national television.[30] There was also a story circulating that while he was serving in Geneva as the chief U.S. arms negotiator, Tower had cavorted with a woman who, unknown to him, was a KGB agent. Many of those on Bush's team professed to have firsthand knowledge of his aberrant behavior. They argued against his being given a position that called for being alert and available at all times.

But Tower's troubles went deeper than his personal life. Treasury secretary-designate Nicholas Brady, who had witnessed Tower's behavior firsthand while serving as an appointed senator from New Jersey, reported to the president-elect that despite their public protests, Tower was far from beloved by his former colleagues on the hill.[31] Napoleonic in bearing, he eschewed compromise for confrontation; he simply had few friends in the Senate, and many members on both sides of the aisle wanted to see him "get what was coming to him." One individual close to the process remembered that during the confirmation hearings, he heard that Tower was visiting the Pentagon and having his picture taken. The individual's response was, "I've spent enough time in the Senate to know there's nothing they resent more than presumptuousness."[32]

The new chairman of the Senate Armed Services Committee, which would examine Tower's credentials and make a recommendation to the full Senate, was Sam Nunn (D-GA), hardly a Tower supporter. He met with Bush and told him that this was not the job for Tower—a job where one would "have to be with it" twenty-four hours a day.[33] There were also concerns about Tower's connections to defense contractors, some of whom he had worked for as a consultant after his resignation from the Senate (administration documents suggest that between 1986 and 1988, Tower had earned $1,028,777 from his consulting services).[34] And there were rumors that Tower had improperly used leftover funds from his previous Senate campaigns for his personal benefit following his retirement. Added to this was the resentment on Capitol Hill from the Iran-Contra investigation, of which Tower had been a part (William Webster, then Bush's director of Central Intelligence, recalled that Congress was "just full of bitterness as to how they had been hustled").[35] The Tower nomination was in trouble from the start.

Brady, Fuller, and Teeter reportedly tried to come up with a "consensus alternative" to Tower at Defense but failed. It hardly mattered. Bush wrote in his memoirs that he held "some slight reservations" about Tower.[36] If so, he never let them show. Despite the lengthy list of allegations, Bush stayed loyal to his friend. In fact, he seemed to have little interest at all in Tower's personal life. After a delay in announcing the nomination—a delay that many advisers told Bush would weaken Tower's chances—Bush named Tower to Defense on 16 December. Bush told the press, "I am totally satisfied . . . because the investigation was extensive. . . . I believe this matter is now totally concluded."

On 11 January 1989, Ronald Reagan gave his televised Farewell Address to the nation. In a wistful tone, Reagan ticked off what he considered to be the accomplishments of his administration, paying particular attention to the new, close relationship with Mikhail Gorbachev and the Soviet Union that the two men had brokered during the last two years of Reagan's tenure. When referring to the domestic scene, he modestly claimed that "they called it the 'Reagan Revolution,' and I'll accept that, but for me it always seemed more like the 'Great Rediscovery'—a rediscovery of our values." Yet one theme contained a rather ironic warning, given the tone of his presidency—that simple patriotism was not enough to guarantee the survival of the American nation and that Americans also had to depend upon their history: "If we forget what we did, we won't know who we are. . . . I am warning of an . . . eradication of . . . the American memory that could result, ultimately, in an erosion of the American spirit." Reagan left office with the highest approval rating of any American president since World War II.[37]

The new administration formally began on Friday, 20 January 1989. It was the 200th anniversary of the inauguration of George Washington; and to celebrate, Bush rested his hand on the Bible used by Washington, as well as on the Bush family Bible, as he was sworn in as the nation's forty-second president. Wearing a business suit (a small flap occurred when he announced he would not wear the formal morning coat that had been worn during each of Reagan's two inaugurations), Bush had trouble repressing a smile of satisfaction as he read the oath. Surrounded on the dais at the West Front of the Capitol by friends and family, the effusive Bush could not resist saying hello to them; even as the twenty-one-gun salute blasted in the background, the audio feed of the ceremony picked up the new president shouting, "Hey, Jack! Hey, Danny!"

Bush's inaugural address was, for the most part, a labored affair. His delivery was halting, as he often paused for what he seemed to think would bring applause, and when none came, he hesitatingly plowed on. But the speech was a rather well-written piece that highlighted the themes of the transition. After announcing that he was pleased to be talking to the nation on "democracy's front porch—a good place to talk as neighbors and friends," Bush announced that "my first act as president is a prayer," which he read word for word and which had as its chief message the hope that he could "use power to help people . . . help us remember, Lord, Amen." This, and his slow conversational style, helped to emphasize a departure from the Bush of the campaign, as he announced that a purpose of his administration would be "to make kinder the face of the nation and gentler the face of the world."

After perfunctory comments on the successes of the Reagan years (including what soon became a highly ironic observation—that "the day of the dictator is over"), the speech became a thinly veiled criticism of Reagan's legacy, to the point where one observer claimed that Nancy Reagan had to be nudged because her face was betraying so much anger. Bush repeated the phrases "a new breeze is blowing" and "there is much to do" several times, which brought applause. Specifically, he reminded Americans that "we have a deficit to bring down. We have more will than wallet, but will is what we need. We will make the hard choices." He warned that "America is not the sum of her possessions. They are not the measure of our lives." He promised to help the "homeless, lost and roaming" and that his administration would have a "new engagement in the lives of others—a new activism." As part of this engagement, Bush called for a "new bipartisanship" with Congress. In fact, the most boisterous applause came when he observed that his presidency would usher in the "age of the offered hand . . . the American people await action; they didn't send us here to bicker."

Yet for the first weeks of the administration, bickering from Washington was what the American public got. Although the Tower nomination had been in trouble from the start, it nevertheless needs to be seen in the light of Bush's inaugural promise to make his administration more ethical than had been Ronald Reagan's. The *New York Times* nicknamed the Bush administration "The Untouchables" after the incorruptible team of federal agents who chased gangsters during prohibition.[38] In one of his first acts as president, Bush issued an executive order creating a bipartisan commission chaired by ambassador to Uruguay Malcolm R. Willey to examine the laws that governed executive appointees and members of Congress.* And only a few days after the inauguration, Bush had declared a National Ethics Week.[39] There was considerable discussion among Bush's aides as to whether the issue of ethics had been hammered home too hard, thus creating the impression that the administration was challenging the press to find anything wrong.

Problems close to home seemed to confirm that assessment. First, press reports claimed that White House counsel C. Boyden Gray, who had played a role in appointing Timothy Muris to the Federal Communications Commission, had nonetheless kept a financially lucrative chairmanship of the Summit Communication Group, which owned sixteen radio stations and had some 130,000 cable television subscribers throughout the South. Gray, son of a Bush friend who had been a member of the Eisenhower cabinet, had been one of Bush's closest personal aides since the vice presidency. Given the stridency of his position on the subject, however, Bush could ill afford to be seen as tolerating any ethical impropriety, no matter how small, on his staff. When the possible conflict of interest was made public, Gray resigned his chair and put his assets in a blind trust.[40] Not even Jim Baker was immune to scrutiny; after charges of a conflict of interest similar to Gray's emerged in the press, Baker sold all his stock holdings.[41] Maureen Dowd of the *New York Times* wryly observed that the White House was so worried about its ethical image that an aide had told her in all seriousness that the president never cheated at tennis.[42]

Such a climate hardly would be charitable to the Tower nomination. The early part of the confirmation hearings bears out Tower's desire to present himself as a moderate alternative to Reagan's defense secretaries, each of whom had pushed for the arms buildup. Tower testified that he would counsel the new president to abandon Star Wars, noting that it would be impossible to build a shield that "can protect the entire American people from nuclear incineration." He also promised to pare the Pentagon's budget: "I am not such a mindless hawk that I would come to you and ask for a substantial increase in defense expenditures when I know that is not going to happen."[43]

But Tower's stand on defense policy did not interest the Armed Services Committee. Despite the fact that he no longer had any equity interest in any of his former clients, the committee pressed for an accounting of his dealings with defense contractors. In this, Tower did not help his own

---

*The committee's report, issued on 10 March 1989, recommended the tightening of the federal ethics laws. But the report also warned that "laws alone will not do the job. Officials must emphasize ethics and lead by example." After an initial public relations splash, the report was ignored (see *NYT*, 11 March 1989, p. 7).

cause any. At one point, he professed to having trouble remembering whether he had advised a unit of British Aerospace on the sales of military systems to the Pentagon, even though during a 1987 divorce deposition, he claimed that he had.[44] It was, however, the issue of his drinking that was the most damaging. On 31 January, Paul Weyrich, a conservative activist, testified that he had seen Tower drunk on several recent occasions. The next day, in open session, Tower responded to a question from Chairman Nunn as to whether he had a problem with alcohol with a flat denial: "I have none, Senator. I am a man of some discipline."[45] On 7 February Nunn surprised no one when he announced that he would vote to oppose the nomination.

Several of Bush's aides—including, according to one report, Boyden Gray—counseled him at this point to withdraw the nomination. House minority whip Richard Cheney (R-WY) unequivocally told Dan Quayle, "Tower's down the tubes. You've got to find someone to work with Congress."[46] But Bush would not budge. The day after Nunn's announcement, the president met informally with reporters in the Oval Office. One reporter described him as "fired up" and quoted the president as saying, "I have seen nothing, not one substantive fact that makes me change my mind about John Tower's ability to be secretary of defense." Bush also remarked, "I'm not mad. I'm calm and content. I don't get mad."[47] On 21 February Bush wrote a friend in Washington, "I'm going to stand with Tower all the way, and I am confident he will make it. I have never seen such a campaign of innuendo, vicious rumor, and gossip in my entire life . . . [but] I am not considering alternatives."[48] Indeed, Bush had already begun his counterattack. A White House aide went before the press to claim that Tower was limiting his intake of wine on doctor's orders, and Tower's own doctor announced that he had seen no signs of alcohol damage during a recent operation on Tower for cancer.[49]

Nevertheless, on 23 February, by a straight party-line vote, Nunn's Armed Services Committee voted 11 to 9 to give the nomination a negative recommendation.[50] The majority report admitted that Tower "has a substantial understanding of national security policy and international security affairs." However, the committee believed that his "excessive use of alcohol would disqualify him from being assigned to many sensitive positions in the Department of Defense," that his work as a consultant "created the appearance of using inside information for private gain," and, although it evidenced "no findings of liaisons with female foreign nationals, and hence, no security violations that such activities would entail," the committee claimed that it did discover "some examples of personal conduct which the committee found indiscreet and which call into question Senator Tower's judgment."[51]

Bush, however, continued to show no signs of withdrawing the nomination. After the committee vote, he told the press: "I stand strongly with John Tower. I know of nobody else whose knowledge in defense matters can equal his." His immense loyalty to Tower was certainly one reason, as was his desire not to surrender to the Democratic Congress on their first test of strength. And this was not a passive commitment—once the committee recommendation had been sent to the Senate, Bush actively lobbied Capitol Hill in favor of Tower. As one example of Bush's faithfulness, on 28 February, his entire day—from 8:30 A.M. to 6:00 P.M.—was filled with a series of appointments with eleven senators to try to persuade them to vote for Tower.[52] For his part, Tower decided to take his case to the people, but it didn't help. On Sunday, 3 March, in appearances on all three major Sunday morning television political talk shows, Tower promised that if confirmed, he would not take a drink while on the cabinet.[53] Virtually no one believed him. Tower had become a national joke, but Bush still refused to withdraw the nomination.

The brawl then shifted to the floor of the Senate, where minority leader Bob Dole decided that if the nomination was going to be defeated, the Democrats would have to pay. The day of the vote on the Armed Services Committee, Dole threw down the gauntlet: "If you want to kill somebody around here, just start piling up the garbage . . . eventually it begins to smell."[54] For the Democrats, the vote was the first test of the leadership of new Senate majority leader George Mitchell. The Maine native, a former federal judge and former federal prosecutor, had been elected to the leadership post three months earlier. Bush later called him "as fierce a partisan as I've come up against."[55] But for all the rhetoric—and it was as ugly as had been seen in Congress in many a day—the issue was never really in doubt. Mitchell only had to hold his lines. Of the Democratic senators, only Howell Heflin of Alabama, Christopher Dodd of Connecticut (Tower had voted against Dodd's father's censure by the Senate), and Lloyd Bentsen of Texas broke ranks to support Tower. On the Republican side, Nancy Kassebaum of Kansas voted against the confirmation. Thus, on 9 March, the final vote against confirmation was 53 to 47; it was the first time that the Congress had rejected a cabinet nomination since 1959.[56]

The next day, Bush announced that his new choice at Defense was the four-term congressman from Wyoming Richard Cheney. Bush and Baker had both known the forty-nine-year-old Cheney from their days in the Ford White House, where he had served as chief of staff. More hawkish than Tower, Cheney had been a consistent supporter of the Reagan arms buildup and was an outspoken supporter of the Nicaraguan Contras. He had served as the ranking Republican on the House committee that had investigated the Iran-Contra affair and had recently been promoted to a leadership role as House minority whip. A complete contrast to the voluble Tower, Cheney's hallmark was a complete lack of pretention (when his press secretary saw the nameplate "Richard B. Cheney" on the door to the secretary's new office, he remembered thinking that it would have to be changed, because "he's not a 'Richard B.' kind of guy. It would have to be 'Dick'").[57] A careful politician—Colin Powell remembered that he "never show[ed] more surface than necessary"[58]—he was well liked on both sides of the aisle, and quick confirmability was now the number-one priority. When the position was offered him, Cheney jumped at the chance. (He later remembered, "[Did I want] four more years in the minority in the House, or did I want to go downtown and run the Department of Defense?"[59]) The only serious question at the confirmation hearings was about the state of Cheney's health; since 1978 he had had three heart attacks and quadruple bypass surgery. The Armed Services Committee voted unanimously to confirm, and on 17 March the full Senate followed suit, 92 to 0. Cheney was sworn in that day.

Cheney was uniformly accepted as a good choice, but this made the pill that Bush had to swallow no less bitter. One week after the defeat, Bush sent Tower an autographed photo of his original cabinet choices, including Tower, with the inscription: "John: This is the way it should have been."[60]

Thus the "character issue" became the business of the day. Members of the administration stumbled over each other in a race to show that they had divested themselves of any financial conflict of interest, and every major politician pontificated for the camera on the importance of protecting "ethics in government."[61] But for the Republicans, exacting political revenge for the Tower defeat was as real a concern. In the attacks that followed, the nation was treated to an ethical wrestling match on Capitol Hill—a bloodletting of accusation, innuendo, and pious condemnation that had not been witnessed since the days when McCarthyism reigned supreme in the early 1950s. The attack was led by the abrasive and brilliant Newt Gingrich of Georgia. The former history professor and conservative Republican tied his considerable ambition to the issue of ethics. He was particularly interested in ferreting out Democratic violators, declaring that "to do nothing is to surrender."[62]

As the newly, and narrowly, elected replacement for Cheney as house minority whip, Gingrich led the charge against the Republican's first target: "We are going to ask Nunn, 'If you couldn't stomach Tower at the Department of Defense, how do you feel about Jim Wright being second in line to the president?'"[63] Like Tower, Speaker of the House James Wright

(D-TX) was quite vulnerable to attack. In the words of the most complete chronicler of Wright's fall from political grace, "One thread connected all of Wright's life—hubris."[64] Among other accusations, Wright was charged with evading limits on outside income by persuading people who heard him speak to buy copies of his autobiography instead of paying him an honorarium. He was also charged with taking $145,000 in improper gifts from a Texas businessman, listing them instead as gifts to his wife. Wright's defense lasted through the spring (one Republican staffer gloated that "the only thing better than a dead speaker is a weak speaker"), until he finally resigned on 31 May. In a defiant final speech to the House, Wright urged an end to the "mindless cannibalism" that was taking place on Capitol Hill in the name of ethics.

But no immediate end was in sight, as both parties attempted to corner the market on ethical purity in time for the 1990 midterm elections. The new Speaker of the House, Thomas Foley (D-WA), had to defend himself against charges of homosexuality, charges that were brought into the public eye by a memo from the Republican National Committee entitled, "Tom Foley: Out of the Liberal Closet." The memo had been approved by Mark Goodin, communications director at the RNC; many people also believed that Lee Atwater, the new chairman of the RNC, had approved its release. After the memo was made public, a furious Bush, who wanted to maintain good relations with Foley, reprimanded Atwater, and Goodin was forced to resign.[65]

Before the end of the summer, Gingrich found himself in the crosshairs, charged with improperly benefiting from the sales of a videotaped teaching package. In August, Cong. Barney Frank (D-MA) admitted to a reported dalliance with a male prostitute; he was formally reprimanded by the House the following July.[66] In November, as part of the fallout from the Savings and Loan scandal (see chapter 6), five senators were investigated for giving preferential-treatment aid to Charles Keating, the head of the doomed Lincoln Savings and Loan. In May 1990, Sen. David Durenburger (D-MN) faced charges that included exceeding the honoraria limits set by the Senate (in any one year, 40 percent of a senator's salary), converting campaign contributions for personal use, and violating Senate rules on personal travel; he was formally denounced by the Senate by a vote of 96 to 0 that July.[67]

The ethics frenzy of 1989–1990 was more than a tempest in a teapot. It was another part of the saga of the grassroots anger directed at all politicians at all levels that fed support for the candidacy of Ross Perot only two years later. But the immediate problem for the Bush administration was that the ethics battle threatened to obscure the president's attempts to develop a coherent set of domestic and foreign policies. Certainly Bush did not want to continue reading such critics as the *Washington Post* writers David Hoffman and Ann Devroy, who in March 1989 concluded that his administration was a ship without a rudder.[68]

5

★ ★ ★ ★ ★

"A LIMITED AGENDA"

Most observers of the Bush administration have been critical of what they perceive as its lack of a unified social agenda; one political scientist has called Bush's tenure the "free-form presidency."[1] But such criticisms ignore political realities. The obstacles in the way of White House success with its domestic policies were formidable. Primarily, the Democrats had a ten-vote majority in the Senate, and an eighty-nine-vote majority in the House. And even those numbers were soft; congressional Republicans felt themselves to be less beholden to George Bush than to Ronald Reagan, and conservative Republicans, who had never fully trusted Bush, lay in wait to make sure that his agenda did not betray the gains of the Reagan Revolution, particularly when it came to Bush's promise not to raise taxes. But the president faced other obstacles, including a Supreme Court that proved itself to be surprisingly resistant to claims of constitutionality for conservative legislation and the massive budget deficit, which made any broad social agenda simply too expensive to implement.

It would have been foolhardy for Bush to have sent a massive, not to mention costly, domestic package to the hill. So he didn't. Rather than wage a domestic war with Congress to gain passage of a large agenda, he chose to fight isolated battles—in the words of John Sununu, "a limited agenda."[2] There was no domestic or social package even remotely comparable to a New Frontier, a Great Society, or even a New Federalism. Indeed, victories were few on the domestic front for the Bush administration, and when they came they resulted more often from the shrewd use of the power of the veto than from the skillful presentation and defense of a White House initiative.

In a situation where Democrats outnumbered the Republicans on Capitol Hill, the veto was the most formidable weapon in the White House legislative arsenal. In 1989 the majority Democrats needed to have 218 of 262 of their number vote in favor of a measure to pass a bill in the House; in the Senate, they needed 51 of their 57 votes. But Bush needed to keep only 34 of his 43 Republican votes to sustain a veto in the Senate. These numbers were largely responsible for his success in using the veto: in four years, Bush vetoed forty-four bills, and his veto was upheld forty-three times.*

As a result of his successes with the veto, Bush was able to use the threat of it to affect how legislation was constructed. As of 25 July 1991, the White House Press Office had recorded thirty-eight threats of a presidential veto of legislation; the vast majority of the legislation on the list did not ever become law.[3] The administration also recognized that with a veto strategy, timing was everything. Whenever it wanted to threaten a veto of a piece of legislation, it did so quickly, in a memo to the Congress, so that there was time to amend the legislation toward a point of view more acceptable to the administration.[4]

The veto, or threat of same, allowed Bush to put a conservative cast on legislation that was, in its original form at least, marked by the liberal slant of the Democratic Congress. One of the best examples was the fight over the minimum wage. In early March 1989, the Senate Labor and Human Resources Committee, chaired by Edward Kennedy (D-MA), approved a plan to raise the minimum wage from $3.35 an hour to $4.65 an hour.[5] Bush told a *Washington Post* reporter, "There will be no compromise with me on the amount of the minimum wage," and he threatened a veto of any figure over $4.25 an hour.[6] On 23 March the House voted to raise the minimum wage to $4.55; the Senate followed suit in May. Tony Coehlo, the Democratic whip, stated the political stakes: "If he vetoes this, the American people will have to judge whether he is being kinder and gentler toward working people or some other group of Americans."[7] On 13 June, in his first veto as president, Bush sent the legislation back to Congress. The next day, the veto was sustained, falling thirty-seven votes short of the two-thirds necessary to override.[8] The following November, Bush and the Senate agreed on a compromise; the minimum wage would rise to $3.80 in 1990 and to $4.25 in 1991.[9]

Bush's victories with the veto were significant. But on other, much testier social issues, the veto was not enough, as Bush faced not only a recalcitrant Congress but also a Supreme Court that, in a shock to many

---

*The only time that a Bush veto was overridden was on the Cable Television Protection and Competition Act of 1992.

observers, turned out to be an adversary, rather than an ally, of a conservative president.

One cartoon published during the 1988 campaign depicted Bush so tightly wrapped in the American flag that he was gasping for air. Unquestionably, Bush and Atwater magnified the Pledge of Allegiance issue so as to paint Dukakis as a liberal, but no one ever needed to exaggerate George Bush's patriotism. At his Presidential Museum in College Station, Texas, visitors can listen to a tape-recorded message from Bush, which gives them a guided tour of a mock-up of his Camp David study. During that tour, the study's flag is bathed in a spotlight, as Bush, with obvious passion in his voice, tells his audience, "I feel emotional when I see it. . . . This flag symbolizes a lot of wonderful things about the United States of America."[10]

On 21 June 1989, the Supreme Court issued its ruling in *Texas v. Johnson*. In its 5 to 4 decision, the justices declared that burning an American flag during protest is a form of symbolic speech protected by the First Amendment. For the majority, Justice William Brennan wrote that "the government may not prohibit the expression of an idea simply because society finds the idea itself offensive or disagreeable." The ruling invalidated all state flag-desecration laws (all states besides Alaska and Wyoming had one) and galvanized Bush into action. When he heard of the *Texas* decision, Bush reportedly "responded with blunt words" and "simmered" for a week.[11] He then announced that he would seek an amendment to the Constitution protecting the American flag.

With memories of the 1988 election still fresh, many observers were dubious about Bush's intent and charged that he was trying to make the amendment into an issue for the upcoming congressional campaign. Regardless, Bush seemed to be on solid political ground: a poll showed that 78 percent of the public agreed with him. The amendment, however, was opposed by Speaker Thomas Foley, who called it "unnecessary."[12] Foley instead supported the Flag Protection Act of 1989, which called for essentially the same thing as Bush's proposed amendment. The measure passed the Senate, 91 to 9, on 15 October. As a result, interest in a congressional amendment temporarily died, until the following February, when a federal judge ruled the new law unconstitutional.[13] The administration immediately had its solicitor general, Kenneth Starr, appeal the decision to the Supreme Court. On 11 June, in *U.S. v. Eichmann,* the Court upheld the decision of the federal court, thus declaring the Flag Protection Act unconstitutional.

The Court's decision in *Eichmann* led to a renewed public outcry for a constitutional amendment, but Foley continued to oppose the step. As a result of Foley's personal engagement on the issue, and his argument that time would defuse the issue without the need to change the Constitution, the proposed amendment fell to defeat on 21 June, 254 to 177—34 votes short of the two-thirds needed to send the amendment to the state legislatures. Five days later, in its final gasp, the amendment went down to defeat in the Senate, 58 to 42. The only bright spot for the administration was the continued belief that in a replay of 1988, the Republicans would be able to use the flag-burning issue against the Democrats in the upcoming congressional elections. They hoped that the abortion issue would afford them the same opportunity.

A desire to reverse the 1973 finding of the Supreme Court in *Roe v. Wade* had long been the litmus test for the conservative wing of the Republican party. Yet despite the heat of the rhetoric, the rate of abortions did not significantly decline during the Reagan years, and abortion foes privately voiced their concerns over his commitment to the cause. Conservatives were not sure what to expect from Bush on the issue. Early on in his career he had been outspokenly pro-choice, but he had reversed himself on the issue in 1980 at the explicit request of Reagan (Erica Jong quipped that "Mr. Bush apparently changed his views on abortion once, for political reasons, when he joined the Reagan team. He can change them again, and join the human race").[14] In a 1986 letter to John Lofton of the *Washington Times*, Bush protested that "frankly, while I have long opposed abortion, there has been an evolution in my thinking on the legal means by which we protect the sanctity of human life." His solution was the "adoption of a constitutional amendment to overturn *Roe v. Wade* and the effort for a human life amendment."[15] Yet while the 1988 Republican platform was firmly pro-life and Bush's statements on the issue during the campaign were also, there was a nagging doubt in the conservative community that, like Reagan, Bush was not wedded to the cause.

Those fears seemed to become reality when Bush appointed Louis Sullivan, a pro-choice advocate, as secretary of health and human services. Only after Sullivan publicly reversed his position was he confirmed by the Senate, but his nomination seemed to be a sign that Bush could not be trusted on the issue of abortion. Bush attempted to allay conservative fears by contacting leading pro-life members of Congress, telling them that he supported the Mexico City policy, which allowed federal funding for organizations that agreed to provide contraceptive services but refrained from promoting abortion. He also declared that he would not agree to fund the United Nations Fund for Population Activities (UNFPA) as long as those monies continued to support programs involving compulsory abortion.[16]

On 3 July 1989, in one of the most anxiously awaited decisions in modern memory, the Supreme Court ruled in *Webster v. Reproductive Health Services of Missouri*. In deciding to hear a case regarding a Missouri law that legislated strong restrictions on abortion, the Court had its opportunity to reverse *Roe*. It did not do so. In *Webster*, the Court gave back to the states the authority to impose new restrictions on abortions, but it stopped short of completely overturning *Roe*. This was a shock to the conservative community, made all the more troubling because two usually conservative votes on the bench made it clear that they saw no need to overturn *Roe*. Justice Sandra Day O'Connor, the swing vote in the majority, wrote in her concurring opinion that the Court saw "no necessity to accept the state's invitation to reexamine the validity of *Roe v. Wade*." And Chief Justice William Rehnquist argued that "nothing in the Constitution requires states to enter or remain in the business of performing abortions." Nevertheless, *Webster* did open up the very real possibility that the impact of *Roe* would be moderated on a state-by-state basis; *U.S. News and World Report* reported that twenty-seven states were likely to enact more restrictions on abortions.[17]

The official White House reaction to *Webster* was a positive one: "The Court appears to have begun to restore to the people the ability to protect the unborn."[18] But in reality, the Court had rebuffed the administration, which had presented a significant and detailed amicus curiae brief in favor of using *Webster* to overturn *Roe*. The *Webster* defeat prompted Bush to announce his support of an anti-abortion amendment to the Constitution.[19] There was little hope of the Democratic Congress sending such an amendment to the states, and it did not happen.

Indeed, quite the opposite occurred, as Congress began to bombard Bush with legislation designed, within the federal guidelines set by *Webster*, to loosen federal restrictions on legislation. Bush vetoed them all—ten of his forty-four vetoes were of abortion-related bills—and he threatened to veto many more. For Bush, his yardstick was both a moral and a financial one, as he explained in a 4 June 1991 letter to Bob Dole:

> Given the importance of this issue, I am writing to make sure there is no misunderstanding of my views or convictions. I have not reached these decisions easily or lightly. Abortion is a difficult, deeply emotional and very personal decision for all Americans. It is made even more difficult when the underlying issue is whether the government—and ultimately the American taxpayer—is asked to pay for abortions. . . . I will veto any legislation that weakens current law or existing regulations.[20]

His vetoes included the August 1989 bill that would have allowed abortions for poor women whose pregnancies resulted from rape or incest and the District of Columbia Appropriations bill for 1990, which contained a clause whereby appropriated funds would pay for abortions other than those where the life of the mother would be endangered if the fetus was carried to full term. *Ms.* magazine responded on the cover of its August 1989 issue, printing in big red letters, "It's War!" But from the point of view of legislation, Bush won; all his abortion-related vetoes were upheld.

In 1989 the Supreme Court handed down six decisions that severely restricted the ability of employees to control their own destinies on the job. In *Patterson v. McLean Credit Union,* the Court limited how the Civil Rights Act of 1866 could be used to sue for private acts of racial discrimination. And in *Wards Cove Packing Co. v. Atonio,* the Court overturned an eighteen-year-old decision that allowed plaintiffs to charge discrimination by claiming that a business work group did not represent the demographics of the local workforce. This time, the Court's opinion reflected the beliefs of the Bush administration. But the Democratic Congress struck back with the Civil Rights Act of 1990, sponsored by Edward Kennedy, which called for the protection of employees from job discrimination by forcing employers who practiced it to pay significant monetary penalties. Businesses opposed the bill, arguing that it would lead to expensive lawsuits. Even many black leaders opposed it, seeing it as a step back from the civil rights laws of the 1970s. Bush also argued that the threat of lawsuit would lead, de facto, to businesses having to set hiring and promotion quotas for themselves so as to escape litigation. An attempt to broker a compromise measure in time for a state visit from South Africa's Nelson Mandela failed. The Civil Rights Act of 1990 passed the Senate on 17 October, and five days later it was vetoed by Bush, who stated that it would "introduce the destructive force of quotas into our Nation's employment system."

The Civil Rights bill was a white-hot issue in the congressional elections of 1990. Republican Senate incumbent Jesse Helms used it to stave off a strong challenge to his bid for reelection in North Carolina from Democrat Harvey Gantt, the African-American mayor of Greensboro. Helms ran an ad that showed a white man ripping up a job rejection letter ("You needed that job and you were the best qualified, but they had to give it to a minority because of a racial quota"). Also that fall, former Ku Klux Klansman David Duke lost his bid for a Louisiana Senate seat but won 60 percent of the white vote by playing to the quota issue. Republican Pete Wilson used the same issue in his successful race for governor of California.[21] In their wake, Bush was able to defeat an attempt to override his veto, mustering the minimum of thirty-four senators in its support.

Despite Bush's actions against the Civil Rights bill, through most of 1989 and into 1990 his approval rating among blacks was little less than astounding for a Republican president. By March 1990 it reached 63 percent, the highest level of approval for any Republican president in thirty years.[22] John Berlau attributes this support to the measures taken by Bush to reach out to black Americans, despite his opposition to the Civil Rights bill. He cites Bush's appointment of Jack Kemp, well-respected in black communities, as secretary of housing and urban development, the appointment of Colin Powell as the first African-American to head the Joint Chiefs of Staff, and symbolic gestures such as Bush's celebrating Christmas at a black church in 1989.[23] There was also Bush's support of Louis Sullivan, despite pressure to drop him as the nominee to head the Department of Health and Human Services, and Bush's public courtship of Jesse Jackson (Bush invited Jackson to the White House for a second visit in March 1989 and instructed his cabinet members to make themselves accessible to him).[24]

On 20 July 1990, noting that "the strenuous demands of Court work and its related duties . . . appear at this time to be incompatible with my advancing age and medical condition," Justice William Brennan resigned from the Supreme Court, giving Bush his first opportunity to appoint an associate justice to the nation's highest bench.[25] The administration having been rebuffed by the Supreme Court on several major social issues, the choice took on an unusual amount of importance. C. Boyden Gray, a key player in the nomination battle, remembered that Bush originally wanted to appoint Clarence Thomas, then sitting on the DC Court of Appeals, but "both [Attorney General Richard] Thornburgh and I thought Thomas wasn't ready. . . . Bush was very disappointed."[26]

Instead, Bush chose a jurist distinguished by his blandness. David Souter had graduated from Harvard Law School in 1966. He was appointed assistant attorney general for New Hampshire in 1968, then promoted to deputy attorney general by the then attorney general of that state, Warren Rudman. In 1976 Souter replaced Rudman and served as attorney general until his appointment to the Superior Court of New Hampshire in 1978. In 1983 he was once again promoted, becoming an associate justice of the New Hampshire Supreme Court. Souter was well liked by the Reagan administration; indeed, he had been thoroughly vetted for the Supreme Court appointment that eventually had gone to Anthony Kennedy.[27] On 30 April 1990 Bush appointed Souter to the U.S. Court of Appeals for the First Circuit. A bachelor, living the life of a scholarly recluse, Souter's Yankee reticence made him the perfect nominee to face the grilling of the Senate Judiciary Committee. Rob Portman, then an associate counsel to the president, remembered that the White House did indeed view Souter as more confirmable because his personal life was so dull.[28] And, as Chase Untermeyer wrote in his congratulatory note to Souter, "OK, being from New Hampshire helped"—Sununu argued for the appointment.[29]

The White House geared itself up for a battle reminiscent of the last Supreme Court nomination, when Reagan had put forward conservative jurist Robert Bork, and his nomination was picked apart by the Judiciary Committee. Edward Kennedy told the *Boston Globe* that he would be sure to question Souter "to determine whether he possesses a strong commitment to the fundamental values of the Constitution and the Bill of Rights."[30] Kennedy's Democratic colleague on the committee, Patrick Leahy of Vermont, was more forthcoming in his comments to the *Washington Times:* "There will be a lot more to know about him, I guarantee you that."[31]

Leahy was wrong. Branded the "stealth candidate" by pundits, Souter declined to state his stand on abortion to the committee, saying only that he had not yet made up his mind about whether or not he would vote to overturn *Roe*. Supporters of abortion rights asked the Senate Judiciary Committee to reject Souter. There was also a brief hue and cry about a 1988 opinion he had written while on the New Hampshire bench, when his court overturned a rape conviction and ordered a new trial because the woman, who had been portrayed as a barroom flirt, might have "publicly invit[ed] acts [which] occurred closely in time to the alleged sexual assault."[32] But he had impressed the committee; Chairman Joseph Biden (D-DE) told Souter that his testimony had been a "tour de force," and Souter was easily confirmed by the whole Senate.

It was not just the Court or the Congress that hurt Bush's attempts to impact the social arena. Expensive packages, for example, were doomed in a political climate that was so dominated by the budget deficit and the oncoming recession, circumstances that sealed the fate of Bush's education policies.

It is hard to argue that Secretary of Education Lauren Cavasos was understating the case when in May 1989 he released a report saying that education in the United States was "stagnant." The figures were telling: 33.5 percent of the nation's youth did not finish four years of high school; between 1980 and 1985, spending for K–12 education, when seen in comparison to other industrialized nations, had declined. During the same period, the United States had fallen from twelfth to fourteenth place among the sixteen industrialized nations.[33]

The immediate legacy of the Reagan administration to education was twofold. First was the evangelizing style of William Bennett as secretary of education. The second was harsh funding cutbacks; in his final budget, Reagan proposed a freeze in overall education spending. As Bush faced how best to position himself as the "education president" he had promised in his campaign that he would be, he faced a conundrum. This was clearly an area of domestic policy in which he had both a commitment and an interest; however, the budget deficit left him no more room to pay for it than it had left for Reagan.

In a speech to the Joint Session of Congress on 9 February 1989, Bush charged that "when some of our students actually have trouble locating America on a map of the world, it is time for us to map a new approach to education." He called for a $500-million program to reward America's best schools, those he called "merit schools." He also called for the creation of Presidential Awards for the best teachers in every state, the establishment of a new program of National Science Scholars, and the use of magnet schools to allow parents more choice in deciding which schools their children would attend. Throughout the first year, Cavasos and Bush spoke out on the issue of school choice, which the latter had advocated in the 1988 campaign.

Ten years later, Bush could only sigh: "We thought we were pioneering on education—but we couldn't get it through the Congress."[34] Yet this was not the main problem of education reform. Clearly, this was reform on the cheap. Bush simply could not infuse more money into the budget, and he seemed to hope that awards and incentives would make do. But it did not take educators long to begin to fault Bush for not spending money on a real solution to the problem. Further, the emphasis of the plan did not please movement conservatives, such as Gary Bauer, who had served as undersecretary of education before leaving to become one of Reagan's domestic policy advisers: "Without an emphasis on choice, merit pay, values, school discipline, it's going to be hard to win conservatives' support" for the plan.[35]

In an attempt to reinvigorate the issue, Bush took a direction that had not been taken since the administration of Franklin Roosevelt: he turned to the nation's governors. In a 31 July speech to the National Governors' Association, Bush invited the state executives to meet with him in Charlottesville, Virginia, in fall 1989 to discuss educational policy. Only twice before in this country's history had the nation's governors met as a group with a president to address an issue.* The summit, held on 27 and 28 September, was at best a first step. No formal policy plans emanated from their deliberations. Nevertheless, Bush saw the meeting as a triumph. At the end of the

---

*Theodore Roosevelt had met with the governors to discuss the issue of the conservation of natural resources; Franklin Roosevelt had met with them to discuss possible solutions to the depression.

conference, he wrote to one of its attendees, Gov. Bill Clinton of Arkansas: "Well done—oh, so well done. You were a joy to work with on the summit and all our folks feel the same way. I guess partisan politics will strain some relationships in '90 but I really want to keep education reform out there above the fray. I'll try to do that and I know you will continue to do so as well. Great Job. George."[36]

But education was also hostage to the White House's stand on affirmative action. Early in December 1989, the Department of Education ruled that scholarships guaranteed only to minorities were illegal. An explosion occurred in the press, and Cavasos was forced to resign. He was replaced by Lamar Alexander, a former governor of Tennessee who had championed education reform in that state and then gone on to serve as president of the University of Tennessee system. Alexander's appointment was supported by professional educators, who were longing for the days of Bennett's evangelism and were impressed with Alexander's credentials. The appointment seemed to signal a new phase of Bush's education program; but such hopes were premature. Despite reports to the contrary, the

The President's Education Summit with governors, University of Virginia, 28 September 1989. *Left to right:* Booth Gardner (Washington), Terry Branstad (Iowa), Bush, Lauren Cavasos (secretary of education), and Bill Clinton (Arkansas). (Courtesy of the George Bush Presidential Library)

White House refused to back down on its decision to curb college aid that was linked to race.[37]

Just as important was the fact that Bush's education plan, announced in April 1991, was gutted by budget concerns. "America 2000" placed the burden of school improvement squarely on the backs of the localities, who could pledge their desire to reform and be designated an "America 2000 Community." The plan called for voluntary national tests to enforce higher standards and a request to business leaders to raise $150 million to help create at least 535 "break the mold" schools.[38] It received criticism, however, for doing nothing to address the deep issues of segregation and poverty in inner-city schools. But in retrospect, this was not an area that the Bush education plan was designed to address. Again, it was not backed by funds; in virtually every area, the proposed FY 1992 budget cut education spending.[39] Indeed, the letter that Alexander sent to the Senate Appropriations Committee outlining Education 2000, a plan he called a "bold, comprehensive, and a long-term strategy," included a footnote: "No additional amounts are added to the total Department of Education budget to fund America 2000."[40] With no monies at his disposal, Alexander was forced to take to the road to convince Americans that only they could fix their local schools. Alexander claimed that he was leading a "populist crusade"; one critic termed it an "empty public relations exercise."[41]

As with its education policy, the administration's drug policy also had to be fought on the cheap. But in this case, Bush's own political needs had forced him to appoint a "drug czar" who then pushed him to go faster on the issue than he ever wanted to go.

William Bennett, the director of the Office of the National Drug Control Policy, was, in a public forum, the exact opposite of Bush. Garrulous to a fault and eminently quotable, Bennett actively sought out the press, with what many observers at the time felt to be an eye toward a future presidential run of his own. Bennett was also impatient for an instant solution to the drug problem. One reporter remembered that when Bennett was serving as Reagan's secretary of education, he stunned a meeting of the National Drug Policy Board by growling, "Let's send the helicopters into Bolivia again" to destroy any drug sources. An aide called him a "tornado in a wheatfield."[42] Recognizing Bennett's ability but also his desire to find the spotlight, Bush had denied him cabinet status, a slight that by all accounts particularly irked the czar. Bennett had been chosen by Bush because, as Reagan's secretary of education, he had become the darling of the conservative right. Certainly, Bennett's evangelical zeal and hard-line approach to the drug problem appealed to many conservatives who had long felt that Washington—even Reagan—had been too soft on drugs.

It may well have been Bennett's growing celebrity that led Bush to make a public relations blunder of the highest order. When planning his first televised address on the drug issue, Bush himself came up with a gimmick. David Demarest, director of communications and overseer of the speech-writing team, remembers Bush saying; "I haven't seen crack. . . . I bet a whole lot of people haven't."[43] Bush asked David Bates, then his cabinet secretary, to ask the Justice Department to get some legal crack, perhaps from an evidence locker, to use as a prop in the upcoming speech. On 5 September 1989, Bush addressed the nation regarding the release of his first drug plan. Midway through the speech, he held up a small plastic bag: "This is crack cocaine. [It was] seized a few days ago in a park across the street from the White House. . . . It could easily have been heroin or PCP."

The bag did indeed contain three ounces of crack, purchased for $2,400. However, the press soon discovered that four days before the speech, drug enforcement agents [DEA] had lured a suspected drug dealer to Lafayette Park, directly across the street from the White House, so that they could purchase the crack. The president's advisers wanted to be able to say in the speech that drugs were available even within a block of the president's home (even though the park, constantly under the watchful eye of the White House police, rarely saw any drug action). The sale confused even the teen-aged drug dealer recruited from another part of the city by the DEA; when contacted, he reportedly asked, "Where the [expletive] is the White House?" One agent ruefully explained, "We had to manipulate him to get him down there. It wasn't easy."[44]

Almost lost in the press field day that followed the speech was the substance of the drug policy that Bush had outlined. Three areas of Bush's first National Drug Control Strategy represented a significant break from Reagan-era drug policy. The first was an expansion of the criminal justice system by providing funds for larger police forces and increased jail space. Second, the plan called for federal funding to the states for developing alternative sentencing programs for nonviolent drug offenders, including one of Bennett's favorite programs—"boot camps." Third, it advocated a "fresh approach to interdiction"—enhancing border interdiction systems and targeting key individuals and high-value shipments.[45]

The idea of military interdiction particularly appealed to Bush. It is telling that his first major speech on the drug problem came in early March, before the national convention of the Veterans of Foreign Wars in Washington, when he told his audience, "I mean to mobilize all our resources, wage this war on all fronts. We're going to combat drug abuse with education, treatment, enforcement, and, yes, interdiction and yes, with our

Bush addressing the nation on his drug policy, 5 September 1989. (Courtesy of the George Bush Presidential Library)

nation's armed services." In late March, he approved the use of the National Guard in twelve southern and western states to help local law enforcement officials battle the drug trade.[46] Bush even floated a trial balloon when Attorney General Richard Thornburgh publicly suggested that the administration was considering sending troops to Colombia to interdict the drug traffic. However, Bush backed down after it was clear that neither the public nor his drug czar supported such a plan.[47]

Bush's drug policies drew immediate fire from those who believed that the administration should be more concerned with funds for treatment than with funds for enforcement. The administration countered with consistent pleas that there simply was not enough money in the budget to significantly expand both theaters of the drug war. For his part, Bennett agreed with the emphasis placed on enforcement, but he believed that the administration was unwilling to commit the resources necessary for victory. His attendance on the nation's talk shows became ubiquitous, and his outspoken zeal soon put him at odds with the administration, many members of which believed that Bennett was positioning himself for a run for the presidency against Bush in 1992.

In January 1990 Bush asked for a 50 percent increase in funds for the military to control drugs, and the following month he attended a Drug Conference in Colombia, where he promised to consider the request of the Latin American leaders for the United States to subsidize the coca farmers for limiting production.[48] By the end of 1990 the administration had won passage of a bill that offered duty-free treatment for certain articles from Bolivia, Ecuador, Colombia, and Peru.[49] But the drug problem did not disappear. This was hammered home to the public by the January 1990 arrest of Marion Barry, mayor of the District of Columbia, for narcotics possession, and the subsequent public release of FBI videotapes showing Barry smoking crack cocaine in a hotel room with a female acquaintance. In April 1991 the administration declared that the war on drugs had failed in Washington, an assessment with which Bennett took public issue.[50] In November 1990, Bennett left the administration and was replaced by former Florida governor Bob Martinez. Bush announced a new National Drug Strategy in February 1991, which included a proposed 11 percent increase in the budget for health incentives.[51] However, the appropriation was soon taken out of the budget.

Two laws have been listed by Bush supporters as undeniable victories for the administration. One, the Americans with Disabilities Act, was a measure for which the administration deserves less credit than it has to date received. But the other, the Clean Air Act Amendments of 1990, shows

George Bush at his policy-making best and was clearly the administration's most significant victory in the domestic sphere.

The nation's disabled (classified by the government as individuals who have a physical or mental impairment that "substantially limits one or more of [their] major life activities")[52] had not been explicitly covered by the Civil Rights Act of 1964. Of the estimated 43 million Americans with disabilities, a congressional study estimated that the vast majority of them had faced either segregation or discriminatory actions.[53] In the mid-1980s, the National Council on the Handicapped began to push for the Americans with Disabilities Act (ADA), and legislation drafted by Connecticut's Lowell Weicker was already in Congress when Bush became president. The four-part bill forbade employers to discriminate against qualified people with disabilities and required employers to provide adequate access to their businesses for patrons with disabilities. It also called for expanded access to transportation services and required the Federal Communication Commission to provide equivalent telephone services for the speech-and-hearing impaired.[54]

Despite the fact that the ADA was not an administration initiative, Bush strongly supported the bill (several people close to him suggest the reason was that one of his sons had dyslexia and had been subject to discriminatory practices while in school). Bush spoke out in favor of the ADA in his Inaugural Address and early in the administration told the assembled staff of the Department of Housing and Human Services that it was one of his highest domestic priorities.[55] Despite the cost—and it was costly, thus bringing a host of criticism from the businesses that would have to enforce it— Bush was unwavering in his support. On 26 July 1990, he signed the ADA into law.

Boyden Gray later called the ADA "in a sense, the first welfare reform."[56] Certainly there is a point to be made here, and it bears noting that the bill stood to make more active consumers of America's disabled by giving them unfettered access to businesses. Yet the act can also be seen as the first real civil rights reform—in the face of business opposition—supported by a Republican administration since the successful desegregation of southern public schools under Nixon.

In terms of protecting the environment, George Bush was more active than any of his twentieth-century predecessors in the White House, save one. John Turner, the president of the Conservation Fund, claimed that "no president since Teddy Roosevelt has done more to protect the wild heritage of America than George Bush."[57] And the claim is justifiable. Bush was a sportsman who was deeply committed to environmental issues. His professed disgust at the state of Boston Harbor in September 1988 had the ring of truth. Many times during the campaign he voiced a desire to be the "environmental president," and one of his first acts as president-elect was to call a working meeting of thirty of the nation's leading environmental experts.[58] Bush appointed William Reilly as the first professional conservationist to head the Environmental Protection Agency (EPA). In 1989 the agency announced an almost total phaseout of all uses of asbestos by 1991. Bush set aside ninety-three new national wildlife refuges; protected or restored 1.7 billion acres of wetlands; doubled funding for parks, wildlife, and outdoor recreation; and tripled funds to the states under the Land and Water Conservation Fund. His support was the driving force behind the Omnibus Water bill of 1992 to protect the Grand Canyon. And without the support of the Bush White House, the most important piece of environmental legislation of the postwar period—the Clean Air Amendments of 1990—would most likely have stayed mired on Capitol Hill.

In 1970, facing a serious electoral challenge from environmentalist Edmund Muskie, Richard Nixon had created the EPA. Not to be outdone, Muskie called for a bill that would require the automobile industry to make a 90 percent reduction in its total emissions by 1 January 1975 and that would direct the EPA to set air-quality standards for industry and limits on toxic pollutants. The Clean Air Act of 1970 was passed, but there were immediate concerns, not the least of which came from industries worried that they could not meet the government's timetable. Nevertheless, with the support of the Carter administration and the newly elected Democratic Congress, those requirements were extended in 1977, as automobile manufacturers were mandated to reduce nitrogen oxide emissions in cars to a minuscule one gram per mile.

But virtually no major urban community or industry was able to meet the deadlines, which were first extended to 1982 and then to 1987. As Richard Cohen, author of the standard book on the subject, points out, there were several attempts during the Reagan years to amend the 1970 act once again; but they were opposed by John Dingell (D-MI), whose constituents in the Detroit auto business stood to lose millions of dollars if any further restrictions were placed on emissions, and by Robert Byrd (D-WV), whose constituents feared that any further restrictions on factory emissions would reduce the demand for West Virginia bituminous coal. By 1988 a bill had been crafted in committee, but there seemed to be little hope of its passage, except, perhaps, in a severely gutted form.

In his confirmation hearings, Reilly made it clear that the first item on the administration's agenda was legislation to strengthen the Clean Air Act.[59] The administration's desire was inadvertently helped by an environmental tragedy. On 24 March 1989, more than 10 million gallons of oil spilled into Alaska's Prince William Sound when the oil tanker *Exxon Valdez* went aground. The spill affected 6,000 square miles of ocean, stained 800 miles of shoreline, and killed countless seabirds and deer. Bush designated Secretary of Transportation Samuel Skinner as his personal liaison to the cleanup efforts. Skinner's personal involvement was heavy, as he traveled to and from the disaster site many times in spring 1989. *U.S. News and World Report* dubbed him the "firefighter in chief . . . [Bush's] unlikely star."[60] Skinner kept the pressure on Exxon to hold to its responsibilities for the cleanup, which led to criminal charges being brought against the company for its complicity in the accident. Although some environmentalists criticized the administration's role as being too slow and deliberate, the cleanup was terminated on 15 September 1989. It had employed some 11,000 people, 1,400 vessels, and over 100 aircraft and treated some 1,000 miles of shoreline.[61]

The *Exxon Valdez* disaster thus contributed to a climate more favorable to environmental legislation. Sig Rogich wrote Bush that the "public response to the assistance in Alaska has been outstanding here in the West. I think it is setting a broad environmental tone for the administration."[62] Looking to take advantage of the momentum, Bush charged a small working group, which included domestic policy adviser Roger Porter, Boyden Gray, William Rosenberg of the EPA, and Robert Grady, the associate director for resources at OMB, to craft a bill that would break the congressional logjam on Clean Air. On 12 June 1989, the administration announced its proposal to the public.

Yet its passage was not guaranteed. However, George Mitchell, Bush's nemesis from the Tower nomination, took on the challenge. When he became majority leader in 1988, amendments to the Clean Air Act were just as much a priority for Mitchell as they were for Bush. Cohen contends that Mitchell's shepherding the bill to passage was "a personal tour de force rarely matched in Senate history."[63] In the House, much of the credit belonged to New York Republican Sherwood Boehlert, who brokered the compromise measure.[64] But both men were helped at several stages of the effort by threats of a Bush veto, threats that sped the process along.[65] The committee compromise passed the House on 22 October, passed the Senate on 1 November, and Bush signed it into law two weeks later.

The Clean Air Act Amendments of 1990 were a landmark piece of legislation. In a tribute to the administration's lobbying efforts, the legislation as it was passed by the House and the Senate contained the central features of Bush's June 1989 proposal. It detailed provisions to bring all cities into compliance with the National Air Quality Standards for ozone, carbon monoxide, and other pollutants; called for an acid rain control program that would achieve a permanent reduction in sulphur dioxide emissions of 10 million tons by the year 2000; and called for a program to reduce industrial emissions of hazardous air pollutants by 75 to 90 percent in the first phase, using technology-based controls.[66] It boasted advances in tailpipe emissions, controls on local air, and the first constraints on midwestern industrial pollution from coal-fire burners that emitted acid rain. It also cataloged 189 toxic chemicals for which the EPA had to set public health standards to decrease their pollution of the air and offered the first steps for dealing with global warming and the depletion of the ozone layer.

6

★ ★ ★ ★ ★

PAYING FOR REAGANOMICS

By 1989 the bills of the Reagan years had come due with a vengeance. The budget deficit was $2.7 trillion; service on the debt itself was $200 billion a year.[1] At the same time that Bush was struggling to articulate a social and a world vision, he was hamstrung by the need to find a way to balance the budget. And he had promised that he would not raise taxes. But as New Hampshire senator Warren Rudman observed in February of that year when a reporter asked him if he thought there would be a tax hike: "Obviously no promise is forever, none that I know of."[2]

As Robin Toner wrote in the *New York Times* in January 1989, "The business of the 101st Congress is, in a way, painfully simple: the Federal budget and its deficit will drive nearly every issue this year, from the modernization of the land-based leg of the nuclear triad to child care to the savings and loan troubles."[3] The budget deficit hovered as a pall over any attempts by the Bush administration to articulate a domestic and social agenda; it was directly responsible for the administration's disappointments in education policy. Bush's early proposals for narrowing the budget gap offered little hope of success. During the campaign, he had called for a "flexible freeze"—letting spending increase but only at the inflation rate; then, when the economy began to grow faster than inflation, the budget would naturally balance itself. Few people, if any, truly believed that it would work; most believed that the budget could not be balanced unless Bush reneged on his promise not to raise taxes. Both Gerald Ford and

Jimmy Carter, during separate meetings with the president-elect in November, told him as much.[4] Three weeks after the elections, the General Accounting Office publicly stated that new taxes would be needed as a part of any "credible" effort to lower the deficit; one House Democrat referred to Bush's policies as "deja voodoo."[5]

Publicly, at least, Bush refused to discuss the possibility of a tax hike. In fact, in the early months of 1989, he argued for a 50 percent cut in the capital gains tax—taxes levied on the profits made by the sale of stock and other assets—down to 15 percent. Yet at the same time, he could not bring himself to slash discretionary federal spending to make the deficit more manageable. Thus, the prospect was quite real for an imbalanced budget into 1990. But because of the Gramm-Rudman-Hollings Act of 1981, there was a catch: if the White House and Congress could not agree on a budget that kept to deficit reduction targets aimed at a balanced budget by 1993, there would be a mandatory sequester on 1 October 1990, which would require a shutdown of many government services.

Bush later remembered that he "didn't really want to" abandon his pledge not to raise taxes and that he did so only because he felt he had to in order to balance the budget.[6] Many administration alumni ascribe Bush's willingness to accept a tax hike to the influence of Richard Darman, his director of the Office of Management and Budget. Darman's belief that spending cuts alone would not balance the budget were demonstrated by his actions during the Reagan administration. He reportedly helped convince the president to abandon the 1981 tax cut and to adopt "revenue enhancements" to bring the deficit into line. It is likely that Darman gave the same advice to Bush. But Bush wanted to get through at least the first year's budget cycle without raising taxes. On 24 April 1989, Michael Boskin, the chairman of the White House Council of Economic Advisers, hinted at the president's plan:

> We're going to see what happens when we get into negotiations for 1991. . . . We have said all along that we don't see the merits of a tax increase. We're willing to hear that case made in negotiations and discuss it on its merits. The president has said he wanted to make sure he kept that pledge the first year and he is hoping to be able to keep it over a longer period, to the extent that's possible.[7]

The president was successful in keeping his pledge for the first year, thanks to a series of bipartisan congressional negotiations (a new tactic recommended by Darman) and to Bush's calling in of a political marker. After a private meeting, chairman of the House Ways and Means Committee and Bush friend Dan Rostenkowski (D-IL) promised to wait a year before he pressed for a tax hike.[8] As a result, Bush's first budget was completed and passed by the Congress in record time. Abandoning the "flexible freeze," the budget for the 1990 fiscal year, as it was finally approved by Congress, estimated federal spending at $1.16 trillion, with a deficit of $91.1 billion. But analysts immediately began to look forward to the next budget cycle. Don Feder of the *Boston Herald* asked Bush in May 1989 if his no new taxes pledge was only good for one year or, "as many of us expected, the life of the administration?" Bush replied, "It was just a flat pledge, is what I'd say. And I don't think—the way this budget agreement worked out, we don't need a tax increase."[9]

But the battle was far from over. The economic picture continued to darken, making Bush's hopes for a second brokered budget compromise seem very difficult to attain in 1990. By year's end, the Democrats were trying to paint Bush into a corner. Also, George Mitchell made it clear that he would not agree to any cuts in the capital gains tax; New York's senator Daniel Patrick Moynihan called for eliminating Social Security from the budget and reducing the Social Security tax, thus making a balanced budget all but impossible.[10] Moreover, Bush was about to face the prospect of a particularly expensive bailout of the nation's badly mismanaged banking system.

Savings and Loans (S&Ls), or Thrifts, are financial institutions that, like banks, accept deposits and pay interest on them. Unlike most banks, however, S&Ls invest most of their funds in home mortgages. As the market in real estate, especially in the Southwest, boomed throughout the late 1970s and early 1980s, the S&Ls made huge profits for their depositors. However, when the real estate market faltered, as it began to do by 1985, S&Ls began to show signs of trouble, and many began to fold.

Yet it was not just the free market that doomed the Thrifts. Reagan's solution to the oncoming crisis was to deregulate the S&Ls, arguing with Hooverian logic that without government interference they would be able to save themselves. This left them to the mercies of unscrupulous directors and managers who invested depositors' money into get-rich-quick real estate schemes. Many members of Congress were intimately involved with S&Ls in their home districts, and it must also share in the blame. The Garn–St. Germain Act (1982) allowed the S&Ls to expand their lending capabilities beyond home mortgages. It also increased the Federal Deposit Insurance limit from $40,000 to $100,000. Thus, when the banks began to fail, the Congress had made the government a full 150 percent more responsible for the bailout of depositors. In the words of L. William Seidman, head of the Federal Deposit Insurance Corporation (FDIC) under Reagan, the government was "a full partner in a nationwide casino."[11]

By the end of the Reagan administration, the scope of the crisis was astounding. By 1989, 350 S&Ls had gone under. The majority of them were located in New England, where the real estate market had taken a particularly hard beating since 1980, and in the Southwest—147 of the failed S&Ls in 1989 were in Texas alone. Some observers were predicting that the problem would be solved only by massive infusions of federal monies, perhaps between $50 billion and $100 billion. Of course, these figures could be counted on to widen the already cavernous budget deficit.[12]

Bush's initial steps toward dealing with the problem gave the first hint that he was willing to use new taxes to solve the financial crunch. Just before his inauguration, he proposed an annual fee of twenty-five cents for every $100 of insured deposits placed in the custody of an S&L. Sununu and Brady argued that these fees were not taxes, but their arguments lacked credibility. The proposal not only violated Bush's no new taxes pledge, but it clearly would not generate the amount of revenue needed to resolve the problem. Facing bipartisan opposition to the plan, Bush backed away quietly from it.[13]

A more complex plan, one that Bush hoped would lead to the banks themselves paying for most of the bailout, was announced by the president in a 6 February 1989 press conference. It called for raising $50 billion in thirty-year government bonds to help the failing Thrifts. The interest on the bonds—estimated in February at some $36.4 billion over the first ten years—would be shared by both the public and by increasing the insurance premiums paid by banks. The Federal Home Loan Bank Board (FHLBB), which had been the rather ineffective regulator and insurer of the Thrifts, was dissolved. The FHLBB's role as insurer was transferred to the FDIC; its regulatory role was given to a new agency, the Office of Thrift Supervision (OTS).[14]

It bears noting that Bush's plan for saving the S&Ls involved a massive layer of new federal regulatory agencies: this from a president who had both chaired a committee on deregulation as vice president and had campaigned in favor of deregulation in 1988. Nevertheless, the plan offered too little, too late. Within only two weeks' time, the administration was forced to admit that the cost of the bailout would exceed $39.9 billion over the next ten years, and it announced that the government would soon have to spend an additional $24 billion to shut down all the S&Ls that would be closed in the 1990s. Treasury Secretary Nicholas Brady informed Bush that more than 722 banks and 1,037 Thrifts were in danger of closing; by summer, private projections given Bush for the bailout were exceeding $200 billion.[15] Faced with a disaster of unprecedented proportions, Congress passed the Financial Institutions Reform, Recovery, and Enforcement Act in August 1989, but not before it had stripped Bush's original proposal of its bonding plan, thus requiring that the monies come straight from the Treasury. As a result, the bailout plan increased the deficit by $50 billion over three years.[16]

By the end of 1989, the talk around Washington had turned to the inevitable recession, with its resulting high prices and high unemployment. Constrained by a Federal Reserve System that continued to pursue a tight-money policy, the economy was starting to falter. Inflation was creeping up; it had reached 5 percent, up from 4.8 percent in 1988, 3.7 percent in 1987, and 1.9 percent in 1986, the lowest rate in the decade.[17] Smelling blood, congressional Democrats refused to meet with Bush to discuss the budget until he put forth his proposals for FY 1991. That year would see the deadline for sequester and a government shutdown as well as a congressional election that would place a political imperative on the process.

The situation was made even more urgent by a grim reminder of how shaky the economy had become. On Friday, 13 October 1989, investors in the stock market finally reacted to the unstable economic climate. The Dow Jones Industrial Average plunged 190 points, its worst nosedive since 1987. The following Monday, the market recovered about one-half its losses in heavy volume, as the Dow rose by 88.12 points, only to go down another 30 points the next day.[18]

Bush submitted his FY 1991 budget to Congress on 29 January 1990, in the wake of the stock market crash. It called for total expenditures of $1.23 trillion—roughly the size of the entire West German economy. It also called for the reduction of the deficit to $64 billion, the target mandated by the Gramm-Rudman-Hollings Act. Bush proposed to accomplish this without cutting Social Security, with a 2.6 percent reduction in defense spending, and with a reduction in the capital gains tax. However, the administration had quietly included as potential income some $14 billion in "users fees."[19] Though these were technically not taxes, it was clear that Bush was willing to consider some sort of income enhancement in order to get the budget closer to the deficit level required by law. On 11 March Rostenkowski put forth his promised counterproposal: a freeze on all cost-of-living increases in all spending categories, and a fifteen-cent-per-gallon tax hike on gasoline.[20]

On 6 May the congressional principals in the budget negotiations— Speaker of the House Thomas Foley, House majority leader Robert Michel, Senate majority leader George Mitchell, and Senate minority leader Bob Dole—as well as Darman, Sununu, and Brady, attended a talk at the White House given by presidential historian David McCullough. At a prearranged time after the conclusion of the lecture, they quietly retired upstairs to the president's living quarters. The subject was the impasse on the budget. Darman tried to impress upon the group the problems that would be caused by a sequester. Mitchell asked Bush if he was prepared to negotiate on taxes; Bush said yes. Mitchell requested that Bush release a statement to that effect, and Bush agreed. The White House press release declared that the budget talks would begin "with no preconditions." Bush made this point even clearer after a 26 June meeting with the congressional leadership, when he agreed to the need for "tax revenue increases."

In a 1998 interview, Bush was certainly correct when he told me that breaking his promise on taxes "played right into the hands of the opposition, as well as those critics" on the right in his own party.[21] The reaction was both immediate and hostile. The *New York Post* ran the headline, "Read My Lips: I Lied." Conservatives were furious, treating the announcement as the ultimate denial of Reaganism. When he was informed of the decision by Sununu, House majority whip Newt Gingrich angrily hung up on him.[22] From within the administration, the most vocal opponent of the decision was Vice President Quayle, a former member of the Senate Budget Committee.

Meeting on the budget, 6 May 1990. *Left to right:* John Sununu, Richard Darman, Bob Dole, George Mitchell, Robert Michel, Thomas Foley, and Bush. (Courtesy of the George Bush Presidential Library)

In most accounts, Darman is given either the credit or the blame for convincing Bush to adopt new taxes in FY 1991.[23] Darman argues in his memoirs that he tried to convince Bush to commit to new taxes earlier, and he lists several meetings where he gave the president that counsel. [24] The question, however, was never whether Bush was going to change his mind; from the earliest moments of the administration, he had resigned himself to new taxes in FY 1991. And just as important was the fact that there was unanimity on this point within the negotiating group; even Gingrich was reported to have proposed a five-year deficit-reduction package tied to new taxes.[25] However, one can question the timing of the administration's announcement that it would support new taxes. It is arguable that had Bush moved earlier, he might well have been better able to deal with the inevitable political fallout. Darman suggests that the way that the release was worded hurt. He concedes that "we allowed the president to make his biggest possible concession publicly without, at the same time, announcing a complete substantive compromise."[26] Bush had allowed himself to go into the budget negotiations having already taken the full public blame for the new taxes. As the administration and Congress began to haggle over the final details of the budget, this position seriously weakened the president's hand.

Darman described the final stages of budget negotiations, with the summiters holed up at Andrews Air Force Base, as "tragicomedy . . . a farce."[27] Perhaps. But the political stakes had never been higher. The end of the fiscal year would come on 1 October; if it came without a budget agreement, the federal government would technically have to shut down. Moreover, the congressional elections were but four months away, and Republicans and Democrats alike were beginning to distance themselves from a budget process that had by then met with virtually unanimous criticism in the press.

For his part, Bush detested the acrimony and viciousness of the negotiations, so he delegated the duty. In his diaries, he wrote, "I much prefer foreign affairs. I salute Sununu and Darman for doing it."[28] For the most part, Sununu and Darman presented a unified front, with Brady taking a minor role. Not surprisingly, it was Sununu who served as the administration's lightning rod. The day after the White House announced that a tax hike was on the table, the *Washington Post* reported that a "senior White House official traveling on a plane from Costa Rica to Washington"— Sununu—claimed that this development meant that the Democrats could propose new tax increases, but Bush would simply veto them.[29] Press Secretary Marlin Fitzwater hastened to assure the press that there were no preconditions to any negotiations, and the congressional leadership wailed about the breach of trust. But none of this seemed to matter to Sununu. He reportedly threatened Republican congressmembers, hinting that Bush would campaign against fellow Republicans if they did not get into line. For example, after Trent Lott (R-MS) questioned the president's decision on taxes, only to be upbraided by the negotiating team, Sununu declared, "Trent Lott has become an insignificant figure in this process." Democrats privately referred to Bush's negotiating team as "Nick, Dick, and Prick."[30]

Bush tried to hasten the distasteful process by using his bully pulpit. He indicated his strategy in his diary on 7 September: "I just hope that Iraq and the country's unity can now be parlayed into support for the budget agreement."[31] On 10 September he spoke to the Congress regarding the 2 August invasion of Kuwait by Iraq, and the status of the American buildup in the region, by this point code-named DESERT SHIELD. After reporting on the status of American forces in the Persian Gulf, Bush shifted gears, proclaiming that domestic policy was inexorably tied to foreign affairs—"a woven piece, strongly bound as Old Glory"—and declared, "We must address our budget deficit—not after election day, not next year, but *now*." He continued, "The Gulf situation helps us realize that we are more economically vulnerable than we ever should be. . . . It is high time we pull together and get the job done right. . . . This is no time to risk America's ability to defend her vital interests." While this section of the speech was met with sporadic applause from the assembled legislators, close observers noticed that Foley, sitting behind Bush in the Speaker's chair, did not applaud once.

It would take more than an appeal to patriotism to break the impasse on the budget. On 25 September Bush told reporters that if there was no budget agreement "with real spending reduction and real process reform by the end of the week, I will have to veto it."[32] But this time, the threat of a presidential veto did not work. The next day, despite later attempts to spin the budget deal as a compromise, it was clear that it was Bush who had surrendered. On 26 September the budget summiters gathered in the Rose Garden to announce the fruit of their labors. The proposed budget agreement would, they claimed, cut $119 billion from entitlement and mandatory programs and $182 billion from discretionary programs (taken primarily from defense, which would be reduced by $67 billion over three years). It also called for a cap on all discretionary spending and a "pay as you go" system that required new programs to be paid for at the time that they were initiated. But the plan also called for an increase in tax revenues of $134 billion; the largest portion would be raised by a phased-in increase in gasoline taxes, starting with a five-cent-per-gallon hike in the first year. Bush protested, "I do not welcome any such tax measure. . . . However, this one does have the virtue not only of contributing to deficit reduction, but also, over time, of decreasing America's dependence on foreign oil—an objective whose importance has been made increasingly evident in the face of the Iraqi invasion of Kuwait." The next day Bush signed a continuing resolution to keep the government going, pending the passage of a budget resolution that reflected the summit agreement.

Darman later pointed out that the tax increase called for in the 1990 budget agreement was less than one-half of Reagan's 1982 tax increase.[33] This was true enough, but it was hardly the point. By the time the agreement was announced, Republican conservatives were fully up in arms against the tax hike. Gingrich deserted the process (he refused to come out to the Rose Garden and stand with the rest of the leadership when the agreement was announced to the press) and began to actively construct a coalition against the package.[34] Embittered, Bush recalled in his memoirs: "Years later [Gingrich] told me that his decision was one of the most difficult he had made in his life. Maybe so, but it sure hurt me. His support could have eliminated the flak I took on the tax question and on my credibility."[35] Led by Gingrich, conservative Republicans flocked en masse to join House Democrats in opposing the measure. On 5 October, the Congress rejected the budget plan. The next day, the House passed a second continuing resolution, and Bush immediately vetoed it, telling the press: "Three dozen continuing resolutions—business as usual—and we can't have it."

It was past the 1 October deadline set by the Gramm-Rudman-Hollings Act, and Bush's veto kicked in the mandatory sequester. For three days the government was shut down. This affected mostly tourist attractions such as the national parks; the military buildup in the Persian Gulf was specifically exempted. Nevertheless, the public was furious, and it directed its anger—not entirely fairly, since the process was then in congressional hands—at the White House. Bush was forced on 9 October to sign a second continuing resolution, providing the funds for the government to operate through 19 October. Over that two-week period, Congress jettisoned most of the gasoline tax provided for in the summit agreement and replaced it with a hike in income taxes for the most wealthy Americans (from 28 percent to 31.5 percent). Congress passed this budget—the Omnibus Budget Reconciliation Act of 1990—in late October. But even with these changes, the Gingrich-led conservatives were not placated; only one-quarter of the Republicans in both houses backed the measure.[36] On 27 October, Bush signed it.

Bush tried to put the best face on what had been a humiliating defeat. He told the press, "It was a good plan. It got done what I wanted done, which was a $500 billion reduction over five years—real enforcement. Didn't get everything I wanted. Had to compromise." A White House Fact

Sheet claimed that the "only thing that went right" in the process was Bush's determination to "hold the line." It noted that the $500 billion in deficit reduction included $355 billion in spending cuts—"the largest cut in history"—and that Congress "agree[d] to put itself on a pay-as-you-go plan, and reduce the rate of spending growth with the first five-year curb on spending *ever*." But such rationales meant little to most Americans, a large portion of whom were unfamiliar with the details of the budget deal. They only knew that their taxes were being raised, and for the rest of his administration, they took it out on Bush.

As the nation went to the polls in the off-year congressional elections of 1990, it faced the very real possibility of war in the Persian Gulf. That fall, however, it was the budget that was the most important issue. Ed Rollins, the cochair of the Republican National Committee, called the budget deal a "disaster" and counseled congressional candidates to "take the pledge" not to vote for higher taxes (writing in a memo, "do not hesitate to distance yourself from the President").[37] Bush was so incensed by this act of political treason that after the election, he had Rollins fired.[38] But the public needed little coaxing from Rollins, or anyone else, as they resisted the temptation to validate Bush's actions in the Persian Gulf and instead sent him a clear message on how they felt about higher taxes. The Republicans lost ten Senate seats, twenty-five House seats, and two governorships; in Georgia, Gingrich almost lost. Bush had targeted his own campaigning on sixty-two close races; thirty-five of those candidates lost.[39] It had been an experience that conservative Republicans would not forget.

Nor would Americans soon forget Bush's change of mind on taxes. It crippled him in his upcoming attempt at reelection. It even permeated the popular media. A March 1991 episode of *L.A. Law*, one of the top-rated television dramas of the day, told the story of a man who was arrested when he refused to pay his taxes. When his lawyer asked him why, he mumbled "George Bush."

7

THE *PAUZA,* "PARTNERSHIP," AND PANAMA

On 7 December 1988, Ronald Reagan and George Bush met with Soviet president Mikhail Gorbachev on Governor's Island in New York Harbor. The press, long smitten by Gorbachev's charm and media savvy, reported that the meeting was a pleasant one, with both the president and the president-elect assuring Gorbachev of their support for perestroika and glasnost.[1] But insider reports of the meeting point to far testier exchanges. In his memoirs, Bush writes that Gorbachev "genuinely flared up when Reagan innocently asked him about progress in reform and perestroika" and responded "Have *you* completed all the reforms you need to complete?"[2] Michael Beschloss and Strobe Talbott, in their book on the relationship between the United States and the Soviet Union between 1989 and 1991, paint a story of conflict, but between different combatants. According to their version, it was Bush who became defensive during the meeting, demanding of Gorbachev, "What assurance can you give me that perestroika and glasnost will succeed?" Gorbachev snapped in response, "Not even Jesus Christ knows the answer to that question!" Then Gorbachev lectured Bush: "You'll see soon enough that I'm *not* doing this for show. . . . I'm engaged in real politics. . . . It's going to be a revolution nonetheless. . . . Don't misread me, Mr. Vice President."[3]

Much was expected of George Bush in foreign policy. He was, after all, the "resumé candidate" who had held an ambassadorship, headed the CIA, and traveled the world as vice president. A *New York Times*–CBS poll taken immediately after the 1988 election showed that 82 percent of those asked believed that Bush would be able to improve relations with the Soviet Union. And by 1989 those relations were already significantly warmer. Reagan had come to office proclaiming the evils of the Soviet Union and demanding an arms buildup; he was leaving office a comparative lamb, working toward détente with Gorbachev and having achieved a treaty banning intermediate range nuclear missiles. Many members of the press observed that Reagan's legacy as a peacemaker was assured; most assumed that Bush would continue his predecessor's courtship of Gorbachev.

In his memoirs, Bush claims that the day after the Governor's Island meeting, he told Brent Scowcroft that he "wanted to come up with something dramatic to move the relationship with Moscow forward."[4] But this did not mean that Bush would be rushed into making that move public. He had agreed with little of Reagan's foreign policy. He had opposed both Reagan's hard-line position toward the Soviets during his first term and his abrupt about-face toward Gorbachev and acceptance of disarmament in the second term. Unquestionably, Bush would have to deal with the Soviets. Yet in an effort to avoid making a blunder from which he could not recover—or to avoid backing a Soviet leader whose radical ideas might any day cause his downfall—Bush initially chose, in the words of Beschloss and Talbott, "to apply the brakes to the Soviet-American relationship, pull over to the side of the road, and study the map for a while."[5] The center-piece of this strategy was an internal policy review that was not fully completed until the Malta Summit of December 1989. According to Jack Matlock, then the American ambassador to the Soviet Union, "Our marching orders are clear: Don't do something, *stand there!*"[6] The Soviets called it the *"pauza"*—the pause.

In his desire for a cooling-off period with the Soviets, Bush had the support of his closest foreign policy advisers. In a 1997 interview, James Baker protested that "my political experience pretty much ended" after his service as Reagan's chief of staff, but this view is somewhat disingenuous.[7] Self-described as "more of a man of action than reflection," and once quoted as saying "I'm more interested in the game than in philosophy," Baker kept Bush's political future in mind throughout his tenure.[8] Baker knew that Bush could ill afford to be seen as being "soft" toward the Soviet Union and still hope to keep the support of his party's right wing; its memebers had already criticized Reagan for his policy of détente with Gorbachev. Moreover, Baker thought that Reagan and George Shultz, his secretary of state, had given too much away in their negotiations; waiting out Gorbachev would bring a better deal.[9] In this view Baker was joined by his deputy, Lawrence Eagleburger, who became an important administration envoy to the Middle East.

Bush's National Security team also agreed with the *pauza*, although on the whole they were more pessimistic about its chances for success than was the State Department. Brent Scowcroft, the administration's National Security Adviser, had long established himself as an opponent of Reagan's foreign policy. He remembered in a 1997 interview that the Reagan administration had gone "from a posture of extreme hostility . . . to the point that they were virtually declaring by 1988 that the cold war was over. . . . [But] the fundamentals hadn't gone near as far as the rhetoric."[10] In his memoirs, Scowcroft implied that the *pauza* was the "bold move" that Bush was looking for.[11] Yet Scowcroft saw it more as an opportunity to plan a strategy that would entail a harsher line toward Moscow. He was supported in this assessment by Chief of Staff John Sununu, a member of the newly created Principals Committee of the NSC, and by Robert Gates, Scowcroft's deputy at the NSC and his representative on the Deputies Committee, who was even more anti-Gorbachev than was his boss. Gates's hawkishness troubled Baker; in October 1989, Baker barred a speech proposed for delivery by Gates because he viewed it as too pessimistic regarding Gorbachev's chances for success.[12] But on the whole, there was little of the infighting that had so typified Reagan's National Security team. Baker's later assessment—that Bush "made the national security apparatus work the way it was supposed to work"—is an accurate one.[13]

In a speech delivered in 1997, Gorbachev claimed that he was "surprised" at the initiation of the *pauza*. If that was indeed the case, he shouldn't have been, given the combative tone of his exchange with Bush on Governor's Island. Nevertheless, Gorbachev remembered that he expressed his concern about the situation to British prime minister Margaret Thatcher "in rather stark terms," and his concern found its way to the White House.[14] Gorbachev tried to push the United States toward détente by unilaterally cutting his missile stockpile and making large cuts in his defense spending.[15] But Bush and his advisers suspected that these moves had as much to do with the imploding Soviet economy as with Gorbachev's desire to continue warm relations with the United States. Bush believed that as the Soviet Union continued toward internal weakness, the United States could negotiate from strength. There was, in his mind, no need to be rushed.

The go-slow policy was fraught with dangers of its own. With no great foreign policy statements coming from the White House, Bush opened himself up to further criticisms of his lack of "vision." He also had to endure (and by all accounts, it was quite difficult) the stories in the press that lauded Gorbachev's personal popularity. Moreover, he was under pressure from his Western allies, particularly Thatcher, to do something.

But perhaps most important was the fact that the conservative wing of his own party thought that Bush was missing a golden opportunity to use this moment of weakness and instability in the Soviet Union to press Gorbachev for concessions that he might not otherwise have been willing to make.

Bush must have had these concerns in mind as he planned the commencement speech at Texas A&M University for 12 May. Billed as his first major statement on foreign policy, this speech was a particularly important one for Bush; in his markup of the seventh draft, he wrote, "I think we need a Noonanism or two more. Perhaps we can salute the Soviet people a little." Then he added the line, "I stand ready to hold out my hand, our hands, to the people of the Soviet Union."[16] But it was another phrase, already in the draft, that the press latched onto: "Containment worked. And now it is time to move *beyond containment* to a new policy for the 1990s." While warning that America's foreign policy "must be based on deeds," he nevertheless articulated what he called a "sweeping vision" of a Soviet Union—with drastically cut troop strength in Europe, serious economic and political reforms, and a commitment to human rights—as a part of the world community of nations. In an attempt to demonstrate his seriousness, Bush floated a plan he called "Open Skies." First suggested by Dwight Eisenhower in 1955, it called for both the Soviet Union and the United States to allow each other the freedom to fly over the other's territory to observe defense capabilities. Scowcroft remembered that the Open Skies proposal "smacked of gimmickry"; Bush, more accurately, observed that it was a "no-lose proposition from our side. Gorbachev, committed to glasnost, would find it hard from a public-relations standpoint to reject it."[17]

Bush took another small step toward Gorbachev during the fortieth anniversary meeting of the North Atlantic Treaty Alliance (NATO), held on 28 May in Brussels. Since March, Bush had been considering a Scowcroft recommendation: the unilateral withdrawal of both U.S. and Soviet ground forces in Europe. Secretary of Defense Dick Cheney was leery of the proposal, and Baker recommended first cutting back on tanks. As the recommendation was staffed out, it was scaled down. At the summit, Bush proposed that both the Warsaw Pact and NATO limit their conventional ground forces (CFE) to about 275,000 for each side, a total cut in combat manpower for NATO of some 350,000 men. Perhaps more important was Bush's use of the word "partnership" in describing the relationship.[18]

Bush was moving forward, but at his own pace. However, world events conspired in a way that caused him to move much more quickly. His dilemma arose from events unfolding in China.

Bush was better prepared for the intrigue that underlay policy with the People's Republic of China than had been any president since Richard Nixon. While serving as the American envoy to the PRC, Bush had come to know Deng Xiaoping. They had visited each other several times since then; Deng even made a pilgrimage to Houston in 1979. James Lilley, who became the American ambassador to the PRC in April 1989, remembered that "both [Bush and Deng were] practical men . . . down to earth . . . human beings who enjoyed each other."[19] In 1989 Deng was the premier of the PRC; Bush believed him to be a man with whom he could deal.

One of Bush's first goals as president was to make a triumphant return to China. He traveled to the PRC in March 1989, but Lilley remembered that the trip was "quite negative. . . . [Bush] was quite disappointed." A large measure of his disappointment resulted from the case of Fang Li Zhi, a noted dissident who was hated by the Chinese leadership, particularly by Deng. Fang had been invited to the banquet held for Bush, but the Chinese leadership announced that they would not attend if Fang did. When Fang arrived, guards stopped him, and the leadership did not come in until they were sure that Fang had left the building. Recognizing that his life was clearly in danger, Fang asked for and received refugee status in the American embassy.[20]

The episode over Fang clearly indicated how worried the Chinese were over the burgeoning dissident movement in their country. Made up mostly of students, the Chinese reformers wished to be freed from the yoke of communist rule. Their anger peaked on 15 April, with the death of a Chinese leader who had been sympathetic to the dissidents. Thousands of students occupied Tiananmen Square, at the heart of Beijing's government district. On 26 April, Deng delivered an address, branding the students as "counterrevolutionary." His words only inflamed the situation; hundreds of students began a hunger strike, in full view of the world press.

One explanation of the timing of the protests is that Gorbachev's promise of perestroika and glasnost had inadvertently opened a window for the Chinese opposition.[21] On 15 May, Gorbachev arrived in China on a state visit; the next day, hundreds of thousands of students marched in Tiananmen Square, carrying Gorbachev's picture and screaming their support for perestroika. As he was being driven around the streets to his meeting with Deng, Gorbachev muttered, "Who the hell is in charge here?"[22]

His question was soon answered. After Gorbachev left for Shanghai on 18 May, the students stayed in Tiananmen Square. The next day, the government declared martial law to deal with the situation. On 4 June the army moved in to clear the square, firing submachine guns at those who refused to move. In the ensuing bloodshed, some 3,000 protesters were killed and 10,000 more were wounded. Broadcast live on television, the picture of a single student dissident, standing with an upraised hand in front of an oncoming PRC tank, became a worldwide symbol of nationalist resistance.

Baker remembered that "in considering our response to the massacre, there was simply no dispute that we had to strike a delicate balance between the need for decisive steps and the need to safeguard the underlying strategic relationship to the fullest extent possible."[23] The Chinese did not help much; their parading of arrested students, with shaved heads, in front of a kangaroo court only inflamed world opinion. Perhaps more important, as Lilley remembered, was that after the massacre, the Chinese had cut off communication with the United States: "When the Chinese get into a situation like this, they don't talk to you. . . . They hunkered down."[24]

For his part, Bush agonized over Tiananmen. He could hardly condone carnage, but he loathed the idea of a social upheaval that would jeopardize the stability of the region. Also important was the economic relationship with the PRC; only three weeks before the massacre, the White House had approved an extension of Most Favored Nation (MFN) status with the PRC.[25] In his memoirs, Bush wrote, "While angry rhetoric might be temporarily satisfying to some, I believed it would deeply hurt our efforts in the long run."[26] Scowcroft later remembered that Bush was "determined that a single incident, no matter how horrible," would not destroy the relationship between the two nations.[27] But the difficulty Bush had in maintaining such a balancing act was evidenced by meeting notes taken by press secretary Marlin Fitzwater as the president tried to develop a response to the massacre: "Difficult. Don't set aside passion or caution. . . . I am trying [my] best. Not love affair with Deng. . . . Democracy has its root. . . . We must walk our way through this."[28]

Sanctions were ultimately imposed—Bush cut off the military relationship between the two nations and delayed loans to the PRC from the World Bank. But these steps fell far short for many of Bush's critics, who thought that he was simply being callous toward the memory of the Tiananmen martyrs. A. M. Rosenthal of the *New York Times*, one of Bush's severest critics in the press, grumbled that "at a moment of passion in the story of democracy, [Bush] has been pale and thin."[29] Bush also had problems in Congress. He recorded in his diary: "[Rep. Steven] Solarz [D-NY] on the left and [Sen. Jesse] Helms on the right want to move much more radically. Helms has always detested this relationship."[30] On 28 June the House voted 418 to 0 to impose additional sanctions against the PRC.

Indeed, in his attempt to offer a measured response to the situation, Bush went out of his way to placate the Chinese authorities. On 30 June Scowcroft and Assistant Secretary of State Lawrence Eagleburger were dispatched on a secret trip to Beijing. The reason for the trip, as Baker remembered, was that "the Chinese had to be made to realize . . . that progress was impossible until they ceased their repression."[31] As Eagleburger later told Baker, "They never said so directly, but I think the smarter ones absorbed the message that we can do a lot more for them when they aren't killing their own people."[32] In November the House unanimously passed another bill calling for stronger sanctions. Bush vetoed it, and on 25 January 1990 the Senate sustained his veto by a three-vote margin. The following December, Scowcroft and Eagleburger returned to Beijing. In a dinner toast, Scowcroft referred to the "negative forces" in both countries that "seek to frustrate our cooperation."[33] Scowcroft later remembered that he "made a mess of it"—largely because the Cable News Network (CNN) taped the toast; and the moment it was played back on the national news, it became instant ammunition for administration critics.[34]

Despite Eagleburger's and Scowcroft's shuttle diplomacy, the Chinese were still obstinate about releasing the dissidents from their prisons. But Bush still held several financial trump cards. By 1990 Bush had informed the Chinese through diplomatic backchannels that he would not extend MFN status to them unless they gave him something in return. The Japanese also threatened to withhold a Third Yen Loan Package unless the Chinese improved their relationship with the United States. Both moves worked; the Chinese privately promised that their position would soon be moderated. On 24 May 1990 Bush extended China's MFN status. Soon after, the Chinese started to release dissidents from their prisons.[35]

Bush and Scowcroft had allowed the Chinese to save face; and although it had taken a year, the relationship between the two nations creaked back toward normalcy. By 1991 the dissidents were freed, the loans were flowing, and there had even been a new initiative toward mutual scientific and technological development.

The Tiananmen uprising served notice that the pace of nationalism would not be easily slowed. Yet Bush's labored reaction to the massacre shows quite clearly his aversion to change in world politics. Abhorring instability more than any other situation, Bush simply could not unilaterally support any national movements to overthrow a government—communist or otherwise—unless it could promise a stable substitute. But Tiananmen had given new hope to those in Europe who had long been ready to lay down their lives in the cause of liberating their homeland from the yoke of the Soviet Union. By summer 1989, nationalist movements were in evidence throughout Eastern Europe. Poland led the way. In 1981 there had been a violent crisis between the Polish government and nationalist dissidents. But by 1989, thanks in equal measure to the bravery of Lech Walesa, the leader of Solidarity (the first independent trade union in the Soviet bloc), the election of John Paul II as the first pope of Polish origin, and the agreement of the communist leader, Gen. Wojciech Jaruzelski, to lift the official ban on Solidarity, the situation had greatly improved.[36] The Bush administration set up roundtable talks between the Polish government and Solidarity, wherein Jaruzelski agreed to free elections. In return for Jaruzelski's cooperation, on 17 April in a speech at Hamtramck, Michigan, Bush promised economic incentives to the Polish government. On 4 June Solidarity won control of the Polish National Assembly, the gathering that would choose the nation's next president.

Scowcroft told an audience of scholars in 1997 that the administration's policy toward Eastern Europe was that "we supported any satellite that . . . made it difficult for the Russians."[37] This was certainly true with regard to Poland. On his way to economic talks in Paris, Bush stopped in Warsaw and personally persuaded Jaruzelski to run for the presidency. As Bush remembered, "It was ironic: here was an American president trying to persuade a senior communist leader to run for office. But I felt that Jaruzelski's experience was the best hope for a smooth transition in Poland."[38] Jaruzelski was easier for Bush to accept since he was also Solidarity's choice for the presidency, Walesa being ineligible to seek the office. Jaruzelski won but ultimately was unable to form a government.[39]

The situation in the Soviet Union was less promising. Several of the Soviet republics had witnessed nationalistic uprisings, each of which had been met with Soviet military force. Nevertheless, on 18 May 1989 Estonia reaffirmed its Declaration of Independence from the Soviet Union. Lithuania declared its own independence on the same day, and Latvia followed suit on 18 August. These Baltic states demonstrated their resolve— the "Baltic Way"—with an unbroken human chain that went through the capitals of the three nations; it represented a turnout of some 40 percent of the total population of those three states.[40]

Unlike in Poland, in the Soviet Union the Bush administration's policy was geared toward a slowing of nationalistic fervor. The rumblings for reform that had been so present in the Baltic States soon made their way to Russia, the largest Soviet republic. The centerpiece of that fervor was Boris Yeltsin, then a member of the Soviet Parliament but already a formidable critic of Gorbachev's policies. Rather than show any support for Yeltsin, however, Bush initially did his best to ignore him, relegating the 12 September visit of the Russian leader to second-class status. Brought to the side entrance of the White House instead of the front, where diplomats are usually met, and told by a NSC staffer that he had a meeting with Scowcroft and not with the president, Yeltsin pitched a fit. He went inside only when he was told that his meeting with Scowcroft was in jeopardy. Bush stopped by the meeting for only a few minutes. When he met the press afterward, Yeltsin boasted that he had presented a "Ten Point Plan" to Bush to "rescue perestroika." Bush and Scowcroft were furious with Yeltsin's grandstanding; Baker's reported reaction was: "What a flake!"[41]

Indeed, instead of helping the nationalist forces free themselves from the Soviet Union, Bush made Gorbachev an offer that he sorely needed to shore up both his popularity and his power base: the promise of an early summit. Needing at least the appearance of a foreign policy victory, Gorbachev had long been pressing for an earlier meeting than their scheduled 1990 summit. Bush did not want to end the *pauza* just yet. But with the lessons of Tiananmen firmly in mind, and with pressure mounting in the Baltics, he had come to believe that an immediate initiative had to be taken on some level, lest Gorbachev be overthrown. Gorbachev remembers that the invitation to the summit came in a handwritten note from Bush, suggesting a private meeting "without thousands of advisers on our backs."[42] They agreed to hold the summit in December 1989 at a neutral site, Malta. Trying to downplay expectations, the White House began to refer to the upcoming meeting as the "little summit."

Before the summit could convene, however, communism imploded in Eastern Europe. In early October, coinciding with the fortieth anniversary of East Germany's endorsement of communism, thousands of demonstrators took to the streets and began to flood embassies with calls for asylum. Thousands more tried to leave the country for Poland, Czechoslovakia, or Hungary, where they were already permitted to travel freely. But the decision by the government to seal off its borders only caused more rioting. The East German government of Erich Honecker was one of the most reactionary in the Soviet sphere; despite pressure from his own hard-liners, even Gorbachev instinctively knew that it was not worth defending. It is also possible that Gorbachev was not willing to risk American indignation should he roll in troops to quell the uprisings. On 7 October, during a visit to East Germany, Gorbachev shocked many observers—and further angered his own cold warriors—by announcing that policy for East Germany was made "not in Moscow, but in Berlin." Clearly, Gorbachev had written off Honecker, effectively sealing the doom of communism in East Germany.[43] It was the end of the cold war.

On 18 October Honecker resigned and was replaced by Egon Krenz. Gorbachev immediately proclaimed that the Soviet Union had "no right to interfere" in Eastern European affairs.[44] But Krenz fared little better than his predecessor; on 7 November his entire cabinet quit. Two days later, the

Krenz government announced its intent to end its travel ban and to open its borders in the near future.[45] But the promise was no longer enough; it took only a few minutes from the time of the government's announcement for much of the citizenry of East Berlin to race to the Berlin Wall and demand that the guards open the gates to the West. The crowds grew in both size and volume, many of them climbing on the wall and openly taunting the guards at the gates, who had been given no orders to deal with the situation. As night fell, the guards made the only decision open to them—at 10:30 P.M. they opened the gates. As the crowds rushed madly into West Berlin, many of them singing "We Shall Overcome," the Krenz government released an "order" that effectively affirmed the decision made by the guards. Within days, the world saw pictures of German youths scaling the wall, chipping off pieces for souvenirs.[46]

Relieved that Gorbachev had not intervened with troops but still wary of the instability of the situation, Bush's response to the crumbling of the Berlin Wall was characteristically muted. Meeting with the press in the Oval Office, he mused, "I don't think any single event is the end of what you might call the Iron Curtain. . . . I didn't foresee it, but imagining it? Yes." Lesley Stahl of CBS News observed that he did not sound "elated"; Bush responded, "I'm not an emotional kind of guy. . . . I'm very pleased." Dick Gephardt (D-MO) responded for the Democrats: "Even as the walls of the modern Jericho come tumbling down, we have a president who is inadequate to the moment."[47] Bush's later response to Gephardt's criticism: "absolutely absurd."[48]

Gorbachev later contended that the Malta Summit, held in the shadow of the fall of the Berlin Wall on 1–3 December 1989, was "epoch making."[49] Certainly, Malta ended the *pauza*. As the two leaders met on board the cruise ship *Maxim Gorky* in the storm-tossed Mediterranean (the winds were so bad that the press dubbed it the Seasick Summit), Bush made it clear that he was willing to help perestroika succeed. Gorbachev told Bush, "We accept your role in Europe. It is very important that you be there. . . . We shouldn't do anything to undermine it—and we should work together and not lose an opportunity."[50] At Malta, Bush and Gorbachev meshed personally in a way that they had not done a year before on Governor's Island. More important, Bush left their meetings convinced that the success of American relations with the Soviet Union depended upon keeping Gorbachev in power.

At summit's end, both men were hailed by their peers as peacemakers, but Gorbachev was enshrined in the press as a diplomatic demigod. *Time* named him as its "Man of the Decade," hailing him as "a zen genius of

George Bush and Mikhail Gorbachev at the Malta Summit, 3 December 1989. (Courtesy of the George Bush Presidential Library)

survival."[51] But such stories downplayed the fact that in the previous October, Gorbachev had surrendered Soviet control of Eastern Europe and that largely because of this, the fall of communism there was complete by the end of the year. In early December the communist governments in Yugoslavia and Bulgaria fell. In Czechoslovakia, poet Vaclav Havel succeeded Gustav Husak, one of the most entrenched of the communist leaders. These seismic events were largely peaceful and were quickly dubbed the Velvet Revolution. The one exception was in Rumania, where hard-line communist Nicolae Ceaucescu, who had publicly praised the Chinese for their actions at Tiananmen, was executed by a firing squad on Christmas Day.

Fundamental to George Bush's understanding of world events was the experience of World War II. He had risked his life to liberate the world from the grip of Nazi and Japanese dictatorships. This war was not fought against a faceless enemy; it had been personalized. Bush and his comrades were fighting against Hitler, against Mussolini, and against Hirohito. For President Bush to act precipitously against a nation or its leader, he had to see him in the same light as he had seen the dictators of the 1940s—as sinister threats to Western society. If the leaders were not this personification of evil, then Bush was more willing to test the diplomatic waters. If they were, then he was more than ready to throw the entire force of American power behind an effort to unseat them. Not Gorbachev, not the Nicaraguan Sandinista leader Daniel Ortega,* not any other Eastern European leader fit this description of malevolence; thus the president was willing to allow events to take a more deliberate course. But for Bush, Saddam Hussein certainly fit that description. And so too did Manuel Noriega.

An intelligence operative told reporter Seymour Hersh that "Noriega was always scum, but you use scum like him."[52] The Panamanian strongman had been a paid informant of American intelligence since his college years. He sent information on the leftist opinions of his teachers, and for that information he was well paid. The *New York Times* reported that throughout the years, the Central Intelligence Agency and the Pentagon had paid him some $322,000 in cash and gifts. A huge operative in the Latin American drug trade, Noriega was also being used by the Americans as a conduit to get arms to the Contra rebels in Nicaragua. He had also worked every conceivable side of the street, dealing as often with Cuba as he did with the Americans. By 1988 Noriega was incredibly powerful, incredibly wealthy, and well insulated. When the Reagan administration finally indicted him in absentia on drug charges, it seemed to be more shadowboxing than a serious attempt to oust the dictator. Given the circumstances, the new Bush administration had cause to worry about the safety of the 12,000 American military personnel and civilians living in Panama.[53]

On 7 May 1989, Noriega nullified the results of elections that had effectively ousted him as leader. Bush protested that "the Panamanian people have spoken. And I call on General Noriega to respect the will of the people." Noriega not only ignored Bush, but his personal police force, the Dignity Battalions, publicly beat Guillermo Endara, the victorious vice-presidential candidate, with an iron bar until his white shirt was soaked in blood. The grizzly scene, replayed over and over on American television and published in virtually every newsmagazine, clearly had an effect on Bush, who ordered an additional 2,000 troops to the Canal Zone.[54] Bush ordered Adm. William Crowe, head of the Joint Chiefs of Staff (JSC), to put together a plan to oust Noriega and to assist the Panamanians with

---

*Baker had negotiated a bipartisan agreement that called for $50 million in humanitarian aid for the Contra rebels, in return for the administration's abandonment of the Reagan policy of trying to overthrow the Sandinistas. But when a general election was held, Ortega lost and stepped down (Baker, *Politics of Diplomacy*, pp. 47–58).

the task of setting up a new government. The plan, code-named BLUE SPOON, also included a scheme to retrieve Kurt Muse, a captured CIA operative, from a Panamanian prison. On 11 May Crowe and Defense Secretary Dick Cheney presented the plan to the president; on the same day, Bush sent 1,881 more troops to Panama.[55]

Bush had clearly become obsessed with getting rid of Noriega; the situation reminds the historian of the fixation that the Kennedy brothers had with disposing of Fidel Castro. Bush thundered in a 14 May speech at Mississippi State University: "The will of the people should not be thwarted by this man and his Doberman thugs."** The next day, in an interview with Arnaud De Borchgrave of the *Washington Times*, Bush's outrage continued to flame:

> You've had an election that was stolen right out from under the eyes of the people and under the eyes of the world. . . . You have 40,000 American citizens and quite a few American troops in Panama. And we have the vital interests of the Canal. . . . Now, those ingredients are different than what you have in Nicaragua in terms of the abuse of people's rights. . . . That's why we are going to make sure we exercise our rights under the treaty. And that's why I've augmented U.S. force. Because when you see an elected president denied his mandate, and when you see an elected vice president beaten and bloodied by thugs that clearly come under the direction of Mr. Noriega, you have an alarming situation, and one where an American president has to act promptly and prudently.[56]

The situation in Panama offered the first test of Bush's national security team. Dick Cheney, chosen as secretary of defense in the wake of the rejection of John Tower, had quickly exerted more civilian control over the Pentagon than had been seen since the days of Robert McNamara. He had shown himself to be an independent, take-charge leader, but in so doing he had ruffled more than a few feathers. Only days after taking over at the Pentagon he had publicly censured Air Force Chief Larry Welch for lobbying Congress with his own plan on upgrading the air force's missile system.[57] Cheney himself had been reprimanded for a 29 April comment on CNN that Gorbachev would "ultimately fail." The comment threatened the placidity of the *pauza*, and Bush immediately disassociated himself from his secretary's remarks.[58] Not yet a member of the Bush inner circle in 1989, Cheney nevertheless radiated the cool confidence that had initially drawn

---

**Apparently Noriega returned Bush's antipathy. The museum at the Bush Presidential Library has on exhibit a target from Noriega's pistol range. Several holes are shot through it, and the target—human in form—is labeled "Bush."

the administration to appoint him. Jim Baker paid Cheney a high compliment when he remembered that "it's hard to keep your sense of equilibrium in Washington, but the power game has never gone to his head."[59]

Cheney's reproach of Welch was one factor in Crowe's decision not to seek reappointment as head of the JCS. In his place, Bush appointed army general Colin Powell. A decorated veteran of Vietnam, Powell had served as Reagan's national security adviser. During the transition, Bush offered Powell either the post of director of Central Intelligence or deputy secretary of state; Powell instead opted to become the commander of U.S. Forces Command, responsible for all field forces based in the United States.[60] While Powell did not openly lobby for the position on the JCS, Cheney had recommended him to Bush. Bush remembered that he had some reservations about choosing Powell, the most junior of the four-star generals who were eligible for the chairmanship, and wondered if it was "actually the right step for Colin at this stage of his service."[61] In promoting Powell, an African American, Bush had sent a powerful message to the black community, one that was met with overwhelming approval. But Bush had also gained a valuable adviser who was as politically agile as was Cheney. And Powell had a stronger base from which to work. He was the first full-term appointment as chief under the terms of the Goldwater-Nichols Act of 1986, which made the chief the "principal military adviser" to the president. Powell soon used this pulpit to its fullest extent.

Cheney and Powell faced different dilemmas in their different Pentagon offices. One of the most pronounced legacies of the Reagan years was that of increased defense expenditures. As Bush began his administration, the press announced that the Pentagon was entering an "era of lowered expectations," and it was Cheney who was expected to make the cuts in military spending that reflected not only the realities of the post–cold war world but also the political reality of the budget deficit.[62] Powell, on the other hand, had inherited a military that had been largely demoralized by the experience of Vietnam. The oft-cited "Vietnam Syndrome" was the belief that that war had been lost because the government had refused to commit the proper amount of American military force to the battle. Privately, Powell vowed that the next battle would be fought with overwhelming force. But given the prospect of Cheney's budget cuts, it was a promise he could not guarantee.

On 3 October, less than a day after Powell was sworn in as chairman, Maj. Moises Giroldi Vega, an officer in the Panamanian Defense Force (PDF), put in motion a coup against Noriega. He asked the Americans to block the exit from Fort Amador and the Bridge of the Americas across the canal. This they did, but no more. Although the administration was aware that Giroldi was planning something, they simply did not know enough about his plans, and in any case, it was too late to give him any substantial help.[63]

Not that American aid at any hour would have made much of a difference. William Webster, Bush's director of Central Intelligence, was charitable when he noted that "it was not what you would call your best planned coup."[64] Giroldi had indeed captured Noriega, but he did not have a clue as to what to do with him. Despite being told by Max Thurman, the commander in chief of the U.S. Southern Command, that if Giroldi brought Noriega to a U.S. military base they would accept him as a prisoner, the major refused. Indeed, in his book *The Commanders*, a penetrating study of American military decision making during the first two years of the Bush administration, Bob Woodward reports that the conspirators floated to Noriega the possibility of his retiring with a full pension.[65] Incredulously, Giroldi allowed the captured Noriega to use the telephone.[66] He called the PDF, which stormed Giroldi's hideout and reclaimed the Panamanian dictator. Within forty-eight hours, Giroldi had been tortured and killed.

The question of how the administration reacted to the Giroldi coup is still open to debate. One scholar concluded that although Bush was "tempted to move" on the coup, he "hesitated."[67] If there was such hesitation, the principals ascribe it to poor crisis communication. Webster remembered that at the time the coup took place, there was a "senior foreign official" being squired around the White House, and many of the key players were away from their desks. When they finally dealt with the crisis, Webster remembers that they did so by "huddling" rather than through formal strategy sessions. As a result, Webster remembers more "grousing" than crisp decision making.[68] In Baker's assessment, "It was apparent that a prime opportunity to remove Noriega had been squandered. Our reaction had been wholly defensive. . . . It's an understatement to say that administration decision making was less than crisp."[69] Scowcroft agreed: "Our performance was spotty."[70]

Powell, however, offers another point of view on administrative decision making in his memoirs. He suggests that there was no indecision regarding the Giroldi coup in the administration. Indeed, it was quite the opposite. He remembers that Max Thurman believed the coup to be destined to failure; Woodward reported Thurman as saying to Powell: "This is ill motivated, ill conceived—they are going to talk this guy into retirement. . . . Stay out of it big time." Powell recalls that "Cheney, Thurman, and I . . . agreed that the United States should not get involved" and that Scowcroft agreed. As for Bush, Powell remembers that the president never had any intention of giving any serious aid to the coup because "Giroldi had said nothing about democracy. And we would not support him unless he had made a commitment to restore civilian rule."[71]

Whether or not the administration had acted decisively, in the press, perception had become reality. As noted by Herbert Parmet, "The most unfortunate part of the Giroldi affair was the notoriety, which gave it a momentum of its own."[72] The press had resurrected the wimp factor, and Noreiga was publicly berating the masculinity of the United States as he bragged about his near escape. After the affair, columnist George Will, whom Bush despised, accused the president of having an "unserious presidency" and that its symbol "should be a wetted finger held up to the breezes."[73] Bush was also attacked by many members of Congress on both sides of the aisle; Republican Jesse Helms called the administration a bunch of "Keystone Cops." Publicly, the administration admitted only to "bad handling" of the affair. But a furious Bush told his staff that "amateur hour is over."[74] The administration heightened their planning for the moment of retribution, and one of the first steps was to enhance the power of the NSC's Deputies Committee. Unless time refused to permit, crisis decisions would go to the Deputies Committee before going to the full NSC.[75]

The administration had an opportunity to fine-tune its crisis response on 30 November 1989, when word came to the White House of a coup attempt against Corazon Aquino of the Philippines. Bush was at the Malta Summit, and Cheney was in bed with what was later called the flu (Bush remembered that Cheney "refused to come to the White House on the grounds that the vice president was not in the chain of command and such a meeting could not validly take place").[76] In their memoirs, Vice President Dan Quayle and Colin Powell both take credit for assuming control of the crisis;[77] Woodward sides with Powell. He reports that it was Powell who decided to have U.S. planes fly low and buzz the rebel planes on the ground, thus keeping them from taking off—a show of force with a small chance of loss of life—a plan that Bush approved.[78] To most of those close to the process, it was Powell who had proven himself to be a confident crisis manager.

Two weeks later, on 16 December, four American soldiers were heading for a restaurant in Panama City. They got lost and unintentionally drove to the PDF headquarters. As they were stopped by five uniformed PDF soldiers, their car was stormed by a crowd that had gathered there. Fearing for their lives, the soldiers sped away. The PDF fired at the car and hit two of the soldiers. One, Lt. Robert Paz, died fifteen minutes after arriving at Gorgas Army Hospital. One-half hour before the four men were ambushed, navy lieutenant Adam J. Curtis and his wife were stopped at the same PDF checkpoint; they too were lost. They were told to pull over and wait by the curb. As they did so, they witnessed the shooting of Paz and his friend. When the PDF realized that they had inadvertently provided witnesses to their deed, they blindfolded the couple and drove them to another location. Over the next four hours, Curtis was beaten, kicked in the groin and the head, and had his life threatened. His wife was slammed into the wall with such force that her head was bleeding; she was also sexually threatened. After four hours, they were released.[79]

When the story broke, Cheney was quick to respond: "Ultimately it is General Noriega who has encouraged this lawlessness." Although there was a token debate at the White House as to whether the incident was enough provocation for a military strike, Bush needed no convincing (Scowcroft later claimed that Paz and Curtis were "the excuse" for the invasion).[80] Thurman recommended that BLUE SPOON commence; Powell endorsed it for the president, and Bush gave it his immediate approval, along with the approval for troop reinforcements requested by Thurman to give the plan better odds of success (Powell remembers Bush's order: "Okay, let's do it. The hell with it").[81] There had been one small change to the plan, however. Noting that men would not be properly motivated to fight and die for a spoon, Thurman changed the name of the plan to Operation JUST CAUSE.

At 12:39 A.M. on 20 December, Guillermo Endara was sworn in as Panama's new president. Fifteen minutes later, American paratroopers descended upon Panama City. In less than an hour, Kurt Muse had been freed from his prison; by 2:40 A.M. Noriega's headquarters, the Commandancia Building, was in flames. By 9:00 A.M. the military action was over. There later were some questions about the performance of U.S. military hardware, particularly the much maligned Stealth bomber, which mistakenly bombed a basketball court and a saloon.[82] But on the whole, the Pentagon could breathe a sigh of relief. American losses were comparatively light: 23 dead and 394 wounded.[83]

But the Americans had not yet captured Noriega. Despite Powell's protests to the press ("He's not running anything because we own all the bases he owned eight hours ago"), the mission as planned was not complete without what the military called the "snatch": having Noriega in American hands. (This was quite unlike Operation DESERT STORM, which never had capturing Saddam Hussein as a goal, stated or otherwise.) On Christmas Eve, a disguised and frightened Noriega showed up at the home of Msgr. Sebastian Laboa, the papal nuncio—the pope's representative in Panama City—where he was granted asylum. The Americans blasted rock music at the building at earsplitting volume, and they purposely landed and unloaded troops where Noreiga could see.*** It was not until 3 January 1990 that Noriega finally surrendered, apparently convinced by the nuncio. He was brought by helicopter to the United States to stand trial. On 9 April 1992 Noriega was found guilty on eight of ten charges, including cocaine trafficking, money laundering, and racketeering.

The Panamanian episode was both a military and a political victory for Bush. For the moment, at least, the wimp label had disappeared. R. W. "Johnny" Apple of the *New York Times* wrote, "Whatever the other results of this roll of the dice in Panama, it has shown [Bush] as a man capable of bold action."[84] Bush's approval polls shot up. At the end of 1989, his 76 percent approval rating was second only to John Kennedy among modern presidents at the end of a first year in office.[85]

Baker later remembered that one of the most important results of the Panamanian episode was to show the world that the United States was not afraid to act unilaterally ("the surest test of a great power").[86] Yet the invasion had not been undertaken in a vacuum. In Panama, Bush reaped the first fruits of his policy during the *pauza* and the new relationship he had begun to forge with Gorbachev.

It was noteworthy that little came from the Soviets in the way of public criticism of America's actions in Panama. A large reason for this was that Gorbachev did not want to rock the boat when he was making headway toward American aid. But he also had his own problems to deal with that December. One realm of crisis was with the Germanies. By 1990 it was clear the reunification of East and West Germany was inevitable. The loss of East Germany from the Warsaw Pact would only worsen Gorbachev's relations with Kremlin hard-liners; thus, Gorbachev called for a confederation between the two Germanies. Great Britain's Margaret Thatcher was also opposed to permanent reunification; she believed that a united Germany could dominate Europe. In the Bush administration, Scowcroft sided with Thatcher, but Baker convinced Bush to press ahead slowly with reunification. Bush agreed to Baker's plan for what was called the "Two Plus Four Negotiations." The two Germanies, plus the four World War II victors (the United States, the Soviet Union, Great Britain, and France), would begin negotiations, but all would agree that the eventual goal was a permanent

***One of the people who contacted the White House with a plan for getting Noriega out of the nuncio's residence was Ross Perot. His cooperation was graciously declined (see Bush to Perot, 4 January 1990, Bush PR, Fitzwater Files, Subject, Alpha File, box 21, Perot folder).

reunification. Throughout the early part of 1990, Bush used the full force of his personal diplomacy to persuade all the leaders—including Thatcher and Gorbachev—to agree to work toward this goal.

Gorbachev's second problem was in the Baltics. As the new year began, he faced increased trouble in Lithuania and in the Caucasus republics of Armenia and Azerbaijan. On 4 February, some 300,000 protesters marched to the Kremlin to demand that the communist party relinquish its power.[87] The question of the use of force by the Soviets in these regions hung as a pall over the new partnership with the Americans. Gorbachev's reaction to the crisis was a mixture of repression and reform. After an initial show of force in Azerbaijan—a crackdown that the Bush administration publicly supported (Fitzwater: "We understand the need to restore order where order has broken down"[88])—Gorbachev promised Bush that there would be no more violence. On 5 February, in a speech to the party's Central Committee, he called for the communist party to give up "any legal and political advantages it might have" and proposed a comprehensive reorganization of the party.[89] But this move only served to anger party hard-liners, and it did nothing to stop the desire for independence in the republics. By mid-February, elections in the republics had begun; on 11 March Lithuania reaffirmed its declaration of independence from the Soviet Union. Gorbachev vowed not to negotiate with the Lithuanians until they revoked their declaration. In April, in an attempt to force the issue, Gorbachev placed an economic embargo around the republic and cut off its oil supply. Despite pressure from both the press and some members of Congress to intervene, the Bush administration was, in the words of the *New York Times,* "artfully silent."[90]

As Gorbachev arrived in Washington on 29 May for the "big summit" with Bush, he was once again the supplicant. According to Beschloss and Talbott, he virtually begged Bush to sign a trade bill, despite congressional protest over his handling of the Lithuanian situation, so that he could bring home a victory. Bush did so (Gorbachev, beaming, told the Americans, "This really matters to me").[91] But in secret, Bush made it clear that he would not send the trade package to Capitol Hill until Gorbachev had lifted his embargo on Lithuania. The price Gorbachev paid for this agreement was immediately evident. He lifted the Lithuanian embargo, and after returning home, announced that he would withdraw his objections to a unified Germany, whose troops could remain in NATO without a corresponding role for the East Germans in the Warsaw Pact. Formal reunification would take place on 3 October, with elections scheduled for 3 December. These concessions only exacerbated Gorbachev's poor relations with his hard-line generals, several of whom openly disagreed with him during the summit, an act that only two years earlier would have been unthinkable.[92] But Bush had won a major victory; his gradual approach had paved the way to a reunified Germany.

It is interesting that in 1996, Bush looked back on the first part of his policy with the Soviets and recalled in an interview, "We should have hit the ground running."[93] But it is clear that the *pauza* had reaped terrific benefits. Many observers, then and now, saw his actions from 1989 to 1991 as nonactions; for their part, the conservative right was furious at what they perceived as Bush's abandonment of the republics. Yet Bush had manipulated the situation so that he could negotiate with Gorbachev from strength, and in so doing he had won major concessions from the Soviets. Moreover, he had done so without compromising a good relationship with Gorbachev, a relationship that made itself evident in the muted Soviet response to the Panamanian episode. That new relationship was about to pay its most important dividend—on 2 August 1990, Iraqi troops poured into Kuwait.

8

★ ★ ★ ★ ★

DESERT SHIELD

Iraq, a nation approximately the size of the state of California, had in 1990 a population of 16.5 million. It also had the fourth largest army in the world, the personal property of the nation's president for life, Saddam Hussein. Saddam had been a fixture in the bloody and unpredictable politics of Iraq since the early 1960s. His brutality and self-confidence had long become legendary. Of the many examples available, one will suffice: in 1969, he added a law degree to his pantheon of honors simply by showing up in the examination room with a pistol in his belt and flanked by two armed bodyguards. He immediately passed the exam.[1] Head of the Ba'ath party and the nation's military strongman throughout the 1970s, he was named president of Iraq in July 1979. Later that year the Shah of Iran was overthrown; Saddam invaded Iran in fall 1980. The war lasted eight years and completely destroyed both nations' economic infrastructure. The war had cost Iraq about $250 billion, and Saddam faced a foreign debt of about $80 billion.[2] Moreover, he could no longer count on oil exports, which once made up 95 percent of Iraq's postwar income, to help pay the debt because the price of oil was falling precipitously at the end of the 1980s, thus putting the macrostructure of the Iraqi economy on even shakier ground.[3]

This situation led Saddam to court moderate Arab nations such as Egypt, European nations, most notably France, and the United States. The Reagan administration was particularly receptive to Saddam's entreaties. Brent Scowcroft was blunt in a 1997 interview: the Reagan policy was to "aid the weaker, which was Iraq."[4] Hoping that Iraq would provide a check to Iran in the region, the United States provided Saddam with agricultural commodity credits. By 1987 Iraq had been given $1 billion in Commodity Credit Corporation credit guarantees by the United States—the largest loan of its kind to any nation in the world.[5] The Reagan administration had also approved export licenses for Saddam so that he might buy military technology.[6]

Saddam was a troublesome business partner. Immediately following the end of the war with Iran, he turned his attention toward ridding himself of the Kurds, an ethnic minority in the north of Iraq, and he enforced his desires with chemical weapons. There was also evidence that American money borrowed by Saddam for food had actually gone toward the purchase of military material used against the Kurds. The Bush administration, however, was loathe to rock the boat in the Middle East by openly criticizing Saddam. In October 1989 the administration increased the number of agricultural credits to Iraq but protested Saddam's use of the money for military purposes, limiting the extent of its objections to Saddam's methods. Indeed, it consistently opposed congressional attempts to impose sanctions on Iraq, the last time coming only two days before Saddam's attack on Kuwait.[7]

If the administration truly believed that agricultural credits would buy stability in the Persian Gulf, it was sorely mistaken. Obsessed with a fear of assassination, Saddam reacted to the fall of communism in Europe—particularly to the bloody execution of Romania's Nicolae Ceaucescu—with a paranoia of suspicion regarding the intentions of his neighbors. This may well have led him toward developing a nuclear ability for Iraq, which was, by late 1989, in its earliest stages.[8] He was especially terrified of Israel, particularly since the fall of communism had led to a glut of Soviet Jews emigrating there. Early in March 1989 Saddam began to construct six fixed launchers for Scud missiles at a point on the Jordanian border within range of Israel, a fact that the *Washington Post* later reported to be known by American intelligence.[9] Despite these moves, Saddam was well aware, as he reportedly told the Saudi ambassador to Washington, Prince Bandar bin Sultan, that if Israel attacked Iraq, "I would not last six hours."[10] Always believing that the best defense was a good offense, Saddam raged in a 1 April 1989 address to his armed forces, "By God, we will make fire eat half of Israel if it tries to do anything to Iraq."[11]

Saddam's "eat fire" speech caused considerable concern within the Bush administration; Baker remembered that after the speech, "our strategic calculation changed irrevocably."[12] Recognizing that fact, Saddam summoned Prince Bandar to Baghdad for the express purpose of asking him to convey to Bush that he would never attack Israel. According to one report, Bush was skeptical, remarking to Bandar (who delivered Saddam's message personally), "If he doesn't intend it, why on earth does he have to say it?"[13] The following month, the administration decided not to go through with the next installment of the loan to Iraq. With the end of the loans, Saddam had to look elsewhere for the money to rebuild his war-ravaged economy.

Saddam saw both the solution to his dilemma, as well as one of its major causes, in his neighbor to the south. The Emirate of Kuwait, a nation roughly the size of New York State with a population of approximately 1.7 million, had gained its independence from Great Britain in 1961. Immediately, Baghdad moved troops to the Kuwaiti border, only to be stopped when the British, following a Kuwaiti request, sent troops to the area. Facing the inevitable, Iraq tacitly recognized Kuwait's right to exist in 1963 by acquiescing in their membership in the Arab League—but only after receiving a sizable cash payment from the Emir of Kuwait in return.[14] The cold war between the two nations continued, however. Saddam had long demanded access to the oil fields on the islands of Warba and Bubiyan. This demand was then joined with charges that the Kuwaitis had been "slant-drilling" into the Rumaylah oil field, the majority of which lay in Iraqi territory.[15] Then came the issue of oil prices. When most of the member nations of the Organization of Petroleum Exporting Countries (OPEC), including Iraq, agreed to cut back production of oil so as to force prices up, Kuwait refused to do so. This action perturbed many of the nations in the oil cartel; to many leaders, the Kuwaitis were seen as little more than mercenaries who were more concerned with lining their own pockets than they were with the welfare or the stability of their nation. For his part, Saddam saw their action simply as, in his words, "a kind of war against Iraq."[16] Add to this affront the fact that Saddam owed Kuwait some $10 billion that it had borrowed during the war with Iran, and more than enough reason, from Saddam's point of view, existed for a military solution.

On 15 July 1990, the U.S. Defense Intelligence Agency (DIA) learned that a division of the select Iraqi Republican Guard troops had begun to move southeast to the Kuwaiti border. Within four days, some 35,000 Iraqi soldiers from three divisions were within ten miles of the border with Kuwait. Colin Powell remembers that this prompted him to order Gen. Norman Schwartzkopf, the commander in chief of the Central Command (CENTCOM), to prepare a plan of attack.

In the words of Rick Atkinson, one of the most thoughtful reporters of the Gulf War, "H. Norman Schwartzkopf was the most theatrical American in uniform since Douglas MacArthur."[17] The recipient of three Silver Stars in Vietnam, Schwartzkopf was equal parts prima donna (described by Atkinson as a man who could "swagger sitting down"[18]), tyrant, and master motivator. For many people, the general came to personify American heroics in the Gulf War. It might not have been so. Atkinson reports that because of Schwartzkopf's unpredictable tirades against his staff and his "yen for imperial trappings," Secretary of Defense Dick Cheney considered firing him, and Powell hints in his memoirs that he had "a replacement in the back of his mind."[19] But Powell worked hard in the handling of the volatile general, not always to Schwartzkopf's satisfaction.

In response to Powell's request, Schwartzkopf produced a plan that was a two-tiered response. One tier would provide a retaliatory option if Saddam committed what Powell called a "minor border infraction"; the other tier was a response in case of a full-fledged invasion of Kuwait.[20] The second-tier plan, code-named OPERATIONS PLAN 1002–90, called for an expeditionary force of between 100,000 to 200,000 military personnel, and it was estimated that it would take about a year to establish that force in such a manner that it had a chance of expelling Saddam from Kuwait.[21]

But OPERATIONS PLAN 1002–90 was to be held in reserve. Virtually no one believed that Saddam would use his troops for anything more than a brief surgical strike and withdrawal, if that. Schwartzkopf told the Joint Chiefs of Staff as much when he briefed them on 1 August.[22] Bush was also told this by Egypt's Hosni Mubarak ("Let us handle it within the Arab family"), Jordan's King Hussein ("There is no possibility for this"), and American ambassador to Iraq April Glaspie, all of whom had met with Saddam in July.[23] They believed that he was most likely looking for more bribe monies from the emir and that then he would stand his forces down. (William Webster remembered that at the height of the crisis, the White House was concerned that the Kuwaitis "were ready to write checks over there . . . sometimes an Arabian solution."[24]) Indeed, the Kuwaitis had not mobilized their own forces; they seemed unconcerned, so it was difficult for the Americans to show any alarm.[25] Nevertheless, American intelligence reports continued to offer evidence of an Iraqi buildup to invasion strength; but in the glow of Mubarak's and Glaspie's reports, these estimates were downplayed at both the Pentagon and the White House.

By the time that Saddam moved his troops into a clearly offensive position on the morning of 1 August, there was nothing that the 10,000 CENTCOM troops stationed in the region could do, except watch events unfold. As Scowcroft remembered, "Our approach to averting conflict—to warn against belligerent behavior, to make clear we would stand by our friends, yet continue to offer good relations for good behavior—had failed."[26]

On 2 August 1990, with Saddam claiming that Iraq was responding to calls from a revolutionary government working for the overthrow of the emir, some 140,000 Iraqi troops and 18,000 tanks rolled into Kuwait. The 16,000-man Kuwaiti army was hopelessly outmatched. Within three-and-one-half hours, the invaders had reached the kingdom's capital at Kuwait City; within twelve hours, it had fallen to Saddam. Although the Iraqis failed to capture the emir, who had fled to Saudi Arabia (Saddam hoped to put him on trial as a war criminal), the Iraqi leader not only controlled Kuwait but also 21 percent of the world's oil supply. Saddam proclaimed that Kuwait had ceased to exist and that it had become the "Nineteenth Province, an eternal part of Iraq."

Bush certainly knew the terrain—his Zapata Oil Company had built Kuwait's first offshore oil well in the 1950s—and he responded quickly.[27] Within hours of the invasion, Bush followed the advice of the NSC Deputies Committee and signed an executive order freezing the approximately $100 billion in Iraqi property and assets in the United States and overseas, an action somewhat offset, as it were, by the fact that the Iraqis were able to plunder Kuwait at will and by all reports did so. Bush also moved the USS *Independence* Carrier Battle Group (two carriers, one guided missile destroyer, two frigates, and one ammunition ship) into the Persian Gulf from the Indian Ocean.

Immediately, Bush's predilection for personal political diplomacy took over. Within hours of learning of the invasion, on 3 August, he worked the phones and spoke to every leader of the Western Alliance, building what soon became known as a coalition of world leaders against Iraqi aggression. The United Kingdom, France, West Germany, Japan, and seven other nations quickly joined the United States in freezing Iraqi assets. Keeping an appointment to speak on cold war diplomacy at the Aspen Institute, Bush nevertheless continued to work the phones from Air Force One. Egypt's Mubarak and Jordan's Hussein, who apologized for inadvertently misleading Bush regarding Saddam's intentions, urged him not to act precipitously, still holding out hope for an Arab solution. In Aspen, Bush met with British prime minister Margaret Thatcher, who, in a joint press conference following their meeting, was unequivocal: "What happened is a total violation of international law."

Saddam undoubtedly was stunned by the surprising unity in the international community against his actions. For the first time since its inception, thanks to a timely shove by an American president who had also served as UN ambassador, the United Nations lurched forward and gave the strongest show of unanimity in its forty-five-year history. The Security Council met within hours of the invasion; by the end of that evening, UN Resolution 660—denouncing Iraq's invasion, calling for its immediate withdrawal, and promising sanctions if it did not comply—had been unanimously passed (with one abstention: Yemen). It was only the fifth time in its history that the Security Council had issued such a threat. On 6 August the UN passed Resolution 661, calling for a complete prohibition of trade with Iraq and authorizing nonmilitary measures to enforce the sanctions. Yet had the UN not acted, the upcoming scenario might well have been the same. Scowcroft was clear in his memoirs: "Never did we think that without its blessing we could not or would not intervene."[28] But the UN had indeed provided Bush with significant political cover; on both votes, the United States was supported by the Soviet Union.

The Soviet Union was key to Bush's coalition. It was the first test of the new partnership that had been forged at Malta. Bush needed Gorbachev either on his side or scrupulously neutral, if for no other reason than to ensure that there would be no trouble in the Security Council. For his part, Gorbachev was reluctantly creaking into line with the rest of the international community against his former client in Iraq. But he was facing mounting opposition. Despite the promise of a trade pact with the United States, Gorbachev's hard-line opponents, particularly in the Soviet military, were still seething over what Gorbachev had conceded to get that pact: agreements to end the Lithuanian embargo and to tolerate a unified Germany. Gorbachev's cold warriors were also concerned about the possibility of a permanent American presence in the Middle East and argued for sending Soviet aid to Saddam.

But by the end of 1990, the Soviet economy had further crumbled into disarray. The food situation was getting close to desperate, and Gorbachev was forced to once again ask Bush for aid. He knew that if he was ever to hope for any further American economic support, he would have to join Bush's coalition against Iraq. Besides, he and his closest advisers saw Saddam's invasion as both foolhardy and as a violation of international law. Thus, Gorbachev had to walk a tightrope during the crisis, torn as he was by his own belief in the necessity of joining the coalition and the demands of his military hard-liners to help Saddam.

On the day of the invasion, Baker had just left the Soviet Union after a visit with Foreign Minister Eduard Shevardnadze and was on his way to Mongolia for a previously scheduled state visit. While in Mongolia, Baker worked out the details of a joint statement with Shevardnadze. On 3 August Baker joined the foreign minister on the tarmac of Vnukovo II airport, just outside Moscow. In their statement, the Soviet Union took the unprecedented step of joining with the United States in calling for "an international cutoff of all arms supplies to Iraq."[29]

Shevardnadze's announcement was a critical, if not the most important, moment in the whole of the Persian Gulf crisis. It was now clear to the world that Saddam could not count on the normal U.S.–Soviet cat-fighting over Middle East policy to help him to quietly consolidate his gains. Over the next several weeks, largely due to the cajoling of Baker, the Soviet Union joined in the UN resolutions. However, the Soviets continued to couch their support with calls for Bush to resist using any kind of force in the region. It was, as Bush later called it, a "new world order." For the first time since 1945, the United States and the Soviet Union were fighting on the same side.

Out of gratitude to Gorbachev's response, as well as from a desire to keep the coalition together, Bush agreed to travel to Helsinki on 5 September for a third summit with Gorbachev. Bush was even willing to appear as the supplicant, and during the summit he agreed to an international conference on the Middle East, an implicit admission that after the conflict, in a stunning reversal of over forty years of policy, America would agree to a Soviet presence in the Middle East.[30] Terrified at the prospect of completely losing the support of the Soviet Union just as the Americans were threatening a counterstrike, Saddam sent his foreign minister, Tariq Aziz, to Moscow to try to soften up Gorbachev. It was to no avail. At Helsinki, Bush and Gorbachev issued a joint statement: the two nations would act "individually and in concert" to see to it that Saddam unconditionally withdraw from Kuwait, "even if that cannot be accomplished by peaceful means." With the Soviets on board, it would be impossible for Saddam to find any European allies. The *New York Times* called it "Bush and Gorbachev, Inc."[31]

After the fall of Kuwait, Bush's attention immediately turned to protecting Saudi Arabia. There was ample reason for Saddam to invade that nation—if he took Saudi Arabia, he would control 40 percent of the world's known oil reserves. From the opening moments of the crisis, Bush was inclined to place American troops in Saudi Arabia to protect that nation. But the Saudis had every reason to be skeptical of American promises of protection; they had heard it all before. After the fall of the Shah of Iran in 1979, Jimmy Carter had promised to send F-15s to Saudi Arabia as a show of power and then had reneged. Saudi memories were also fresh of Reagan's withdrawal of the marines from Lebanon in 1984. And there were concerns about an American presence in their nation, particularly around their holy sites. But Bush held some cards of his own. Saddam had lied to Saudi King Fahd about his plans for Kuwait, as he had lied to Jordan's Hussein and Egypt's Mubarak. Further, Bush had built up a close relationship with King Fahd during his years as CIA director. Perhaps most important was that military intelligence showed the distinct possibility that Saddam's next move would indeed be against Saudi Arabia.

On the afternoon of 3 August, Bush told Scowcroft to invite Prince Bandar to the White House to make a case for allowing American troops to deploy in Saudi Arabia. After the meeting had begun, Bush came into the office. He told Bandar that the Kuwaitis had not asked for help until it was too late and that Fahd should not wait until the last minute. Bush then ordered Colin Powell to fully brief Bandar on Schwartzkopf's two-tiered plan. Powell did so, and he also showed the Saudi ambassador secret satellite photos that demonstrated that Saddam had increased his military strength in Kuwait to the point where an attack against the Saudis was a real possibility. When Bandar asked how many men the Americans were thinking of placing in Saudi Arabia, Powell replied "about one hundred thousand," an understatement of Schwartzkopf's estimate. Still, Bandar was stunned by the force that Bush had in mind; he smiled and replied to Powell, "Well, at least it shows you're serious."[32] Bandar then excused himself to dispatch the news to his uncle, King Fahd.

The next day, during an NSC meeting at Camp David, Bush was more fully briefed on an expanded version of Schwartzkopf's plan. He was also informed that intelligence reports strongly suggested that the Saudis continued to be disinclined to accept any long-term American presence on their soil. As Scowcroft's notes of the meeting show, Bush was clear: "Our first objective is to keep Saddam out of Saudi Arabia. Our second is to protect the Saudis against retaliation when we shut down Iraq's export capability. We have a problem if Saddam does not invade Saudi Arabia but holds on to Kuwait." The meeting led to Bush's approval of the plan, subject to the approval of the Saudis.[33] After the meeting, according to Bob Woodward, Bush met with Scowcroft alone and decided to immediately send Cheney and Schwartzkopf to present the Pentagon's plan to Fahd.[34]

Whether the next event was a result of Scowcroft's convincing Bush, as Woodward's reporting implies, or of Thatcher's prompting, as Powell implies, remains an open question.[35] On Sunday, 5 August, after disembarking from his helicopter from Camp David, Bush announced to the press that "this will not stand, this aggression of Kuwait." Powell was astonished; this clearly changed the focus of the American response from giving up on Kuwait and protecting Saudi Arabia to protecting Saudi Arabia by evicting the Iraqis from Kuwait.[36] It is, of course, highly possible that Bush's statement was designed primarily to impress the Saudis with the irreversibility of the American commitment. If that was one of the goals of Bush's statement, it worked. The next day, Cheney and Scowcroft arrived in Riyadh to explain the extent of the American commitment to Fahd. The delegation was astounded at the king's immediate positive reply.[37]

On Wednesday, 8 August, Bush addressed the nation, announcing the deployment of the Eighty-second Airborne Division as well as two squad-

rons of F-15 fighters to Saudi Arabia. He later remembered that as he prepared his speech, he wanted to make it clear to the American people that
"this time I wanted no appeasement."[38] Proclaiming that "a line has been
drawn in the sand," Bush said that what the Americans sought was nothing less—or more—than "the immediate, unconditional, and complete
withdrawal of all Iraqi forces from Kuwait." He also stated, "The mission of our troops is wholly defensive . . . [but] they will defend themselves, the Kingdom of Saudi Arabia, and other friends in the Persian
Gulf." By the end of August, there were 80,000 coalition troops in Saudi
Arabia, part of what was by then code-named DESERT SHIELD. Saddam
immediately reinforced his own army to a strength of some 200,000; on
21 August Bush responded by calling up 40,000 reservists to help trans-
port troops, the first call-up of the reserves since the Tet Offensive of 1968.
On 19 November Saddam added 250,000 more troops, giving him a
ground contingent of approximately 680,000 men.[39] The *Washington Post*
severely understated the case when it noted that "a happy ending does
not appear imminent."[40]

In the weeks that followed Bush's announcement of DESERT SHIELD, the
allied coalition became both larger and more fully committed to the American cause. Much of this was due to Saddam, who had embarked on a program of "Zionizing" the conflict. In an attempt to win Arab support, he
intimated that he would withdraw from Kuwait if Israel would withdraw
from its occupied Palestinian territories. But Saddam had worn out his
welcome with his Arab neighbors. After a 10 August meeting of the Arab
League, both Syria and Egypt joined forces against Iraq. In fact, it was
Mubarak, who felt personally betrayed by Saddam, who made the first
reference to the Iraqi leader as "the new Hitler, since he has become a danger to the region, to the Arabs, and to the world."[41]

Yet the key to keeping Arab support on the side of the budding coalition against Saddam—and the most difficult task that Bush had in the entire war—was keeping Israel out of the coalition. There had never been any
love lost between Bush and the Likud government of Yitzhak Shamir. Baker
and Bush held the prime minister responsible for holding up the Middle
East peace process by continuing to build settlements on the disputed territory of the West Bank, even as the Palestine Liberation Organization (PLO)
had taken a major step in 1989 by acknowledging Israel's right to exist.
However, from the point of view of Washington, Israel could not be a part
of the coalition. If it entered the war, neighboring Arab states would be
forced to decide whether to declare war on the hated Israel, a quandary
that Saddam hoped would present itself. But Shamir turned out to be the

voice of reason in his cabinet. In the days after the invasion, he promised that Israel would restrain itself unless attacked.

Bush was also shrewd enough to understand that he needed to win commitments of financial support from the coalition, if for no other reason than that the cost of American intervention was incredibly expensive; one estimate suggests that by the end of August, the Americans were spending $28.9 million a day to keep U.S. troops in Saudi Arabia.[42] There were also early warning signs of the recession to come, not only in the United States but also abroad. In terms of financial underwriting, Bush concentrated his efforts on Germany and Japan. Neither nation could be expected to commit troops; both had constitutions, drafted by the United States after World War II, that severely constrained what they could do with their troops off their own soil. Moreover, there were domestic political considerations. Germany was only weeks away from its first elections as a unified nation since 1945, and in Japan leaders of several of the minority parties argued against sending aid of any kind. But the two countries could afford a financial commitment, and both Helmut Kohl and Toshiki Kaifu eventually convinced their respective governments to send money.[43] By the end of the operation, Kuwait, Saudi Arabia, and the United Arab Emirates (UAE) paid for 62 percent of the costs; Germany, Japan, and Korea another 26 percent. Over 70 percent of the foreign commitment came in cash.[44] In addition, Bush asked for, and on 10 April 1991 received, a supplemental defense appropriation from his own Congress of $15 billion in budget authority to support DESERT SHIELD.[45]

If persuading the world community to support American intervention in the Gulf financially was an act of political legerdemain—and it was—convincing the other members of the coalition to send troops for the purpose of ousting Saddam from Kuwait was actually much easier. The hawkish Thatcher's support came effortlessly (in the words of Freedman and Karsh, "Fighting aggressors can appear as almost a national calling in Britain").[46] Squadrons of Tornado fighters and the Seventh Armored Brigade were sent to Saudi Arabia. Even France, which had been closest to Iraq of any Western nation, eventually sent 4,200 troops.

As coalition troops began to arrive on Saudi soil, they were particularly vulnerable to Iraqi attack. One estimate suggested that it would take until the end of September for the troops to be ready to withstand an assault. War, then, could not come too soon. Yet on 22 August it almost did. Saddam challenged the UN embargo policy by sending an Iraqi tanker, the *Khaneqan*, toward Yemen, one of Saddam's few remaining allies. An American frigate fired warning shots across the bow of the tanker; Saddam warned of "grave consequences" if any more shots were fired. Bush originally favored an immediate retaliation, and Powell, Cheney, and Scowcroft agreed.

Baker protested, however, pointing out that the Soviet Union made it clear that it was not in favor of an attack on the tanker. Baker won; he called Shevardnadze and said that Bush would not fire on the ship, but only if the Soviets agreed to a new UN resolution that would allow the coalition to enforce the embargo—by force, if necessary. Gorbachev agreed. Bush allowed the tanker to pass (Thatcher, angry at what she perceived to be Bush's weakness, told the president on the phone, "This is no time to go wobbly") and pressed the UN to be more definitive in its statement on the embargo. On 25 August that body passed UN Resolution 665, giving the coalition the right to search, and if necessary disable, ships that were suspected of attempting to run the embargo.[47]

In his memoirs, Bush claims, "I don't know exactly when I became resigned to the fact that it would come to war."[48] Observers of the Bush administration, both contemporary and historical, have also struggled with this question, trying to decide when Bush's intentions turned from a defense of Saudi Arabia and toward a plan for expelling Saddam Hussein from Kuwait, in Operation DESERT STORM.

Bush's actions during fall 1990 strongly suggest that he never really thought that economic sanctions would work and that from the beginning of the crisis he was planning to use DESERT SHIELD troops in an offensive manner to dislodge Saddam from Kuwait. Powell himself cites an instance in mid-August when Bush turned to him and said, "I don't know if sanctions are going to work in an acceptable time frame"; Powell concluded that Bush "did not sound like a man willing to wait long for sanctions to work."[49] Indeed, throughout Powell's account, Bush is depicted as a person who is simply waiting for the right moment to launch an offensive attack. This conclusion is made even more certain by the tone of the four chapters in Bush's memoirs dealing with DESERT SHIELD. Bush relates that as early as 23 August, when he was fishing with Scowcroft at Kennebunkport, he "asked impatiently when we could strike."[50] Scowcroft remembers that from the very beginning of the crisis, with Bush's approval, he undertook to push the NSC to take a tougher stance on the issue of the possible use of force to dislodge Saddam.[51] Apparently Bush never doubted that he would be sending more troops; the mindset of "incrementalism" had taken over: Schwartzkopf would have enough men to do the job. In Cheney's words, Bush had adopted the post-Vietnam, "don't-screw-around school of military strategy."[52] Indeed, Bush admitted as much to the American people on 10 September, in a speech to a Joint Session of Congress, when he quietly but pointedly said, "Iraq will not be permitted to annex Kuwait. That's not a threat or a boast. That's just the way it's going to be."[53] On

22 September Bush wrote in his diary: "I am wondering if we need to speed up the timetable."[54]*

Nevertheless, Bush had to deal with the fact that by October, the economic sanctions as set by the United Nations showed signs of working. Saddam had control of 20 percent of the world's oil supply, but he could not sell any of it anywhere; indeed, on 10 September he began giving it away to any developing nation who dared to run the blockade.[55] His hopes of affecting the world market had also fallen flat. The oil lost by Kuwait was made up for, and rather quickly, by increased production from Saudi Arabia, Venezuela, the United Arab Emirates, and Nigeria.[56] The coalition could keep food from Iraq—a nation that imported 75 percent of its foodstuffs—but it could not be seen to be starving children as a war aim.

No one knew for sure how soon the sanctions would begin to affect not only Saddam but the members of the coalition. The Western economies, including that of the United States, were already on shaky ground. The recession that played such a large part at the end of the Bush administration was only a few months away, and even before the invasion the economy had already begun to show signs of a slowdown. It was doubtful whether the economies of the Arab members of the coalition would survive the two years that some analysts predicted it would take for the sanctions to bring Saddam to his knees; indeed, the CIA was telling Bush that the sanctions might never work.[57]

Since the beginning of the crisis, Bush had been meeting regularly with a group that was dubbed the Gang of Eight—Dan Quayle, James Baker, John Sununu, Brent Scowcroft, Richard Gates, Dick Cheney, and Colin Powell. Baker and Powell urged the president to continue the containment route, at least until that time when economic sanctions and diplomacy had been given enough time to work.[58] But Scowcroft, Gates, and Cheney advocated an offensive option that would expel Saddam from Kuwait. That military option had been in the pipeline since early August. On 8 Au-

---

*In his memoirs, James Baker offers a different point of view, one that deserves to be quoted at length: "Some critics have fixed on this statement ["This will not stand"]—and the resolute manner in which the President issued it—as an indication of the President's intention from the very beginning to go to war. That, however, would be a serious misreading, both of George Bush the man and of the situation in which the United States . . . found itself that August. The President's statement reflected his instinctive sense, very early on, that this was no ordinary crisis. . . . His statement also showed his determination to undo Iraq's aggression. . . . And with every decision, the world community would be one step closer to ejecting Iraq from Kuwait. What the President's statement did not reveal was how he would go about doing that" (Baker, *Politics of Diplomacy*, pp. 276–77).

gust, the day that Bush announced the deployment of DESERT SHIELD, Schwartzkopf asked for assistance in developing an offensive plan. That initial plan, code-named Operation INSTANT THUNDER, called for the targeting of key Iraqi military and technological installations for air bombardment. It also called for an intensive air bombardment of Iraqi command and communications and then a ground war, with coalition troops attacking straight into the teeth of the Republican Guard. Nevertheless, the prediction of the planner was succinct: "National leadership and command and control destroyed. Iraq's strategic offense and defense eliminated for extended period."[59] Powell was briefed on the plan on 11 August, and he ordered it to be expanded to include options for expelling Hussein from Kuwait, should it come to that.

The plan was presented to Bush from 6 to 8 October, but it satisfied no one. It virtually guaranteed high losses, and the military felt that they were being pressured into providing an offensive option too soon, before the DESERT SHIELD troops were even safely in place; the civilians in the room saw only poor planning. Ordered to present a new offensive strategy that would guarantee success, Schwartzkopf returned with a plan that called

"The Gang of Eight." *Left to right:* Richard Gates, John Sununu, Dick Cheney, Dan Quayle, Bush, James Baker, Brent Scowcroft, and Colin Powell. (Courtesy of the George Bush Presidential Library)

for the doubling of the DESERT SHIELD troop commitment. These reinforcements would be necessary to guarantee the success of the bold plan, which called for an initial attack against the heart of Saddam's forces and then a strike against the Iraqi flank to the west—a "left hook"—that would encircle the fleeing Iraqi army.[60]

When presented in October with the revamped INSTANT THUNDER plan, Bush immediately favored reinforcing the DESERT SHIELD troop commitment. But politically, his hands were tied; the congressional elections were coming up, and Bush did not want to send more troops to the Gulf until they were over. He approved the doubling of forces on 31 October but did not announce it until after the election.[61] On 8 November Bush revealed that he was doubling the American force in Saudi Arabia from 230,000 to more than 500,000 troops in order to create an "offensive military option." Bush also added more than 1,200 M-1 tanks to those already in Saudi Arabia. The new reinforcements, in numbers approximately equal to those stationed in Europe at the height of the cold war, represented the largest American military deployment since the Vietnam War.

Bush justified his decision to move toward an offensive option on the grounds of saving the world from a brutal bully. By the end of 1990, he was making regular comparisons between Saddam (whose name he continually mispronounced, a serious slight to an Arabic male and one that it is possible Bush did deliberately) and Adolf Hitler.[62] He also frequently used terms like "rapist," "evil," and "madman" to describe the Iraqi leader. Bush used the Wilsonian rhetoric of righteousness; in his 1991 State of the Union Address, he bluntly asserted, "Our cause is just. Our cause is moral. Our cause is right."

Yet Bush's most impassioned utterance in this regard was part of an interview, first broadcast to the American people on 2 January 1991. British journalist David Frost had been given access to Bush for a program analyzing the first two years of his presidency. Not surprisingly, the crisis in the Gulf dominated the program—particularly since on the day he was interviewed, Bush had read an Amnesty International report that outlined a host of Iraqi atrocities. Bush told Frost that the report "should be compulsory reading [for] anyone who thinks we have all the time in the world." He then listed several examples from the report, the most gruesome of which was the torture and rape of a handicapped child. As he continued, Bush's lips tightened and his face flushed with anger. He called Saddam "primeval" and "the rapist of Kuwait" and promised that "we will prevail. There's no question about it."[63]

Bush was completely sincere in his hatred of Saddam; it was easy for him to equate the Iraqi dictator's actions to those of the 1940s' dictators whom he had risked his life to defeat. But there was an equally important national security reason for Bush's actions, one that James Baker highlights in his memoirs: "We *had* responded to a clear violation of international law . . . and we *were* dealing with a megalomaniacal personality. But it was also true that we had vital interests at stake. . . . We had to make sure we could maintain a secure supply of energy."[64]

For half a century, the United States had clearly stated that keeping the Middle Eastern oil pipeline flowing—and keeping the price of crude as low as possible—was in its vested national security interests. Yet Bush did not articulate the economic ramifications of Saddam's actions nearly as well, or as passionately, as he expressed his belief that Saddam was basically an evil man. Bush left the oil argument up to Baker to explain, which the secretary of state did on several occasions. The most notable came after a 13 November press conference, when Baker declared, "We cannot permit a dictator such as this to sit astride that economic lifeline. And to bring it down to the level of the average American citizen, let me say that means jobs."[65] Baker later argued that it was the "rhetorical confusion" of the administration—sending too many mixed messages in an attempt to justify the military actions—that played into the hands of a growing movement in opposition to DESERT SHIELD.[66] Just as likely is the explanation that Baker never should have mentioned the oil issue publicly, for that was the aspect the antiwar activists pounced on.

The announcement of troop reinforcements, and the administration's heated rhetoric about Saddam's actions costing American jobs, brought a wave of antiwar protests both in the United States and around the world. In New York City, a parade of marchers six blocks long rallied at Times Square, chanting "Hell, no, we won't go—we won't fight for Texaco."[67] A group that called itself Out Now ran an advertisement in the liberal magazine the *Nation;* they asked for contributions for future ads so that they might continue to broadcast their message: "Must we trade body bags for oil? Why not Give Peace a Chance? Speak Out Now—Remember Vietnam. . . . Out Now—Bring Our Troops Home."[68]

More troubling from a political point of view was the fact that many Republican conservatives, who presumably would support the president's actions, were instead opposing the move toward war, claiming that Bush was involving the nation in another Vietnam-like morass for no real purpose. Chief among these critics was conservative columnist and television talk-show host Pat Buchanan. In August 1990, the former Nixon speechwriter had written an editorial, "How the Gulf Crisis Is Rupturing the Right." In it, he claimed that "neoconservatives" like Bush supported a war "that has quagmire written all over it. . . . Saddam Hussein is not a madman; he is no Adolf Hitler; while a ruthless menace to his neighbors, he is no threat to us. . . . Have the neocons thought this through?"[69] And Buchanan was by no means the only conservative critical of Bush's policies. In January 1991, the Cato Institute ran a conference "America in the Gulf: Vital Interests or Pointless Entanglement?" The papers presented make it clear that the participants overwhelmingly sided with the latter interpretation.[70]

The public support for Bush's actions, which had been high at the beginning of the crisis, slowly ebbed throughout the fall. In August Bush's popularity rating had been at 75 percent in favor of the job he was doing as president; by October it had dropped to 59 percent, and immediately after the congressional elections it was at 50 percent.[71] This drop was caused not only by his moves toward an offensive option but also by his decision to support a tax increase. With Bush's tumble in the polls, the opportunity presented itself for the Democratic Congress to make some political hay before the November election. The Senate Armed Services Committee, chaired by Sam Nunn, began a series of hearings on the Gulf crisis. They gained instant notoriety because of the testimony of a young girl who claimed to have seen Iraqi soldiers snatch Kuwaiti babies from the incubators in the hospital where she worked, leaving them to die on the floor. The witness, however, was the daughter of the Kuwaiti ambassador to the United States who had been prepared for her testimony by an American public relations firm.[72]

As the administration prepared to expel Saddam from Kuwait, no one helped Bush's cause more than Saddam himself. Foremost was his taking of hostages. Saddam's treatment of the thousands of Western civilians (including over 3,000 Americans) living in Kuwait or Iraq, whom he refused to allow to leave after the outbreak of the crisis, can only be described as bizarre. Although calling them "human shields," they were nonetheless treated well, housed in hotels in Baghdad, and then paraded in front of television cameras with Saddam so that they might testify to the humaneness of their treatment. The strategy, if it was one, backfired. Westerners were appalled at pictures of five-year-old British hostage Stuart Lockwood, riveted with fear, standing next to Saddam as the Iraqi leader patted his head and asked him, "Are you getting your milk, Stuart, and your corn flakes, too?" Thatcher mocked Saddam for "hiding behind women's skirts."[73] For his part, Saddam ignored the rumbling of world opinion against him, and on 22 September he issued a statement urging all Iraqi citizens to prepare for "the mother of all battles."[74] The UN responded on 29 November by passing Security Council Resolution 678, giving him a deadline: it agreed to support the use of "all necessary means" by the coalition forces to expel Saddam from Kuwait if he did not withdraw his forces by 15 January 1991.

The day after the UN vote, Bush surprised many observers when he announced that he was willing to go the "extra mile for peace," and he offered to send Baker to Baghdad and to receive Iraqi foreign minister Tariq Aziz in Washington. The decision was less a diplomatic move than it was a political one. Baker's political radar told him not only that there was a great deal of support in the country for the idea but also that even if Saddam spurned the invitation, as the administration seems to have assumed, then the mere act of extending the olive branch would help defuse the rapidly growing antiwar feeling at home. As Baker recalled, it would show that "we weren't cowboying this."[75]

The plan almost backfired on Bush when Saddam found reasons to reject each American request for a meeting. On 14 December, in remarks to the press on his way to Camp David, Bush chided his opponent: "It is simply not credible that he cannot, over a two-week period, make a couple of hours available for the secretary of state on an issue of this importance—unless, of course, he is seeking to circumvent the United Nations deadline." Eventually, Saddam agreed to a meeting between Baker and Aziz in Geneva on 9 January 1991.

The meeting was both tense and confrontational. Baker presented Aziz with a letter from Bush, to be delivered to Saddam. Dated 5 January, it was stark and blunt. Bush told Saddam that "we stand today at the brink of war between Iraq and the world," a war that "can only be ended by Iraq's full and unconditional compliance" with UN Security Council Resolution 678. Bush also made it clear that the time for negotiating was over and that if Saddam used chemical or biological weapons—which he had done against Iran—or if he destroyed any of the Kuwaiti oil fields, "the American people would demand the strongest possible response." Bush closed the letter by saying that he had not written "to threaten, but to inform."[76] Aziz, who apparently believed that the meeting was for the purposes of negotiation, refused to accept the letter from Baker. Clearly, Baker had not come to negotiate but to deliver Bush's ultimatum. Baker wanted to make sure that Saddam understood the gravity of the situation; he looked at Aziz and quietly declared, "Don't let your military commanders convince you that your strategy against Iran will work against us. You are facing an entirely different kind of force. . . . Because of the superiority of our forces, we will dictate the terms of the battle, not you." Aziz responded, "We accept war." After the meeting broke up, Baker told the press, "Regrettably, I heard nothing today that suggested to me any Iraqi flexibility."[77]**

The final hurdle to war was on Capitol Hill, where the Congress stood poised to claim authority given it under the War Powers Act and to debate Bush's authority to send troops into combat. Bush decided to co-opt the process and to formally ask Congress for its support before such a debate could begin. This decision was made despite the advice of C. Boyden Gray, who believed that "as a question of international law, we were on solid ground deploying the troops" (a conclusion heartily shared by Bush),[78] and of Cheney, who did not want to take the risk that Congress would reject the measure. But Bush was adamant; as he later remembered, he wanted "to send a signal to Saddam Hussein that it wasn't just a trigger-happy president" but that he had the American nation behind him.[79] And there was another consideration; as Gray remembered, "If it went sour, [Bush] wanted Democrats with him. . . . He wanted a unified government. . . . It's a military, constitutional, moral, and political thing."[80]

The debate was civil, but lines had been drawn. Antiwar resolutions were introduced in both houses of Congress, and for most of 10 and 11 January, the debate on the issue was nonstop. Senate majority leader George Mitchell (D-ME), who with Nunn had sponsored the antiwar resolution in the Senate, argued that although "it may become necessary to use force to expel Iraq from Kuwait . . . because war is such a grave undertaking, with such serious consequences, we must make certain that war is employed only as a last resort." Edward Kennedy proclaimed that "there is still time to save the president from himself." In the House, minority leader Robert Michel argued, "Either we stop [Saddam] now, and stop him permanently, or we won't stop him at all."[81] Several times, debate had to be suspended

---

**The possibility that the administration did not "regret" the outcome of Baker's mission is strongly suggested by the reaction of those in the cabinet room, including Bush, immediately following Baker's press conference. John Gravois of the *Houston Post*, acting as that day's pool reporter for the White House Press Corps, observed, "There was much whooping and loud noises . . . suggesting something positive was afoot, but it turned out to be a somber-looking bunch when the writers and photogs entered." Bush told the reporters that he was not encouraged by Baker's report but that he was "not giving up on peace at all" (Pool Report, 9 January 1991, Bush PP, WHPO, Lower Press Office Pool Reports, box 14, dated folder).

because visitors in the gallery were shouting antiwar slogans. The vote in both chambers promised to be close.

But Baker's gamble in Geneva paid off; the administration was able to say that it had gone the extra mile and been spurned. Both the House and the Senate voted on 12 January. In the House, the conservatives who had abandoned Bush on the budget only weeks before returned to the fold; the vote was 250 to 183 against an antiwar resolution. In the Senate, the vote was closer. Mitchell and Nunn worked hard to hold the Democratic ranks together. However, minority leader Bob Dole did a better job of holding the Republican feet to the fire. The final vote was a razor-thin 52-to-47 defeat of the antiwar resolution. Nine Democrats, including Al Gore Jr. of Tennessee, had defected to support the president; only two Republicans, Charles Grassley of Iowa and Mark Hatfield of Oregon, voted no. Following the defeat of the antiwar proposals, both houses voted, by the same tally, in favor of House Joint Resolution 77, the Authorization for Use of Military Force Against Iraq.

As with the earlier support of the UN, however, the vote of Congress was, though welcome, hardly deemed by the White House to be absolutely necessary. In a later interview, Bush made it clear that "I know I would have" ordered troops into combat, even without a resolution of support from Congress.[82] From the earliest moments of the crisis, the die had been cast.

Three days after the congressional vote of support, Bush signed National Security Directive 54: "Pursuant to my responsibility under the Constitution as President and Commander in Chief, and under the laws and treaties of the United States, and pursuant to H[ouse] J[oint] Resolution 77 and in accordance with the rights and obligations of the United States under international law," the president was initiating military hostilities against Iraq. The directive was clear in its statement of war aims:

    a. To effect the immediate, complete, and unconditional withdrawal of all Iraqi forces from Kuwait.
    b. To restore Kuwait's legitimate government.
    c. To protect the lives of American citizens abroad, and
    d. To promote the security and stability of the Persian Gulf.

Bush was also clear about when those military operations would end: "Only when I have determined that the objectives set forth . . . above have been met."[83]

9

DESERT STORM

On 31 December 1990, after he left a family celebration at Camp David, Bush wrote a letter to his children.

> I hope I didn't seem moody. I tried not to. . . . I have thought long and hard about what might have to be done. As I write this letter at year's end there is still some hope that Iraq's dictator will pull out of Kuwait. I vary on this. Sometimes I think he might; at others I think he is simply too unrealistic—too ignorant of what he might face. I have the peace of mind that comes from knowing that we have tried hard for peace.
>
> I look at today's crisis as "good vs. evil"—yes, it is that clear. . . . Principle must be adhered to—Saddam cannot profit in any way at all from his aggression . . . and sometimes in your life you have to act as you think best—you can't compromise, you can't give in.
>
> So, dear kids, better batten down the hatches.[1]

At 3:00 A.M. Iraqi time, 17 January 1991 (7:00 P.M. eastern standard time, 16 January in the United States), one day after the deadline set in UN Resolution 678, Operation DESERT SHIELD turned into Operation DESERT STORM. The first strikes came from AH-64A Apache antiarmor attack helicopters, which flew into Iraq and knocked out key early warning radar systems. They were followed by attacks by F117A bombers—the Stealth bomber—and F-15C fighter bombers, which struck at targets in the heart of the city of Baghdad. Within the first fourteen hours of the war, over 1,000 sorties were flown, and forty-five key targets in the capital city were hit.[2] The bombing runs were supported by Tomahawk missile attacks from destroyers in the Gulf—one of the support carriers was Bush's old ship, the USS *San Jacinto*. That first night, Americans were glued to their TV screens, as CNN, which had three reporters holed up in a hotel in Baghdad, broadcast terrifying live shots of Tomahawk missiles descending upon the city, then exploding only yards from where the reporters were stationed.

After five-and-one-half weeks of near constant air bombardment, and several attempts by Saddam to end the war without withdrawing from Kuwait, the land war began on 24 February. Feinting an amphibious marine landing just outside Kuwait City, the First and Second Marine Divisions and the Tiger Brigade of the Twenty-second Armored—already some ten miles inside Kuwait before the attack order was given—smashed into the teeth of the Iraqi front-line defenses. However, the marines moved so quickly that they engaged the Iraqis in Kuwait City before they could be joined by the Twenty-eighth Corps and the Seventh Corps advancing from the west (neither Gen. Norman Schwartzkopf in the field nor Gen. Colin Powell at the Pentagon thought that the army was advancing anywhere near fast enough). As a result, within twenty-four hours Iraqi troops poured out of Kuwait City, taking the road north to Basra. On 27 February, more than 1,500 coalition tanks, led by the Seventh Corps, shattered the heart of the Republican Guard defensive position at the Battle of Medina Ridge (tank commander to his forward positions: "Understand we are engaging the Medina Division?" Response: "Negative sir. We are *destroying* the Medina Division").[3] In about forty minutes, 300 Iraqi tanks were lost; one American was killed. The next day—six weeks after the beginning of the air war, and exactly 100 hours after the beginning of the ground war—a cease-fire was declared. On 3 March at Safwan, Iraq, Schwartzkopf met with the Iraqi military leadership and dictated the terms of the cease-fire. The Americans had lost 148 killed in action and 458 wounded (more Americans were murdered in the United States during that 100-hour period than were lost in combat in Iraq); the rest of the coalition lost some ninety-two soldiers. Iraqi reports, although still disputed, suggest some 22,000 Iraqi dead.[4]

My purpose here is not to offer a full military history of the Persian Gulf War. Indeed, the literature on the subject is vast, and beginning with Rick Atkinson's exceptional *Crusade: The Untold Story of the Persian Gulf War*, surprisingly good, given that at this writing much of the government material on the war continues to be security classified. My goal, rather, is to look at the impact of the war on the nation as a whole and on the Bush administration in particular.

With that in mind, several points need to be made. First, the point that is the most often made on the Gulf War: the outcome was never in doubt.

Outnumbered and with no air support, Saddam knew that he could not win. The only strategy open to him was to dig in his lines and hope that he could repel the coalition advance long enough for the American people to tire of the war, just as they had in Vietnam. However, this strategy played right into the coalition's hands. With superb intelligence, the coalition knew that the Iraqi forces were dug in; thus, the Iraqis were sitting ducks. When the bombardment began, it was so easy for the coalition forces that airmen christened a new sport: "tank plinking."[5] Moreover, this entrenched Iraqi army was so chained to its eastern trenches that when the ground assault came, the army had no chance. After the left hook began, reports circulated of American tanks simply rolling over and burying Iraqi soldiers who had no way out of their trenches.

Over the five-and-one-half weeks of the air bombardment, the coalition flew more than 100,000 sorties. Saddam's tiny air force was both unable (most of the 800-plane air force was destroyed on the ground early in the offensive; during the entirety of the conflict, a total of seventy-six American planes were shot down) and ultimately unwilling to respond. Few Iraqi sorties—toward the end of the bombardment, virtually none—were flown to meet the allied offensive. American Stealth bombers were never touched by Iraqi defenses, and they operated at will over Baghdad. During the ground war, the marines advanced so quickly against only token opposition that they reached Kuwait City before the flanking attack could catch up with them. When the left hook finally met the Republican Guard, there was absolutely no contest. Iraqi T-72s were simply no match for the new American M1-A1s; coalition soldiers called it a "turkey shoot."

Added to this situation was the fact that the Iraqi military leadership was completely incompetent. Let one example suffice: the Iraqis marked their way through their own minefields with concertina wire in a path that was clear to the invading coalition tanks. As one tank commander put it, "Once we found that, the only thing missing was a neon sign saying 'start here.'"[6] Iraqis surrendered by the thousands, chanting "M–R–E" (the American serviceman's slang for "Meals Ready to Eat") and flashing victory signs rather than white flags (final military guesstimates say that the coalition captured some 80,000 Iraqi prisoners of war). The president's Office of Communications was so optimistic about a quick victory that on 14 January, a full three days before the war began, it sent Chief of Staff John Sununu a full plan, including the setup for lights and teleprompters, the length of the address, and sequencing for the "presidential announcement of the liberation of Kuwait."[7] The staff was overly confident, but not wrong. For the Americans, Operation DESERT STORM was always a no-lose proposition.

Another key point that had long-lasting effects for Bush's New World Order was the role that Israel played during the Gulf War. Saddam's only real offensive weapons were Scud missiles, 14,000-pound liquid-fueled rockets, with an accuracy of one mile (to improve its range, the Iraqis welded two rockets together). For all intents and purposes, the Scud was useless as a tactical weapon and useful only for inflicting civilian terror.[8] On the second night of the war, Saddam began to indiscriminately lob Scud missiles into Israel. Property damage occurred, but initially there were no fatalities. Certain members of Yitzhak Shamir's cabinet, most notably Minister of Defense Moshe Arens and Minister of Housing Ariel Sharon, argued for immediate retaliation.

Key to Bush's success at holding together the coalition had been his ability to keep the Israelis out of the conflict. With the launching of the Scuds, however, Bush had to up the ante. The DELTA FORCE, a counterterrorist commando unit, was infiltrated into Iraq to try to ferret out and destroy any Scuds as well as their launchers.[9] Bush also sent two Patriot missile batteries to Israel, the largest airlift of American military weaponry to Israel since the 1973 Yom Kippur War. And he agreed to inform Shamir in real time, by way of the newly installed secure satellite line between the White House and Tel Aviv, code-named HAMMER RICK, of any confirmed Scud launchings toward Israel. Iraq continued to lob Scuds into Israel; a total of forty were fired at Israel and forty-six at Saudi Arabia. The total death toll from this counterattack was 31 dead and 400 injured.[10] Israelis lived with gas masks within their reach: puppet performers on the children's television program *Kippy of Rechov Sumsum* also wore gas masks to calm the fears of their little viewers.[11] But Shamir did not retaliate. A grateful Bush remembered Shamir's restraint in the months following the war, with important ramifications for the Middle East peace process.

During the war, the American press stressed the impact of the new technology on both strategy and offensive capability. It was dubbed the Nintendo War, after a popular video game of the time; and stories abounded of the technological marvels that gave the United States an overwhelming military superiority—the term "unbeatable" was omnipresent in press reports of the conflict. Certainly since World War II's mass-destruction bombings of Germany and Japan, the air force had developed technologies of precision guidance that allowed it by 1990 to pinpoint its targets with amazing accuracy. Few people who watched the drama unfold on television were not awed by pictures taken from within the cockpit of an F-15 fighter, showing a missile zoom down an airshaft and destroy a building.

The surgical nature of America's air power might have given the impression to many observers that the war was bloodless. It often seemed to the American public that the key to the war was the skill of a military technician who sat behind a computer, punched in coordinates, and launched missiles that simply erased the enemy from memory. American bombardiers apparently never missed. Bush himself perpetuated this perception, calling the bombing "fantastically accurate"; Schwartzkopf's chief of staff, Robert Johnson, declared, "I quite truthfully cannot tell you of any reports that I know of that would show inaccurate bombing."[12]

It is now clear, however, that the Americans were far less accurate with their precision bombing than was portrayed by either Washington or Riyadh. Rick Atkinson recounts that of the 167 laser-guided bombs dropped by F-117s during the first five nights of combat, 76 missed their targets completely, a fact that was not acknowledged to the press by either the Pentagon or the White House.[13] One bizarre example of this inaccuracy was an F-15 attack on what was purported to be seven mobile missile launchers. When the cockpit tape was played back for CIA analysts, however, they immediately saw that the destroyed targets were not missile sites; some thought them to be oil tankers, others believed them to be milk trucks (the error was not revealed to the public).[14] There were other examples. On 22 January, coalition bombing destroyed what CENTCOM claimed was a factory that made biological weapons; Iraqi claims at the time, broadcast by CNN's Peter Arnett, suggest that the factory actually made baby formula.[15]

Along with accusations of targeting errors came reports of problems with the Patriot missile. A postwar army investigation claimed that the greatest single loss of American life in the war—twenty-eight American soldiers killed—resulted from a Scud hit on an army barracks. The Scud had sneaked through coalition defenses due to a computer failure that shut down a Patriot missile's capacity to intercept it.[16] The problems of the Patriot were kept from media and public scrutiny, as was the astoundingly high number of coalition deaths resulting from errant bombardment by their own forces. Thirty-five coalition soldiers, 23 percent of the total, were killed by friendly fire—"fratricide," in military parlance. In comparison to past wars, this percentage was much higher, and it took the Pentagon some five months to inform their families of that fact.[17]

The "bloodlessness" of the war can also be challenged by the number of civilian deaths. The most publicized tragedy took place on 13 February. The coalition had been closely monitoring a building in the Al Firdos section of Baghdad that had been labeled Public Shelter Number 25. But the allies believed that the bunker had become, in the words of the attack plan that sealed its doom, an "activated, recently camouflaged command-and-control bunker." Available evidence suggests both that the coalition had evidence that showed this assessment to be true but that this evidence—a newly camouflaged roof, captured radio messages, and a new protective fence—was hardly irrefutable. Nevertheless, the bunker was destroyed, killing 204 civilians, many of them children, who had been sleeping in an air-raid shelter in the bunker. Administration and military planners remain convinced to the present day that somewhere in the bunker there had been a command-and-control center. But the tragedy, quite aside from the human loss, took on a political life of its own. In order to avoid any further public-relations disasters, CENTCOM was ordered to choose its bombing targets in Kuwait rather than in Baghdad. Some analysts argue that this decision lengthened the air war and gave Saddam badly needed time to regroup.[18]

In a postwar study, the group Human Rights Watch evaluated the civilian death toll during the war and largely exonerated the American military: "In many if not most respects the allies conduct was consistent with their stated intent to take all feasible precautions to avoid civilian casualties."[19] The evidence suggests that this assessment was quite accurate. Nevertheless, one must also agree with Atkinson's assessment: "The sanitary conflict depicted by Bush and his commanders, though of a piece with similar exaggerations in previous wars, was a lie."[20]

This lie was perpetuated, although not willingly, by the press. Unlike in Vietnam, where television shots of ravaged bodies became daily fare for the nightly news, in the Persian Gulf the military constricted the operations of the some-1,600 reporters to the point where they got little film footage other than what the central command wanted them to have. The U.S. Armed Forces Joint Information Bureau decided which reporters actually got to visit, and film, the front. The wire services and a few newsmagazines, television networks, and radio outlets were given priority in the field, and even those lucky enough to get into the pool were most often fed information by the armed services and taken only where the army wanted them to go. Other reporters were, in their parlance, "corralled" behind the lines, left to file their stories largely from watching CNN reports and from attending official military press conferences. As one reporter put it, "For most journalists, coverage of the war has been by invitation only."[21] As a result, Americans saw more video clips of successful bombing raids than they saw human beings in combat; they saw virtually no casualties and heard few references to coalition errors.

The press, smitten with the impressive show of American technological might, did little to challenge the situation. The general tone of the coverage—particularly on television, and especially on CNN, the most watched network during the conflict—makes it clear that reporters largely accepted CENTCOM's line at face value. Reports such as those from the *New York Times* on 21 January claiming that American Patriot missiles "intercepted most or all of [the Scuds] and knocked them from the sky before they could hit their targets" were the norm.[22] With remarkably few exceptions, the Gulf War was sanitized for popular consumption.

Perhaps the biggest controversy arising from the Gulf War revolved around Bush's decision as to when it would end. His decision to stop it before the left hook had completely encircled the Iraqis, thus completely cutting off their path of retreat, was for him an easy one. He had been clearly told both by Powell and Cheney that Saddam's capability to make war had been obliterated by the end of the first day of the ground war, and Powell argued for ending the fighting as soon as possible. The road out of Kuwait City north to Basra—the line of retreat for the occupying Iraqi army—became known as the Highway of Death. As coalition forces bombed the fleeing Iraqis at will, Bush found himself appalled at the slaughter. NSC Deputy Robert Gates recalled that Bush used the word "unchivalrous" to describe the infliction of any further carnage on the Iraqis.[23] Powell summarized the situation: "You don't do unnecessary killing if you can avoid it."[24] Bush agreed with him. Put simply, when faced with the choice between any further bloodshed or ending the war ahead of schedule, Bush did not hesitate to end the war.

Powell remembers that when he got the news, Schwartzkopf responded, "I could live with that."[25] Atkinson reports that Schwartzkopf "seemed neither upset nor surprised" at Bush's decision (when one of his staffers asked why they were not being allowed to encircle the enemy completely before the cease-fire, Schwartzkopf replied, "Because that's what the commander in chief wants. The president says we've accomplished enough").[26] In his memoirs, Powell writes that "every member of [Schwartzkopf's] policymaking team agreed" with the decision.[27] Scowcroft later agreed: "There was no dissent."[28] In a later interview with David Frost, however, Schwartzkopf asserted that Bush had been too hasty: "Frankly, my recommendation had been, you know, continue the march"—an assertion that made Powell, in his words, "mad as hell."[29] Schwartzkopf's statement, made during the 1992 presidential campaign, gave fodder to Bill Clinton and Ross Perot, both of whom charged the administration with ignoring the supposed recommendation of its field general to end the war one day later, a recommendation that, as it turned out, was never made. The tempest prompted Powell to issue a statement on 27 August 1992, which read in part, "General

Schwartzkopf and I both supported terminating DESERT STORM combat operations at 12 P.M., 27 February 1991 (EST), as did all the president's advisers. There was no contrary recommendation. There was no debate. . . . Those who claim that another twelve or twenty-four hours of fighting *without a cease-fire* would have fundamentally changed the residual capability of the Iraqi army are mistaken."[30]

Indeed, if anyone was responsible for letting Saddam's army "escape," it was Norman Schwartzkopf. During the cease-fire meeting at Safwan, his generosity to the Iraqis was pronounced. He promised that American forces would not long remain in Iraq, but he went even further. Through his generals, Saddam claimed that he needed to keep his armed helicopters because the Americans had destroyed most of the bridges and roads. Without obtaining the permission of Washington, Schwartzkopf acquiesced. The cease-fire allowed the Iraqis to continue to fly armed helicopters over their territory, an arrangement that soon came back to haunt other Iraqi opponents. To be fair, everyone in the White House did not initially see the danger in Schwartzkopf's largesse. Scowcroft wanted to reverse Schwartzkopf's decision, remembering in a later interview, "I didn't care whether the country was administered that way or not and it gave [Saddam] a great loophole." However, Scowcroft was overruled.[31]

On 6 March 1991, Bush went before a Joint Session of Congress, each member having been given a miniature American flag to wave. In the most dramatic moment of his presidency, Bush turned to face the Kuwaiti ambassador, sitting in the House gallery, and announced to a standing ovation: "Ambassador Al-Sabah—Kuwait is free." Bush then recalled the CNN footage of an American soldier who was guarding several Iraqi prisoners, softly and carefully telling them, "You're all right." When Bush remembered that moment, to thunderous applause, he took out his handkerchief and dabbed his eyes. At the end of the talk, he gave Colin Powell a hug.

Certainly, one outcome of the war was a tremendous surge of patriotism, typified for many Americans by the near-constant radio airplay of Lee Greenwood's signature song, "God Bless the U.S.A." For others, it was the pageantry of the 8 June victory parade held in the streets of Washington. Norman Schwartzkopf was immediately enshrined as the first American military hero since Eisenhower; Dick Cheney and Colin Powell were christened overnight as presidential contenders. Fred Barnes, one of Bush's most severe critics, declared in his column in the *New Republic:* "I can't think of another president who could have pulled this off."[32] For George Bush, these accolades were quite quantifiable; those people expressing faith in the Bush administration increased from 43 percent in September 1990 to 67 percent at war's end.[33]

Bush speaking to the Joint Session of Congress, 6 March 1991. (Courtesy of the George Bush Presidential Library)

When I asked Brent Scowcroft if the United States won the war with Iraq, he did not hesitate for a moment when he answered in the affirmative. Yet he later mused that "very few geopolitical problems are solved by any one action."[34] Despite the many bits of evidence that pointed to an overwhelming American victory in the Persian Gulf War, by mid-1991 one point had begun to gnaw at many Americans. Despite the success of the coalition at expelling Saddam Hussein from Kuwait, he was still very much alive and in control of Iraq's destiny. He had also escaped with a full one-third of his army intact.

It is important to note that nowhere in his public statements—or anywhere in the available records of the administration or in the memories of any of the individuals present in the decision-making loop—did George Bush (or the United Nations, which specifically and carefully avoided any such reference in any of its resolutions on the crisis) ever call for the overthrow of Saddam from his position of power in Iraq. For Bush, the potential political ramifications of an operation designed to catch and overthrow Saddam were staggering. Uppermost in the president's mind was the Panama Syndrome; how could an army that could not catch one Panamanian dictator dislodge Saddam Hussein? Moreover, such a strategy would necessitate marines fighting in the streets of Baghdad, guarantee thousands of coalition casualties, and ensure a protracted military commitment, possibly an army of occupation after the war, none of which was acceptable either to the Pentagon or Bush, for whom "escalation"—reminiscent of Vietnam—was abhorrent. Also important was the same issue that had guided Bush's temperate response to the fall of communism in Eastern Europe in 1989: a completely smashed Iraq, leaving a power vacuum in the Gulf area that either Iran or Syria could quickly exploit, was not in the best interests of the United States. Thus, throughout the conflict, the president's goal, as clearly stated in press briefing notes dated 2 August 1990, was to "get Iraq out of Kuwait and Kuwait back to the status quo ante."[35] As Scowcroft bluntly put it, getting Saddam out of power was "never a goal—only a hopeful byproduct."[36] Privately, Bush reportedly told his aides that he hoped "some kind of Ceaucescu scenario" would befall the Iraqi dictator.[37] But the hoped-for coup did not emerge. Indeed, Saddam had expanded his power base by declaring that he had stood up to everything the Americans could throw at him, and he had survived. Bush and Scowcroft had both hoped for a Battleship *Missouri* surrender, reminiscent of the Japanese unconditional surrender to the Allies on an aircraft carrier at the end of World War II. This, due to Schwartzkopf's miscalculations at Safwan and to Saddam's survival, they did not get; and ethnic minorities in Iraq soon paid the price.

Sensing an instability in Saddam's regime, Shi'ite Muslims, a religious minority located in southern Iraq and longtime vocal critics of Saddam's claim that he headed the one, true branch of the Muslim faith, rose up in revolt in early March. Saddam and his helicopters were brutal in their response, and the Shi'ites suffered terrible losses. Citing earlier promises of American support, the Shi'ite rebels fully expected American help. They did not get any. Robert Gates was blunt: "Therein lay Vietnam, as far as we were concerned."[38]

The same fate awaited the Kurds, an ethnic minority living in the north of Iraq who had been systematically denied a political homeland of their own for almost a century. Bush may well have inadvertently called for a Kurdish uprising when he said that "the Iraqi military and the Iraqi people should take matters into their own hands, to force Saddam Hussein, the dictator, to step aside."[39] Regardless, Saddam used his helicopters to wreak havoc on the Kurds, who tried to flee to refugee camps in nearby Iran and Turkey. When they pleaded for Western assistance, however, they were spurned.

According to one source, during one Oval Office meeting on the subject, Powell spelled out a "precise military case against" intervention.[40] In his memoirs, Powell was clear: "Neither revolt had a chance. Nor, frankly, was their success a goal of our policy."[41] More interested in getting American troops home from the Gulf than in embroiling them in another conflict, postwar America took on a decidedly isolationist tinge. Newspaper editorials were clear in their advice: "Iraq: The Limits of Sympathy"; "A Blood Bath Beyond Our Grasp"; "Caution on New War With Iraq"; "The Quicksand in Iraq."[42] Baker paid a pro forma visit to a Kurdish refugee camp but spent only seven minutes there.[43]

Perhaps the greatest legacy of the Gulf War was that it rejuvenated the peace process in the Middle East. In his diary, Bush wrote that despite Israeli intransigence, "We kicked Saddam Hussein and solved their security problem in the area . . . [so now] they're going to have to move on the peace process."[44] Thanks to Baker's postwar shuttle diplomacy, all affected parties—including, in a breakthrough of gigantic proportions, the Israelis, the Syrians, and the Palestine Liberation Organization—agreed to the international conference on the Middle East that Bush had promised Gorbachev in Helsinki. But the Soviet leader was not a major factor at the conference. He had just survived a coup attempt and was but a month away from resignation when the conference convened in Madrid on 30 October 1991. Indeed, little of substance emerged from Madrid; little had been expected.[45] But its symbolic effects were nevertheless earth-shattering. For many observers, the conference was the most tangible sign of Bush's New World Order—for the first time in decades, age-old enemies had all sat together and talked in the same room.[46]

10

★ ★ ★ ★ ★

PRESIDENT BUSH

Despite Americans' latent affection for Ronald Reagan, long before 1988 they had become troubled with his hands-off, detached approach to presidential leadership. In George Bush they found Reagan's polar opposite. Bush's style of executive leadership was characterized by indefatigable energy. Indeed, the words "energetic" and "hyperactive" damn Bush with faint praise; by any definition, he was a workaholic. No one had thrown himself into this job with this amount of vigor since the last Texan to occupy the White House. Jim Baker later remembered that Bush has "the finest manners of any man you'll ever meet. But somewhere along the way he never learned to sit still."[1] Bush's staff continually complained (or boasted, depending on whom they were talking to) about the long hours and the phone calls in the middle of the night from a boss who just wanted to talk. There was no question that Bush loved his work; Herbert S. Parmet has observed that he "never did get over how special it was to be president of the United States."[2]

Bush's high energy level on the job stemmed from his naturally competitive personality. Fred Malek, one of Bush's campaign managers in 1992, most accurately observed in a television interview, "This was a guy who above all else wanted to do *everything* well."[3] All forms of outdoor activity were treated not as restful recreation but as serious competition. In comparison to Reagan, who had been characterized in the press as a dottering grandfather-type, there were pictures of Bush taking his daily jog, leaving the press corps in his wake (prompting cute headlines about how Bush was always "'running' for president"). As the White House Press Corps, hardly athletic by nature, tried its best to keep up, it could not help but be impressed with the president's stamina (the *New York Times'* Maureen Dowd, a pronounced Bush critic, marveled, "This President relaxes by wearing the others out").[4]

Whether fishing at Kennebunkport, playing golf, or playing tennis, Bush kept score; and his former aides make it clear that the boss was not so much a fool that opponents could "let him win" just to impress him. Horseshoes was the most serious business. Bush had new pits installed at the White House, and he was so eager to try them out that he took off their covers and pitched a round before the paint was dry. Every foreign dignitary of consequence was compelled to be taught the finer points of the game. This led to one of the most comic moments of the Bush presidency. During the May 1990 summit, Mikhail Gorbachev, who had never before played the game, pitched a ringer on his first—and only—try. Bush was astounded (some aides remember that he was angry) at being outshone by a rookie at his game. Nevertheless, in the spirit of good sportsmanship, Bush had the offending horseshoe framed and presented to Gorbachev as a gift.

One might expect that it would be easy for a man as energetic as Bush to discard the wimp image when he became president, simply by allowing himself to be seen as he truly was, a rough and tumble man's man. Indeed, Bush seemed to be, in the words of an admiring aide, "the real Ronald Reagan."[5] After all, the casual Reagan, to the delight of the media and the citizenry, had dressed as a cowboy and chopped wood—hardly, as evidenced by his biographers, the true Ronald Reagan. But even though Bush was a more genuine outdoorsman and man of energy than his predecessor—a true hunter, fisherman, and horseshoe player—the prevalent perception of him as a rich, elitist snob dogged him both during and after his presidency. For example, David Mervin has characterized Bush as "a rather cold-blooded and uncaring patrician, out of touch with the needs and discontents of ordinary people."[6]

The elitist factor had staying power in part because it was, indeed, an aspect of Bush's rather complex character. Unlike Lyndon Johnson, whose manhood was never in question, Bush was no yahooing Texan in the White House. He was, like many of his friends from the wild-catting days, what native Texans called (and still call) a "transplant." As such, Bush adopted those parts of the Texas lifestyle that he particularly enjoyed, such as pork rinds and country music. These mixed together with a homespun patriotism that was born of World War II but had by the time he entered public service taken on a rural flavor (he kept Oak Ridge Boys tapes in his briefcase to play on the cassette deck in his limousine; and in his diary, he wrote that country music "is just for these times. The flags, patriotism, and someone's praying").[7]

Yet despite spending the balance of his adult life in the Lone Star State, Bush never exorcised his New England prep-school upbringing; nor did he seem to wish to do so. No less an expert on the modern presidency than Hugh Sidey has observed that there was, indeed, a "dimension" of George Bush that separated him from other people but that "he didn't have the least idea about it."[8] In his 1964 congressional campaign, for example, his manager begged him to stop wearing button-down collars; Bush refused.[9] During the 1992 campaign, he entered a store and professed his amazement at a technological tool that he had never seen before—a price scanner, which had been used in checkout lines for over a decade. At one point on a presidential outing, he was confused when he went to buy a pair of socks for himself. Bush was that rare breed of individual who lived in two worlds—the world of the Rich and Famous and the world of a real Texas barbecue. This created a dichotomy in his personality that was effectively captured in the title of Parmet's 1997 biography, *Lone Star Yankee*. The *New York Times* was a bit more direct, classifying Bush as "A Special Mix: Ivy League and Pork Rinds."[10]

Bush might have rid himself of the wimp label had he been able to *allow* his image to be retooled. However, unlike his predecessor, who was willingly malleable and marketable, Bush hated image makers. His director of communications, David Demarest, explained it: "The president does not see himself as the center of national attention."[11] Whether this was, as many of his aides contend, a function of Bush's natural humility, or whether it was a result of a calculated attempt to distance himself from the scripted Reagan presidency, the result was the same. Bush was never able to manipulate his public image to his advantage; the elitist factor remained.

The elitist factor played a major role in Bush's 1992 defeat, as the more homespun Bill Clinton and Ross Perot either were more in touch with everyday Americans or were able to present themselves as such. But this perception should not mask the most frequently cited facet of George Bush's personality: every person who came in contact with him, on either side of the political aisle, pays tribute to his genuine decency. There are very few genuinely nice people in the political arena. Most have become so hardened by the process that they lack any genuineness, any real warmth, except, of course, that which has been created for them in their advertisements. This was never the case with George Bush. It is difficult to find fault with the assessment of Daniel Heimbach, then Bush's deputy assistant secretary of the Domestic Policy Council: "George Bush set a tone in terms of personal example . . . that was focused on doing the right thing for America and as an individual . . . whether the law required it or not."[12] Courtly, almost

Victorian in his mannerisms, Bush showed a genteelness that was innately gracious; when he told me in 1998 that "I'm not the kinda guy who likes to hurt feelings," it was both believable and provable through the testimony of those with whom he served.[13] Generous to a fault, he was willing to make available his personal time for virtually any aide who asked for it. His thank-you notes, written for what one might consider the most trivial of favors, were Washington legends. Republican strategist Ed Rollins, far from a Bush fan or supporter, remembered that he had to tell his wife, a member of the Bush White House, to stop sending Bush a thank-you note for his, or the correspondence would continue forever.[14]

Bush's sense of humor ranged from the droll style of the New Englander to the often uproarious guffawing of the Texan. As vice president, he visited West Germany as the guest of Chancellor Helmut Kohl. At dinner, the head of the anti-Kohl party, a young woman named Petra Kelly, burst in and began to berate Kohl. Bush turned to his host and dead-panned, "Is your attachment to Petra emotional, or is it a physical attraction?" The usually staid Kohl burst out laughing.[15] He also had no problem poking fun at himself. On Halloween 1988, Bush put on a rubber George Bush mask, and strutted through his campaign plane chanting, "Read my lips! Read my lips!").[16] He loved the parody done of his nasal speaking voice by comic Dana Carvey; he even invited Carvey to the White House, where the two men had reporters in stitches as they each tried to sound most like the real George Bush.

Bush the politician was never an accurate reflection of Bush the man. His campaign style was harsh, often shrill, consistently a take-no-prisoners approach. In many ways, Lee Atwater and John Sununu existed to counter Bush's kinder, gentler side, to give him an edge of toughness. Pragmatic to a fault, Bush not only openly courted these individuals to become a part of his campaign team, but he also embraced them, placing little or no distance between himself and their rather vicious way of doing business. Once these prodigal sons were aboard, Bush allowed them to work their political magic, and stayed loyal to them far beyond the point at which other presidents would have let them go.

Indeed, if there is one personal characteristic that best defines George Bush, it is the place that loyalty plays in his life and career. It is absolutely clear that loyalty is what makes him tick. James Baker has written, "Friendships mean a lot to George Bush. Indeed, his loyalty to friends is one of his defining personal strengths."[17] It was also the key to his political choices. Craig Fuller lost his chance to be chief of staff for perceived disloyalty to the Bush family; Bush held on to John Tower and John Sununu out of the same sense of loyalty.

Few observers have bothered to look at how George Bush approached the presidency. Dismissing him as a passive, guardian president, they seem to work under the assumption that he had no overriding philosophy of executive power other than being reelected in 1992. Not given to sweeping, philosophical statements on any subjects, Bush came closest to a specific statement of his view of presidential power on 10 May 1991 in a speech at Princeton University. The speech was largely a criticism of Congress for trying to "micromanage" the executive branch and a reinstatement of his call for a line-item veto ("our founders never envisioned a Congress that would churn out hundreds of thousands of pages worth of reports and hearings and documents and laws every year. . . . [They] waste the time and energy of the executive"). But Bush also spoke to the "real power of the presidency," not the constitutional ones but the power to lead "through example [and] through encouragement."

The Princeton speech suggests that Bush viewed the power of the presidency along the lines set out by Richard Neustadt, in his 1960 masterpiece on the executive mindset, *Presidential Power*. Neustadt emphasized that the real power of the American president was not constitutional in nature but personal—successful presidents were successful persuaders. If one uses this as a barometer, Bush's grades are mixed. In his one-to-one dealings with people, Bush was a master of the persuasive art. He cultivated people not as allies (although they often were used for such) but as friends (according to Maureen Dowd, "There have been some unconfirmed reports that Mr. Bush sometimes spends time alone. But no one believes this").[18] Bush's ubiquitous use of the telephone was representative of his preference for personal dealings rather than the use of backchannels or political aides. For example, Andrew Card, who served in several capacities in the Bush administration, remembers that ten minutes after he called James Baker in 1979 to tell him "I'm on board" for the 1980 election, Bush called him back: "Jimmy tells me you're on board."[19] Two close observers slyly note that when Bush "looked at the globe, he thought of the ultimate Rolodex."[20]

Yet in the area of the public presidency—that part of leadership that requires the president to connect with the citizenry at large—historians will find Bush wanting. George Bush was, to put it charitably, an uninspiring speaker. One White House aide summed up his public pronouncements crudely but accurately: "[Bush] doesn't give speeches. He gives remarks."[21] But it is just as important to understand that Bush never saw his role as a second great communicator. In his memoirs, he wrote, "Some wanted me to deliver fireside chats to explain things, as Franklin Roosevelt had done. I am not good at that."[22] In the role of "chief soother," Bush found difficulty in connecting with average Americans in their time of need. For but one example, in April 1989, forty-seven sailors were killed in an accident aboard the USS *Iowa*. Forced into the limelight of national grief for the first time as president, Bush reportedly called the all-time expert at executive grief management, Ronald Reagan, and asked him, "How do you do this?"[23]

Perhaps this deficit explains why Bush clearly relished crisis situations and was better at managing them than he was at managing the day-to-day demands of being the nation's chief executive officer. In times of crisis, the president can, and most often does, withdraw from the people and then makes his decisions surrounded only by a small number of his closest aides. Here, Reagan was lacking—a born delegator, he would rather make a speech than make a tight decision. As in so many ways, Bush was the opposite of Reagan in this regard. A born crisis manager, Bush listened, quickly sifted through the advice of his staff, and then made immediate decisions. Christopher Buckley was quite correct when he observed, "George Bush is at his best when his dander is up."[24]

These characteristics clearly explain one of the biggest disappointments of Bush's tenure as president: his abysmal relationship with the press. It had never been very good to begin with. The wimp factor, the mud-wrestling match with Dan Rather during the 1988 Iowa primary campaign, the choice of Dan Quayle, and the Willie Horton mess had combined to make the press wary of reporting Bush's human side and led them to treat him as a light-weight—a treatment that exasperated him.

Nevertheless, Bush made a genuine attempt as president-elect to repair his rocky relationship with the Fifth Estate. A key to Bush's "kinder, gentler" transition to the presidency was a genuine attempt to distance himself from his predecessor's rather imperious relationship with the press. Essential to that strategy was the rehiring of Marlin Fitzwater. Fitzwater had earned his bachelor's degree from Kansas State University (1965) and had worked as a reporter and as an advertising executive for several Kansas newspapers. He had served as press secretary to Vice President Bush from 1 April 1985 to January 1987, when he began his service as Reagan's press secretary. His successor on Bush's staff did not fare as well. Bush's press secretary during the 1988 campaign, Sheila Tate, was pilloried by the press for both a lack of availability and an imperious manner; thus, Bush did not keep her into the administration. Instead, he broke precedent and became the first president to retain his predecessor's press secretary.[25]* The modest, affable

---

*In 1963, following the assassination of John Kennedy, Pierre Salinger stayed on for a brief period as Lyndon Johnson's press secretary; however, all concerned knew that that was a temporary arrangement.

Fitzwater was universally seen by the press as a strong press secretary: in the words of Hugh Sidey, he was "honest . . . straightforward . . . not grandstanding."[26] But he was no pushover. He often clashed with Sununu, whom he described in his memoirs as "an overweight Kermit the Frog walking head down with his hands in his pockets. . . . That's John Sununu, only shorter."[27] Fitzwater quickly became one of Bush's most trusted aides.

When asked in a 1998 interview if he hated the press when he was in the White House, Bush diplomatically responded, with a smile, "Well, not the whole time." In his own defense, he remembered that in the early months of his presidency, he "bent over backwards" to provide "availability" to the press.[28] Indeed, in the early going Bush raised accessibility to an art form, oftentimes dropping by the White House briefing room for unscheduled questions and answers. He made himself available for one-on-one interviews that he continued to hold even when the result was an article critical of him or his policy.[29] In his first year as president, Bush held almost as many press conferences (thirty-two) as Reagan had held in eight years (forty-seven).[30] This attitude was quite beneficial for Bush; during his first three months, coverage of the president ran two-to-one positive, compared to the three-to-one negative during the campaign.[31]

But even Fitzwater's affability and Bush's accessibility could not keep the president's relationship with the press from eventually reverting to its campaign-time hostility. Bush and Fitzwater seemed to have believed that increased access alone would lead to better coverage. It did not. Bush did not partake in the good-natured banter with the press that Reagan had so enjoyed; none of the humor, none of the playful reminders of the power structure (Reagan would often cup his ears and pretend not to hear an offending question, much to the enjoyment of the press corps). Bush perhaps met with the press more often, but the press instinctively knew that Reagan liked them more.

The relationship seems to have soured after the failed October 1989 Giroldi coup in Panama, which resurrected the wimp factor. An angry Bush, publicly castigating purported leakers from within his own administration, began to withdraw from the press. For example, on the way to a February 1990 drug summit in Colombia, a visibly angry Bush went back to the press seats on Air Force One. He condemned stories that had been written on his tendency for secrecy and announced that from that point forward, "we've got a whole new relationship."[32] That relationship continued to sour as the press felt itself—rightfully, as the evidence shows—to have been closed out of the field of battle in both the Panamanian and the Persian Gulf conflicts. By 1991 there was an open hostility between Bush and the press that had become difficult to contain. On 4 September 1990 the press was asking the president questions before a cabinet meeting. Helen Thomas of United Press International (UPI) looked directly at Bush and asked, "Who's in charge here?" According to the pool report of the exchange, Bush stared straight ahead, and Baker flashed a glance at Bush. Bush responded, "Some people never learn."[33] By the administration's end, by all accounts, the relationship had gone past thrust and parry; George Bush truly seemed to hate the press, and, in many journalism quarters, the feeling was mutual. It became an important factor in his electoral travails in 1992.

However, one aspect of Bush's press coverage was impeccable. In comparison with her immediate predecessor's and her successor's, Barbara Bush's press coverage was outstanding. Unlike Nancy Reagan and Hillary Clinton, who made no pretense of hiding their roles in helping to shape their husbands' policies, Mrs. Bush supressed her views. Indeed, after a minor firestorm when it was reported that she disagreed with her husband on gun control and abortion, she publicly announced that she would not be speaking out on policy for the rest of the administration.[34] Nevertheless, reports of her private influence circulated throughout the Bush tenure; she was christened by some observers as "the Silver Fox."[35] She wasn't. Barbara Bush carved out two roles for herself. The first was as a tireless advocate for the cause of literacy. She served on the board of Reading Is Fundamental and was a sponsor of Laubach Literacy Actions. In 1990 she wrote her second book, a biography of the First Dog. Called *Millie's Book*, the delightful story depicted the life of the vice president and president as seen through the eyes of a dog. It grossed almost $1 million for literacy.[36]

Her second role was as her husband's "good cop" with the press. Her openness and her wry sense of humor—for example, her appearance at the annual Gridiron Dinner in a red fright wig—offered a stark contrast to Nancy Reagan. Mrs. Bush's mastery of the one-liner quickly became legendary (in 1989, answering a question about her often matronly appearance, she quipped, "My mail tells me a lot of fat, white-haired wrinkled ladies are tickled pink").[37] Speechwriter Peggy Noonan called Barbara "Greenwich granite" and noted that she and her husband were "a good match: a team."[38]

George and Barbara Bush were the proud scions of a massive family, and stories abound of the free-wheeling vacations at the family home at Kennebunkport. Bush's faith in public service was reinforced as he watched two of his sons, Jeb and George W., gingerly take the first steps toward political life while he was still president. He reveled in each opportunity to roughhouse with his grandchildren. His devotion to his wife was completely sincere, open, and loving. Referring to the attempt by the

Barbara Bush. (Courtesy of the George Bush Presidential Library)

Reagan conservatives to co-opt the issue of traditional values, one observer noted, "George Bush was a family man before being a family man was cool."[39]

In many ways, Bush as both a man and as a president are well explained by the Points of Light movement. The concept of rewarding and advancing citizen volunteers, whom he saw as bright, shining stars, had long been in Bush's mind. Long before he won the White House, he was smitten with this imagery. While he was at the United Nations, Bush made a speech in Houston. Handwritten into his notes was a telling comment: "Ideals are like stars. You cannot touch them with your hands but like the seafaring man on desert waters if you use them as a guide they will lead U [sic] to your destiny."[40] He used the metaphor again in his 1988 acceptance speech at the Republican convention, in his 1989 Inaugural Address, and in virtually every domestic-oriented speech as president. This gave him the opportunity to express some of the most spirited rhetoric of his presidency, as in his 1991 State of the Union Address, when he called on Americans to "join the community of conscience" and "do the hard work of freedom."

Once president, Bush moved quickly to set his idea into concrete form, creating the Office of National Service (ONS) in the White House. It was run by C. Gregg Petersmeyer, a friend of the Bush family and chairman of Bush's campaign in Colorado. Despite the problems with the budget deficit, Bush was able to secure a $25-million allocation for the ONS, whose task was to identify and honor community and volunteer groups.[41] According to the reference guide written by the ONS, the criterion for choosing the honored groups was "hands on work," which was focused on "serious problems." The group or organization "had to be replicable," have been in operation for at least one year, and be "working systematically" on a community problem.[42] Six days a week, the ONS would recognize a Daily Point of Light, and Bush often found the time to attend that formal recognition. During his term, he met with representatives of 675 Points of Light, and Vice President Quayle met with another 103.[43] Petersmeyer, clearly an evangelist for the ONS, later remembered that he believed it to be "a movement rather than a program."[44] The zeal of both Petersmeyer and the president for a program that seemed to many observers at the time more symbolic than substantial led the press to treat the Points of Light largely as a joke. However, it had created an instrument for the volunteerism that Reagan had preached but had taken few concrete steps to accomplish. Moreover, in a tribute to its resilience, the program outlived the Bush administration. The nonpartisan, nonprofit Points of Light Foundation, founded in May 1990, still serves to foster the spirit of American volunteerism. At present the foundation has 500 centers around the nation; as late as November 1998 it was sponsoring relief to Honduras, a nation completely devastated by Hurricane Mitch.

When asked by Peggy Noonan, in preparation for drafting his acceptance speech at the 1988 convention, to write a few words that described him, Bush replied: "Others may speak better, look better, be smoother, more creative but I must be myself." He provided for her a list of words that were important to him, including "family, kids, grandkids, love, decency, honor, pride, tolerance, hope, kindness, loyalty, freedom, caring, heart, faith, service to country, fair (fair play), strength, healing, excellence."[45] It can be said that George Bush knew himself well.

11

★ ★ ★ ★ ★

"THE SITUATION IS ABOUT AS BAD AS IT CAN BE"

Whether it is put to scholar, generalist, or citizen, it is the most frequently asked question about the Bush presidency: "How could he have lost the presidency when he won the war?" Most observers have pointed to the 1990 flip-flop on taxes as the primary reason for Bush's 1992 loss to Bill Clinton. Clearly it was a factor; between September and mid-October 1990, Bush experienced a twenty-five point drop in his approval ratings.[1] But with the Persian Gulf War, he made up that deficit and more. In February 1991, at the time of the cease-fire, Bush enjoyed an astounding 84 percent approval rating; however, by the end of the year, his administration was in free-fall. In mid-November it was at 51 percent; December, 46 percent, and 42 percent in spring 1992. By summer 1992, his ratings had hit their lowest point—a mere 29 percent.[2] In fall 1988, 58 percent of the people polled thought that the country was "headed in the right direction"; in fall 1992, that number had plummeted to a microscopic 16 percent.[3]

Clearly, then, the budget crisis was not the only factor in Bush's downfall. Between the time of the cease-fire in the Persian Gulf and the start of the 1992 campaign, his administration faced serious difficulties—largely but not entirely of its own making—in rapid succession. These problems combined to make the reelection of George Bush, only a year before a sure thing, a long shot at best. Small wonder that David Bates, then Bush's cabinet secretary, remembered that in summer 1991, Bush was "talking out loud" about whether or not he should even run for reelection.[4]

151

In retrospect, the beginning of the end of the Bush reelection campaign came on 5 March 1990. Along with several other party leaders, chairman of the Republican National Committee Lee Atwater was making an appearance at a party fund-raiser for Sen. Phil Gramm (R-TX) at Washington's Ramada Renaissance Hotel. The beginning of Atwater's speech was a hit; the guaranteed sound bite—that the 1988 tank ad made Michael Dukakis "look like Rocky the Flying Squirrel"—got a big laugh. Suddenly, Atwater's left foot starting twitching uncontrollably. The spasm moved through the left side of his body, and Atwater collapsed, screaming in pain. Later that day he was diagnosed with a terminal brain tumor and given one year to live. Throughout that year, as Atwater suffered through a new kind of chemotherapy that, at best, bought him only a few extra weeks, the RNC disintegrated into factional feuding. In January 1991, Atwater resigned as its chair. Bush's first choice for the job was former drug czar William Bennett, who turned down the appointment to take a lucrative position in the private sector. Atwater's successor was Clayton Yeutter, previously Bush's secretary of agriculture, but a man with virtually no political experience. It mattered little; the damage had been done. Short on funds (while ill, Atwater had been unable to raise funds and his chief of staff, Mary Matalin, who took over the reins during his illness, had not been very good at it), the RNC had to lay off 25 percent of its staff just before Yeutter arrived. Because of the political fallout from Bush's flip-flop on taxes, the RNC fundraising machinery never fully recovered.[5]

The RNC itself never recovered from the beating it had taken during Atwater's year of suffering, and it played a muted role in the 1992 election. There are individuals today who believe that had Atwater remained healthy and in control of the political machinery, the damage from Bush's decision in summer 1990 to embrace new taxes would have been less severe.[6] More important, Bush had lost one of the few people who could pinpoint a campaign strategy. The 29 March 1991 death of Harvey Leroy Atwater turned out to be not just the first but the most important loss to the 1992 campaign. It was followed by the departure of advertising guru Roger Ailes, who refused to participate in the campaign (Rich Bond, who succeeded Yeutter at the RNC, described Ailes as "burnt out in his personal life, [and] alienated from the White House by intrigue." Bond later remembered that as the White House tried to gear itself up for the coming campaign, "the A-Team was missing.")[7]

Two months after the death of Atwater, Bush's own health became an issue. On 4 May 1991, during a jog at Camp David, the sixty-six-year-old president was stopped by severe shortness of breath. Rushed to Bethesda Naval Hospital, he was diagnosed with an atrial fibrillation—a tiny flutter in the small chamber at the top of the heart that controls its rhythm.[8]

Later that week, however, the diagnosis was changed. Bush had Graves' disease, which had led to both the arrhythmia and an overactive thyroid.* Many members of his team began to privately wonder if Bush would have the strength to endure another grueling presidential campaign.

The recent history and development of the position of White House chief of staff makes it clear that the primary role of the job was, in the words of Nixon staffer H. R. "Bob" Haldeman, to be "the president's son of a bitch." But few modern chiefs relished this role more than John Sununu. He had played the part of Bush's bad cop—a necessary task, given Bush's courtly manner—to perfection and had made few friends in the White House as a result. On the same day that Bush's heart flutter was reported, Sununu also made the *New York Times,* quoted in a story about his tenure as chief of staff: "I don't care if people hate me, as long as they hate me for the right reasons."[9] The reasons were varied, but he was certainly hated. Yet though he was reviled by virtually everyone in Bush's inner circle, and even held at arm's length by the president, who valued his service to the administration but rarely allowed him to join in tennis or golf outings, there can be no question that Sununu's power and influence were incredible. More so than any other member of the administration, Sununu was responsible for holding the right wing in line during the many episodes in 1989 and 1990, which strained the conservative alliance with Bush to the breaking point. Even this role became suspect after Sununu's brazen performance during the 1990 budget negotiations, but once again the chief of staff made himself indispensable. During the Persian Gulf crisis, acting under the authority given him through NSD-1, Sununu was a key player in the Gang of Eight that worked the president through the decision of wartime policy. Indeed, for a man with few friends in high places, Sununu's position in May 1991 could not have been stronger.

That month, stories that exposed Sununu's abuse of his White House position began to leak. It was soon reported that he had taken ninety-nine taxpayer-financed flights on air force jets for personal use; several were

---

*Both George and Barbara Bush contracted Graves' disease within a year of moving into the White House. In fact, their dog Millie came down with lupus, which is in the same autoimmune category as Graves. This set off much speculation as to whether or not the White House environment posed a serious health hazard, a debate that was never satisfactorily concluded. See Burton J. Lee, M.D. (physician to Bush) in *Portraits of American Presidents,* ed. Kenneth E. Thompson, vol. 10, *The Bush Presidency* (Lanham, MD: University Press of America, 1997).

for family ski vacations, one for a dental appointment in Boston. It was also reported that the cost of those trips was nearly $500,000, as opposed to the approximately $45,000 they would have cost had he flown first class on a commercial flight.[10] It was also revealed that Sununu had traveled in his chauffeured government limousine to New York City to purchase $5,000 worth of rare stamps at a Christie's auction (he argued that he took the limo because his job required him to stay in constant touch with Washington). *New York Times* columnist William Safire called for his resignation "because he lacks a presidential aide's most essential attribute: political judgment."[11]

Although none of the activities that the press dubbed the "Air Sununu" scandal was illegal, it was certainly indiscreet. It was also the type of story that the White House Press Corps could sink its teeth into. But Sununu dug in his heels, telling Press Secretary Marlin Fitzwater, "I'm not going to give them a damn thing. It's none of their business. Every trip I made was authorized on behalf of the president."[12] Bush could hardly ignore the issue; he himself had made ethical behavior in his administration a hot issue. Thus, Sununu was admonished. He was forbidden to take trips without prior consent from the White House. Then, to add insult to injury, Sununu had to preapprove all his flights with White House Counsel Boyden Gray, who had himself been the subject of an ethics investigation early in 1989 and whose office was under Sununu's in the executive office chain of command.

Yet Bush could not bring himself to take the next logical step, particularly in view of the upcoming presidential campaign, and dismiss Sununu. Fitzwater remembers that the reasons were complex: "[Bush] liked him and his take-charge attitude. Furthermore, he had staked a great deal of his presidency on Sununu."[13] But Sununu repaid this loyalty by getting himself deeper into trouble. In November he accosted *Washington Post* reporter Ann Devroy at a White House ceremony, shouting "You're a liar! Your stories are all lies!" The next day, he admitted on national television that Bush had "ad libbed" a line in a speech. On Sununu's initiative, Bush had inserted a line calling for a lowered interest rate on credit cards. The Senate passed the measure, and the stock market dropped 120 points. Rather than fall on his own knife, Sununu publicly blamed Bush for a gaffe, thus giving the impression that he was criticizing his boss's judgment.[14]

Sununu had become the subject of ridicule, and a reluctant Bush decided he had to go. But the end did not come easily. George W. Bush reportedly tried to get Sununu to resign, but he would have none of it. Indeed, when summoned to Camp David to speak with the president, Sununu surprised Bush by not offering to resign. There followed a series of leaks to the press from Bush's supporters, predicting Sununu's impending demise, a sure sign that he had lost whatever support he might have had left in the administration.[15] Andrew Card, then Sununu's deputy chief of staff, remembered that it was he who told Sununu that the president would accept his resignation, a recollection supported by Fitzwater.[16] On 3 December 1991, Sununu resigned.

On the surface, at least, Bush's choice as Sununu's successor, announced the day of the latter's resignation, was a winner. Thanks to his role in the *Exxon Valdez* debacle and in coordinating the administration's response to the October 1989 San Francisco earthquake that killed over 250 people, Secretary of Transportation Samuel Skinner had earned a deservedly high reputation as the Mr. Fixit of the administration. The polar opposite of Sununu, Skinner was quiet and thoughtful (on himself to the *Washington Post*: "not bad for a guy who went to night law school").[17] It also didn't hurt that Skinner's wife was friends with George W. Bush's wife, Laura, and that Skinner reportedly lobbied the couple on his own behalf.[18] In further staff restructuring, Skinner was joined at the White House by the equally cerebral Clayton Yeutter, who left the RNC to serve as counselor to the president for domestic policy.

However, as Secretary for Veteran's Affairs Edward Derwinski observed, when Skinner came aboard, "the White House bureaucracy collapsed."[19] Virtually all present in the White House at the time remember Skinner as a poor chief of staff. Perhaps Card put it best: "Sununu relished the opportunity to make a decision. . . . Skinner wanted decisions made for him."[20] Skinner simply was not ready for turf battles with savage political operators such as Richard Darman, who, according to several members of the administration, regularly undercut him.[21] For his part, Yeutter had accepted his job only after being promised that he would receive control over the flailing domestic and economic policy shops once belonging to Roger Porter. He abolished those two cabinet councils and created the Policy Coordinating Group (PCG), but it failed to produce any more coherent a policy strategy than had Porter's councils.[22] Yeutter later wrote the epitaph for Bush's policy-making machinery: "The administration had never gotten on top of domestic policy . . . in retrospect, it was too late."[23]

Before Sununu left, however, the administration faced a firestorm of criticism over its second appointment to the Supreme Court. On 28 June 1991, after twenty-four years as the liberal voice of the Court, Thurgood Marshall retired. It was soon clear that Bush would not be able to get away with another "stealth candidate" like David Souter. Marshall's retirement left only one member of the Court who had been appointed by a Democratic president (Byron White, appointed by Kennedy), and though no one believed that Bush would appoint a liberal, the Democratic Congress was ready to pounce if he appointed a cipher. Marshall's resignation also left the Court with no African-American justices, and liberal groups immediately called for Bush to fill Marshall's seat with a person of color.

For Bush, this was a golden opportunity to mend fences with the right wing of his party. He operated from the start on the premise that he would have to nominate a conservative African American. Indeed, the appointment of a moderate, no matter what his or her race, would never satisfy the right wing, particularly since Souter had proven to be a more moderate judge than expected. Sununu had privately promised conservatives that Bush's next appointment to the Court would be a true conservative: a solidly anti-abortion, strict constructionist judge.[24]

On 1 July 1991 at Kennebunkport, Bush announced that he would nominate Clarence Thomas of the Circuit Court of Appeals for the District of Columbia. The *New York Times* bemoaned Thomas as "a conservative Republican with a scanty judicial record on civil rights and abortion."[25] This was an understatement. In his seven-and-one-half years as director of the Equal Employment Opportunity Commission (EEOC), Thomas had opposed both affirmative action and quota hiring, and in 1987 he had praised an article that criticized the Court's decision in *Roe v. Wade*. Thomas's record from the bench was thin, to say the least. He had been considered for the Supreme Court when Justice William Brennan resigned, but it was decided he needed more experience; when Bush tapped him for the Supreme Court, he had served only eight months on the Circuit bench.

In his speech introducing Thomas, Bush referred to the judge as a man with a poor rural past who had pulled himself up and labeled him as a "model for all Americans." When Thomas testified on his own behalf before the Senate Judiciary Committee on 10 September, he emphasized the same themes, outlining in his opening remarks the segregation and poverty that his parents had lived under and how he had come to value hard work as a young man. Like Souter, however, Thomas danced around the issue of abortion, refusing to comment directly on *Roe* (arguing that as a potential Supreme Court justice he would be required to hear arguments on the case, and he did not want to prejudice himself by discussing the case before his confirmation), although he did endorse the constitutional right to privacy.

For the White House, it was to be the Souter strategy all over again, and it initially seemed that it would work. There was more tension than had been experienced at the Souter hearings—civil rights organizations, for example, were solidly against Thomas. But conservative forces were wary of opposing the nomination, lest they be branded in the press as racists. On 27 September the Judiciary Committee voted 7 in favor of the nominee and 7 against but voted 13 to 1 to send Thomas's name to the Senate floor for full debate and a vote on 8 October.

Bush with Clarence Thomas, 1 July 1991. (Courtesy of the Bush Presidential Library)

During the committee's investigations, employees of Thomas had been contacted by the Federal Bureau of Investigation (FBI) and asked for their response to rumors of sexual harassment at the EEOC. One of those employees, law professor Anita Hill of the University of Oklahoma, gave the FBI a detailed statement that not only charged Thomas with harassment but also detailed his affection for pornographic movies and his penchant for discussing his sexual prowess with his female aides. That report was not made public until after the Judiciary Committee had voted to send Thomas's nomination to the Senate floor; it might not have been made public at all had not members of the press obtained copies of Hill's supposedly confidential report.

On 6 October Hill's allegations broke on National Public Radio and in *Newsday*. Faced with the public airing of this report, the members of the Judiciary Committee fell over each other to get their spin before the press. Alan Simpson (R-WY) appeared on ABC's *Nightline* brandishing Hill's telephone records, showing that she had stayed in contact with Thomas, even asking his advice on getting research grants, long after she had resigned from the EEOC.[26] Hill responded to this charge in her memoir:

[This suggests] that I was seeking something I had no right to expect, though I had worked for Clarence Thomas for two years and had performed my job conscientiously. . . . Never would I have considered these solicitations opportunism. I received no personal gain. Besides, I had not been the one to behave inappropriately. So why should I later allow his behavior to deprive me of a job I had rightfully earned?[27]

Arlen Specter (R-PA) and Orrin Hatch (R-UT) criticized the broad nature of the sexual harassment laws themselves, which, in their argument, made it possible for any accuser to smear an innocent party. On the floor of the Senate, John Danforth (R-MO) read a statement in which he claimed that Thomas had sworn in an affidavit that Hill's allegations were false and that he was "terribly saddened and deeply offended" by her charges. Congressional Republicans were in full attack, and Hill had few defenders. The one person on the Judiciary Committee who might have been expected to defend her, Edward Kennedy of Massachusetts, was himself so tainted from charges of womanizing that he could not speak too loudly, lest the press throw stones at his glass house.

After the release of Hill's statement, Thomas's confirmation was in jeopardy. Many conservatives, particularly those from the religious right, were privately urging Bush to withdraw the nomination. But as Bush had done two years earlier with John Tower, he stood by his nominee. On 9 October he told the press, "I've got strong feelings but they all end up in support for Clarence Thomas." Bush had approved a new tactic: reopening the Judiciary Committee hearings. On 11 October Thomas again appeared before the committee and turned his wrath on both Anita Hill and the confirmation process. He called the procedure a "lynching" and "Kafkaesque," claiming, "I never asked to be nominated. It was an honor. Little did I know the price, but it is too high. . . . confirm me if you want, don't confirm me if you are so led. But let this process end." Thomas was excused after reading his statement; then it was Hill's turn. In her statement, she outlined her recollection of Thomas's transgressions and asserted that "telling the world is the most difficult experience of my life, but it is very close to having to live through the experience that occasioned this meeting." For the rest of that day, Hill was grilled as to the validity of her charges. That evening and for part of the next day, Thomas returned to the committee room to deny them all, charging that they played "into the most bigoted racist stereotypes that any black man will face."[28] For his part, Bush told the press, "In my view Judge Thomas made a very, very powerful and convincing statement. This decent and honorable man has been smeared."[29]

The hearings were a media circus, and the senators played to the cameras. Hatch suggested that Hill had concocted her story and waved a copy of the novel *The Exorcist* before the cameras, claiming that it was where the story had come from. Specter accused her of perjury (though the result was inadmissible, the *New York Times* reported on 14 October that Hill had passed a polygraph test).[30] The incivility oozed from the committee room and onto the Senate floor. When Kennedy rose to challenge those who would "tolerate any unsubstantial attack on a woman in order to rationalize a vote for this nomination," Hatch snapped back, "Anybody who believes that, I know a bridge up in Massachusetts that I'll be happy to sell them," a reference to the 1969 incident where Kennedy had driven off the Dike Bridge at Chappaquiddick, drowning his passenger, Mary Jo Kopechne.[31] During a pause in the acrimony, on 16 October, the Senate voted to confirm Thomas by a vote of 52 to 48.

The mangled process of choosing and confirming Clarence Thomas seriously wounded the Bush administration. Once again, Bush was charged with putting loyalty above either competence or political common sense, as many observers claimed that he should have jettisoned Thomas as soon as Hill's charges were made public. Bush had also done little to endear himself to conservatives, who ignored Thomas's opposition to affirmative action and excoriated the administration for nominating a man with a checkered moral past. By opening up sexual harassment as a major political and social issue, the Thomas hearings also lost Bush any hope of winning the women's vote in 1992. And, according to some analysts, the hearings accelerated Bush's loss of the black vote, a defection hastened by his 21 November 1991 signature of a Civil Rights bill that allowed an employer to avoid charges of discrimination if it could be proven that the racial disparity in the workplace had been caused by a valid "business necessity." These were the quotas that Bush had argued against so strenuously only one year before, and black Americans decried the flip-flop more than they did the quotas. Over the three days that Bush agreed to sign the bill, his approval rating among nonwhites dropped to 28 percent. They never recovered.[32]

Judicial politics was hardly the only crisis facing Bush in 1991. In the middle of the Persian Gulf crisis, Mikhail Gorbachev had made a major miscalculation. Believing the Americans to be preoccupied, he cracked down on the secessionist outbreaks in the Soviet republics. On 11 January 1991 in Lithuania, Soviet troops seized several government buildings; two days later, Lithuania was placed under martial law. In the rioting that followed, 15 were killed and about 170 wounded. Gorbachev blamed Lithuania; his former foreign secretary, Eduard Shevardnadze (who had resigned over Gorbachev's policies in December), commented, "He al-

ways thinks he is the master of events."[33] Faced not only with the impera-
tives of the Gulf War, which necessitated keeping Gorbachev in the coalition, but also with criticism from Republican conservatives who accused
him of abandoning the republics, Bush was caught; his response to the
Lithuanian crisis was muted. This prompted Sen. Bill Bradley (D-NJ) to
remark, "It would be a sad irony if the price of Soviet support for freeing
Kuwait was American acquiescence in Soviet aggression against another
illegally annexed country."[34]

After the Gulf War, Bush was being pressured from within the White
House to drop Gorbachev in favor of Boris Yeltsin, whom Gorbachev privately referred to as "that cowboy" but who had been elected to Moscow's
at-large seat in the legislature with 89 percent of the vote.[35] Loyalty to
Gorbachev, as well as a belief that Yeltsin was the less stable choice of the
two, led Bush to continue to support Gorbachev until it was too late (he
recorded in his diary on 17 March: "My view is, you dance with who is on
the dance floor").[36] During the July 1991 summit in Moscow, during which
the START treaty was signed, Bush took the advice of his aides and made
a visit to the Ukraine. Yet even in the capital city of that republic, he could
not bring himself to break with Gorbachev, telling the Ukrainians, "Americans will not support those who seek independence in order to replace a
far off tyranny with a local despotism." Conservative columnist William
Safire dubbed it the "Chicken Kiev" speech.[37]

Despite Bush's support for Gorbachev, his inability to deal with the
republics was the final straw for the cold warriors in the Kremlin who had
long hoped to displace him. On 18 August 1991 Gorbachev was placed
under house arrest at his dacha on the Black Sea. But the coup was poorly
planned and its leadership far from adept. When they appeared on Soviet
television, they were nervous and inarticulate; their leader, Soviet vice
president Gennady Yenayev, was clearly drunk (prompting the *Wall Street
Journal* to call their effort the "Vodka Putsch").[38] For his part, Yeltsin denounced the plotters, shouting outside the Russian Federation Building,
"Aggression will not go forward! Only democracy will win!"[39] Again, Bush
showed restraint, explaining to the press, "It's not a time for flamboyance
or show business or posturing." He voiced his support for Yeltsin's stance
only when he was certain that the coup would fail.

The aborted coup led directly to the passage of resolutions of secession
in eight of the republics, including Russia. Three days after Gorbachev's
return from exile, the communist party was voted out of existence by the
Parliament (the vote was 283 to 29, with 52 abstaining).[40] Gorbachev's days
as Soviet president were numbered. At the international conference on the
Middle East, held in Madrid that October, Gorbachev was, in the words of
one observer, "a shadow of his former self" and did not play a serious role

in the proceedings.[41] On 21 December the eleven former republics formed the Commonwealth of Independent States and accepted Gorbachev's resignation, even though it had yet to be submitted. Gorbachev resigned four days later, two years to the day after Nicolae Ceauscescu of Romania had been executed. By deciding to stand by Gorbachev until the bitter end, Bush had once again angered his party's conservatives and had gained nothing in return.

These factors played into the hands of a Democratic party that hoped to use the reversal of Bush's fortunes against him in the upcoming presidential elections. It was, however, the severe economic downturn that Bill Clinton used as his most potent weapon. A large sign at Clinton headquarters, one that stayed up throughout the entire campaign, kept their focus true: "The Economy, Stupid."

By August 1990 the long-predicted recession had arrived with a vengeance. By the end of the year, the big three auto makers (Chrysler, General Motors, and Ford), had lost a total of $1 billion—their first combined loss since the 1978–1982 recession—and they were predicting that they would lose money in the first quarter of 1991 as well. In that first quarter, the big three had temporarily shut down or slowed production in more than twenty American assembly plants, firing some 60,000 workers.[42] But this recession was not just a working-class phenomenon. Layoffs hit suburbia as well, as large corporations were forced to cut back on their middle management; the term "downsizing" became a grotesque part of the American vocabulary. By June 1991 the national unemployment rate had risen to 7.8 percent, the highest in eight years.[43]

Most contemporary analysts pointed to the Gulf War as the principal cause of the decline. But the seeds for a severe economic slowdown had been sown during the Reagan years. Nevertheless, because of the Gulf War crisis, Bush's advisers tried to keep any talk of an economic crisis on the back burner. Indeed, it was not until December 1991 that, despite all evidence to the contrary, the White House officially admitted that the nation was in a recession.[44] Bush's own economic advisers felt that the downturn would last ten months at most and that the recovery would begin in time for the fall election.[45]

Once the crisis was too large to ignore, Bush took only halting steps. In September 1991, he vetoed the Unemployment Insurance Reform Act because it would "destroy the bipartisan budget agreement" with excessive levels of benefits. The move, though fiscally prudent, played into the hands of Bush's critics, who claimed that he did not understand the depth of the anxiety that the recession was causing working-class Americans. Moreover, the huge deficit made this recession different. To the chagrin of the administration, the Federal Reserve Board refused to take the only step that was open to a debtor economy in a recession—raising the interest rate so as to discourage borrowing. By fall 1991, the explanation of Treasury Secretary Brady sounded weak: "We're in a recovery that's slower than we want it to be."[46] At a dinner with his corporate friends, John A. Young, then the president and CEO of Hewlett-Packard Company, discovered that "probably eight out of twelve" of his colleagues planned to vote not for Bush but for the Democratic governor of Arkansas, Bill Clinton.[47]

As Bush struggled with the recession, he was also faced with a policy dilemma that mixed economic, political, and national security factors. With the fall of the Berlin Wall and the implosion of the Soviet Union came a renewed cry for a reduction in American defense spending. Many people argued that it was the moral thing to do; others argued that it was the fiscally responsible thing to do. The monies that would be saved by defense cutbacks—the "peace dividend"—could help to balance the budget or, in some cases, be applied to expensive social programs. The issue came to a head when the budget agreement of 1990 mandated a $67-billion decrease in defense spending over five years. Defense Secretary Dick Cheney saw the issue in a broader light. He believed that cutbacks would not only have to apply to defense technology and manpower, as many on Capitol Hill were arguing; he resolved that to achieve the cuts mandated by the budget agreement, the nation's defense infrastructure would also have to be drastically reduced.

The Bush administration was not the first to propose the closing of military bases. It had been discussed since 1960, only to be derailed by the Vietnam War and the post-Vietnam boom in defense spending. In the final year of the Reagan administration, which had become besieged with criticism about the deficit, Secretary of Defense Frank Carlucci created a commission in December 1988 that proposed that fifty-five bases be closed. Arguing that the bases were useless parts of an already bloated infrastructure, the commission targeted those that were small, recreational, or largely administrative in nature. Nevertheless, there was a cry of outrage from congressional Democrats, already stung by Bush's victory, who believed that Carlucci had deliberately targeted bases in Democratic districts. Ultimately the bases were closed, but the ad hoc process needlessly raised the hackles of Congress, exacerbating an already acrimonious relationship as a result of the failed Tower nomination.

As the process was revisited in spring 1990, Cheney concluded that the approach had to be different. He strove to make it fairer and at the same time to place some of the burden for the closures on Congress, just in time for the off-year elections. After collecting data on every base that had been marked for extinction over the past decade, Cheney announced that he intended the procedure to follow the guidelines of the National Environmental Protection Act (NEPA), including public hearings, environmental impact statements, and the like. Thus the process would last close to a year and involve congressional testimony both in Washington and in the affected districts. Sensing the political danger, Congress set up the Base Realignment and Closure Commission (BRAC) as part of that year's Defense Authorization bill. Largely the brainchild of Les Aspin (D-WI), chairman of the House Armed Services Committee, BRAC was an independent commission that would critique a list of bases being marked for extinction by the secretary of defense. Using a rigid set of criteria that was defined in the act, BRAC was authorized to add or subtract from the list, and then Congress would vote on its recommendations.

Douglas Brook, then the acting secretary of the army for Financial Management, argued that one of the purposes of BRAC was to "give political cover to Congress."[48] It accomplished this goal; but in the process, the White House gained a political problem of the first degree. On 11 April 1991, Cheney announced his recommendations to close thirty-one major military bases, a move that would eliminate some 70,000 jobs in twenty states by the end of the year.[49] Many observers reacted angrily to the closings, contending they would hurt the American defense position. They argued that it had been the Reagan buildup that had created the military machine that defeated Iraq, and if Bush's closures had come before the Gulf War the United States would not have won.[50] They also argued that the people left unemployed by the closures would have a difficult time finding a job in the recession economy. The lobbying was intense; the Bush papers are full of pleas from both citizens and congressmembers for Cheney to withdraw his recommendation.

Still, the administration was completely wedded to the plan; with only a few exceptions, BRAC approved Cheney's list, and those bases were closed. The political fallout was immense. Seven bases were closed in California and three in Texas, both states Bush needed to win if he hoped to be reelected. Many Republican politicians who had been straddling the fence over other policies abandoned the administration in an effort to save their own political fate.[51]

Bush White House alumni like to point to the fact that by 1992, the economy was improving. They most often cite the statistic showing that by the third quarter of that year—the quarter in which the presidential election was fought—there was a 3.8 percent growth rate, a fact that was not widely carried in the press until after the election. They also note that the growth rate climbed to 5.7 percent in the year's final quarter and became the foundation for what would be billed as the "Clinton prosperity" of the second half of the decade of the 1990s.[52] These arguments are true enough, but the fact of the matter was that Americans did not feel the recovery in fall 1992. It was clearly too little, too late, to help George Bush. An aide of Bush pollster Bob Teeter summed up the matter in March 1992: "Our whole political problem is the recession. . . . We face a twenty month recession, a 78 percent wrong track number, and (likely) a southern conservative Democrat. The situation is about as bad as it could be."[53]

12

"THE PRESIDENT SHOULD
HAVE FIRED US ALL"

Flying on Air Force One late in 1991, George W. Bush was chatting with a reporter about his father's record in foreign policy over the first three years of his term. Bush's son pointed to the instability in the world, particularly in the Soviet Union, which he argued required a steady, experienced hand in order for the United States to avoid becoming embroiled in any further crises. Turning to the reporter, he exclaimed, "Do you think the American people are going to turn to a Democrat *now*?"[1]

This perspective largely mirrored the mood of those in the Bush camp as the nation spun into its 1992 presidential election cycle. They could not bring themselves to believe that the nation would turn to a liberal Democrat to guide the nation through the next four years of economic and international insecurity. Herbert S. Parmet puts it quite succinctly: "Throughout, Bush remained convinced that the American people would, in the end, reward him for his patriotism, dedication, and spotless leadership. He had trouble imagining it otherwise."[2]

This belief was caused, at least in part, by a serious misreading of the mood of the American people in late 1991. The goodwill that Bush had earned during the Persian Gulf War had been squandered in the second half of 1991, until his foreign policy successes were largely forgotten by the public. Instead, he was being pilloried for an economy that had gone south and a domestic policy that seemed to have no vision for the future.

Bush had larger problems than public dissatisfaction with his postwar policies, however. By 1991 many Americans were fed up with what they called "politics as usual." Some observers trace the genesis of this "revolt" of 1992 to the revelations of scandal within the Reagan administration. Others date its beginnings to the first months of the Bush administration, citing the public's disgust with the congressional morality play over ethics. That reaction grew when, during the height of the furor over the Tower nomination, the House of Representatives voted itself a 50 percent pay raise, only to withdraw the decision two weeks later due to intense public pressure. But that November the House voted again, not only to raise the salaries of its own members but also the salaries of top executive branch officials.[3] For many Americans, the last straw was the tempest that hit the front pages in October 1991 when several members of Congress were charged with bouncing checks drawn on the House Credit Union. For others, the defining moment came with Bush's flip-flop on taxes. Whatever the origins of the discontent, by the end of 1991 a large segment of the population was decrying "politics as usual" with a vehemence that had not been seen since the 1960s.*

This contempt for politicians was key in the off-year elections that fall. The most notable races were those in Pennsylvania and Louisiana. Attorney General Richard Thornburgh had resigned from Bush's cabinet to run against Pennsylvania senator Harris Wofford, appointed to complete the term of John Heinz, who had been killed in a plane crash. Wofford played up Thornburgh's insider credentials as well as the issue of health care and won with 57 percent of the vote. Many Bush aides point to this defeat of a candidate that Bush had handpicked as being their first hint of what was to come.

Equally transparent was the gubernatorial race in Louisiana, where former Klansman David Duke excoriated the system, and his own Republican party, in an attempt to defeat Democrat Edwin Edwards. Duke lost, partly because the Republican party disowned his candidacy. But his strong showing in defeat, and the immediate announcement of his candidacy for the presidency, shocked many party observers into a realization of the depth of voter discontent.

The Bush administration attempted to spin this disenchantment as a natural reaction to the economic downturn. But others saw it as a more

---

*I visited Capitol Hill on the day that the check overdraft story hit the press. One Republican congressman was carrying in his pocket a letter that claimed he had not bounced any checks. He was showing it to everyone he met, whether they brought up the subject or not.

global problem. William Greider, former editor of the *Washington Post,* emphasized the feeling in *Who Will Tell the People? The Betrayal of American Democracy.* One of the most important books of the year—a National Book Award nominee and voted one of the ten most notable books of 1992 by the *New York Times Book Review*—its author painted these developments as business as usual: "The most troubling proposition in this book is that the self-correcting mechanisms of politics are no longer working."[4] The *New York Times* called the discontented public "dealignment voters," who could no longer be counted upon to stick to the confines of the two-party system.[5]

This feeling was key to the voter revolt that led to the on-again, off-again candidacy in 1992 of Texas billionaire H. Ross Perot. Where Bush had misread the depth of voter anger, Perot not only recognized but also channeled it as a vehicle for his own considerable presidential ambitions. He understood that the way to make political profit from this anger was to present himself as a national leader who did not really want the presidency but who could be cajoled into accepting it if drafted by the people. A master of the television media, particularly the political talk shows, Perot used such shows as *Larry King Live* to dangle the possibility of his candidacy before the American people, professing to be uninterested unless his band of volunteers got his name on the ballot in all fifty states. In a quixotic storm of grassroots political activism, supporters from all over the political and economic map professed their devotion to Perot and actively worked for his candidacy. His legion of supporters ignored press reports that Perot was getting into the campaign only to gain revenge against Bush, who had refused to sanction the Texan's plan for freeing American soldiers still held captive in North Vietnam (one Perot aide told a reporter, "If [Perot] denies Bush the presidency, he'll be on top of the world. He hates George Bush").[6] Instead, they focused on the message of Perot's television infomercials: that none of the politicians in Washington could be trusted. In the Oregon primary in late May, Perot won an incredible 13 percent of the vote and 15 percent in that state's Republican primary, all of it coming on write-in votes.[7] By June he was running ahead of both Clinton and Bush.

Bush, then, had to convince an angry electorate that he deserved four more years—despite the defection of his party's conservatives, despite grassroots antipathy toward politicians in general, despite the recession, and despite his own natural difficulty with articulating his vision in a public forum. Such obstacles would have been a challenge for any campaign, but one must agree with the assessment of president-watcher Hugh Sidey: "In reelective politics, [Bush] was lousy."[8] Bush's 1992 campaign was as poorly run as his 1988 campaign had been brilliant. This failing left the door open for his opponents—one in a particularly divisive Republican primary campaign and two in the fall election—each of whom seemed to understand the temper of the times better than George Bush.

During the first weekend of August 1991, Bush met with his political staff at Camp David. To no one's surprise, he told them that he would run for reelection. But to everyone's dismay, he made it clear that he would not begin campaigning until the new year, telling them, "I want to postpone politics 1992."[9] When his staff voiced their concern about Perot, Bush reportedly replied, "I'm not worried about him. You guys get paid to worry about him."[10] As late as fall 1991, Bush had formed no committee, nor had he begun any serious polling operation. He had also not raised any significant money. He believed, as he told his staff, that "the longer we wait, the more money we'll have in the end," and he postponed the formal announcement of his candidacy until 12 February 1992.[11]

Many observers felt that Bush had deliberately adopted for his campaign the leisurely timetable of the Reagan juggernaut of 1984. This strategy, however, presupposed that the money and the support of Bush's major base of financial backing—the conservative wing of his party—would still be there in 1992. This assumption was a major miscalculation. Conservatives were abandoning Bush in droves, citing a long list of disappointments, only beginning with his reversal on the tax pledge. In December 1991, the *National Review* formally broke with the president. By the end of 1991, Bush had raised only $10 million and was forced to fund-raise rather than make campaign appearances.[12]

The fury of spurned Republican conservatives fueled the candidacy of Patrick J. Buchanan. A former journalist for the *St. Louis Post-Dispatch* and a speechwriter in the Nixon White House, Buchanan was best known for his appearances on several television talk shows, including a stint as cohost of CNN's *Crossfire*. From those prime-time pulpits, Buchanan had spent much of 1991 lambasting Bush, whom he dubbed "King George," on everything from his support of free trade to his mishandling of the economy. One fellow journalist described Buchanan as "a lightning rod for an angry message."[13] His attacks were made even more difficult to deflect because John Sununu, who had been fired, had served as Bush's chief link with the conservative wing of the party. In the New Hampshire primary, Buchanan finished a startling second, garnering 34 percent of the vote (the reactionary *Manchester Union-Leader*, which had run daily anti-Bush editorials, ran a three-inch headline the day after the primary: "READ *OUR* LIPS"). More important, Buchanan was openly defiant to those who suggested that he withdraw from the race in the name of party unity. He made it clear that win, lose, or draw, he was staying in the race until the convention.

As Bush's reelection bid creaked to a start, his campaign mishandled a golden opportunity to make points in voter-rich California. In April 1992, not-guilty verdicts for four policemen accused of beating robbery-suspect Rodney King sparked a rampage in the streets in which 52 people died, 2,500 were injured, and an estimated $446 million in property damage occurred. Ironically, the administration had been planning for just such an outburst in Los Angeles for almost six months, since Mayor Tom Bradley had come to the White House to discuss such a possibility with Bush. Members of the administration were in Los Angeles within twenty-four hours of the start of the riots (one staffer remembered that when he arrived, "there was still smoke coming out of the buildings").[14]

And yet the press castigated Bush for a tepid and halting response to the LA riots, and in part this criticism was warranted. David Demarest, Bush's director of communications, remembered that it was not until the second or third day of the crisis that Bush told Chief of Staff Sam Skinner that he wanted to go on television. The subsequent staffing out of the drafts of the speech, the dueling over speech drafts, and Skinner's inability to make up his mind lost precious time.[15] It took the president five days to get to Los Angeles to view the destruction and to meet with local leaders, leaving him exposed to charges of being aloof to the crisis.

Yet staff indecision was not the only problem facing the White House during the riots. Vice President Dan Quayle, who had been carving out a name for himself as the administration's most vocal adherent to the conservative line, made a speech in San Francisco on 19 May. In it, he blamed the riots on a "poverty of values" and noted, "It doesn't help matters when prime time TV has Murphy Brown—a character who supposedly epitomizes today's intelligent, highly paid, professional woman, mocking the importance of fathers by bearing a child alone, and calling it just another 'lifestyle choice.'" It was a throwaway line that pleased many movement conservatives. But from virtually every other corner, the remark was met with ridicule and derision. In his memoirs, Quayle writes that Bush called him to express his support. Publicly, however, the White House did its best to distance itself from the vice president's opinions.[16]

Many White House insiders began to lobby privately for Skinner's replacement and for dropping Quayle from the fall ticket. But such palace intrigue missed the point; the public was blaming the president, and his polls continued to drop. In early June, Bush further angered conservatives in an interview on ABC's 20/20. When asked if he would "knowingly" appoint a homosexual to his cabinet, Bush replied that there should be no "litmus test" on gays in his administration.[17] This statement even drew the not-altogether quiet protests of Quayle, who had made his opposition to gay rights clearly known in several speeches. Before the end of the primary campaign, Bush's policies were criticized by both Ronald Reagan and Richard Nixon (who, in a memo that was leaked to the press the day before the Super Tuesday primaries, called Bush's Russian policy "pathetically inadequate").[18]

Such mistakes kept the Buchanan campaign alive long after it should have asphyxiated from a lack of money. His supporters, dubbed "Buchanan Brigades" by their candidate, nipped at Bush's heels in every primary and caucus all the way to the convention. Although there was never any possibility of Buchanan's winning the nomination, his candidacy forced Bush to spend a great deal more money on advertisements in the primaries than he had planned. When the fall campaign began, the Bush campaign was strapped for cash, having spent $27 million to keep Buchanan at bay, while his other two opponents were in good shape. Moreover, Buchanan's campaign made it clear that there was a sizable portion of Republicans who would find it difficult to support Bush in November; Buchanan won a total of 22.5 percent of the total vote cast in all Republican primaries. Political analyst Kevin Phillips quipped, "George Bush is winning and sounds like a loser. Pat Buchanan is losing and sounds like a winner."[19]

Bush's stance on the issue of free trade played into the hands of both Perot and Buchanan. In 1987 the United States had successfully concluded a Free Trade Agreement with Canada. Reagan dreamed of expanding that deal into a comprehensive North American Free Trade Agreement (NAFTA), which would eradicate most tariffs within ten years of its passage. The next logical step was to negotiate a treaty with Mexico. However, it was not until the 1988 election of Carlos Salinas de Gortari to the presidency that the Mexican government was amenable to such negotiations. Thanks to Bush's personal diplomacy and the aid of his close friend Brian Mulroney, then prime minister of Canada, Salinas threw his support behind NAFTA. Negotiations with the Mexicans began in summer 1990.

From Bush's vantage point, NAFTA could not happen fast enough. Both Bush and Secretary of State James Baker wanted to complete the treaty negotiations before 1992, not only because they were philosophically in favor of free trade but also because they wanted to close the deal before the presidential election season. Thus, on 5 February 1991, Bush requested that Congress extend the "fast track" status that had been granted to the 1988 negotiations with Canada. Fast track gave authority to the president to negotiate a treaty in three months; and once it was presented to Congress, that body was given ninety days to vote on its approval, without being able to amend the treaty from the floor.

The debate on Bush's fast track request began the next day. A Mexican observer of the process was quite correct when he concluded, "Arguments against the fast track were really against the concept of a free trade agreement with Mexico."[20] House majority leader Richard Gephardt, at that time mentioned as a possible presidential candidate, led the opposition to the proposal. However, the lobbying blitz, particularly by the American Hispanic community, carried the day. On 24 May the request to extend fast track status was approved by the House, 231 to 192. It then passed the Senate, 59 to 36.

Thus, the debate over fast track, and the subsequent negotiations for NAFTA, were carried out during the heat of the presidential election. The proposed treaty was cautiously supported by Democratic front-runner Bill Clinton but vehemently opposed by Buchanan and Perot, who argued that it would result in the relocation of American industry and the loss of American jobs. In the midst of a recession, their arguments struck home to a large number of voters, and opposition to NAFTA became an anti-Bush rallying cry. The treaty, one of Bush's most notable diplomatic successes, was finally signed on 17 December 1992—not soon enough to keep the issue from exacting a political cost.[21]

Unlike Buchanan, who reveled in the campaign, Bush often seemed listless, as if he were just going through the motions. There was none of the spark, none of the crackle that had accompanied his campaign three years earlier. Bush did not even provide for himself a convention spectacle that would increase his standing in the polls once he had been renominated. In a series of tactical blunders, the Bush team lost control of their own convention. Instead of its being a carefully scripted showcase for the renomination of the president, the Republican convention, held in Houston, became a bully pulpit for Buchanan and his conservative supporters.

The administration virtually ceded the platform hearings to Buchanan, who turned them into a rancorous debate over the issue of abortion. More important than the platform (which Bush would simply ignore in the fall election, as would his two opponents ignore their party's platforms) was the decision—later characterized by RNC chairman Rich Bond as a "flat-out mistake"[22]—to allow Buchanan to speak during the first night of the convention in prime time. Buchanan's speech was a screed designed not to promote party unity but to ignite his brigades into a demonstration of support for conservative principles. He charged that "there is a religious war going on in our country for the soul of America" and then pilloried homosexuals to make his point. Buchanan called the Democratic ticket "the most pro-gay and pro-lesbian ticket in history" and decried their convention ads as "the greatest single exhibition of cross-dressing in American political history." He claimed that the Democratic agenda—which included, according to Buchanan, homosexual rights, gays in the military, and abortion on demand—offered "change all right, but not the kind of change America needs." Buchanan's was but the opening speech in a series of conservative speeches, the next most slashing delivered by Marilyn Quayle, calling for the party to return to its conservative roots. All of these speeches could be taken as tacit attacks on the moderate programs of the Bush administration.

Bush's acceptance speech did nothing to help his own situation. Indeed, in delivery and style of writing, it paled in comparison to Buchanan's. Gone was the defiant tone of his 1988 speech, when he demanded that the nation read his lips. Moreover, Bush further angered conservatives by admitting that "two years ago, I made a bad call on the . . . tax increase." Bush had wanted to use the speech to focus on his fall opponent and to call attention to his foreign policy successes. But the feeling that many listeners got from the speech was that Bush had become embittered about the criticism he was getting ("When the Berlin Wall fell, I half expected to see a headline: 'Wall Falls, Three Border Guards Lose Jobs,' and underneath it probably says, 'Clinton Blames Bush'"). Bush's call to arms—"Here is my question for the American people—who do you trust in this election?"—fell flat. For many Americans, long since soured on the political system, the Republican convention, aptly described by columnist Molly Ivins as "a feast of hate and fear . . . sour, mean, and dull," was the last straw. [23] Many observers viewed both Bush and his party as out of touch with mainstream Americans. Besides, they had found a candidate who, they believed, in his own words, "felt their pain."

In early 1989 the Democratic strategy was simple. As noted by one reporter, the party was "depending on Bush's screwing up and the economy going to hell in a handbasket."[24] Until late 1990, neither had happened, and Bush was riding high in the polls. As a result, the story of the race for the Democratic presidential nomination in 1992 was, initially at least, the same as it had been in 1988: the story of who wouldn't run. A lengthy list of nationally known Democrats—Rev. Jesse Jackson, New Jersey senator Bill Bradley, Georgia senator Sam Nunn, House majority leader Dick Gephardt—once again chose to sit out the race rather than face George Bush who was in early 1991 at the height of his popularity. As he had done in 1988, New York's Mario Cuomo toyed with a candidacy, but once again he refused to commit himself. Exasperated Democrats even approached Colin Powell to run; he turned them down with a not-too-gentle rebuff.

Just as in 1988, with the party's best-known names out of the race, the Democrats were left with lesser-known candidates. Douglas Wilder, the first African-American governor of Virginia, was treated as a stand-in for Jesse Jackson; Wilder withdrew from the race before the first primary. Paul Tsongas, former senator from Massachusetts and author of *A Call to Economic Arms*, was treated as a dull policy wonk, with a one-issue message: "There is no reason why the United States should not be the preeminent economic power on earth. No reason whatsoever. . . . It's not just another issue. It is *the issue*."[25] Like Tsongas, Sen. Tom Harkin of Iowa was earnest in his attempt to turn the national debate to the economy. But, also like Tsongas, his lack of charisma cost him any serious support, and he dropped out of the race three days before the Super Tuesday primaries. Sen. Bob Kerrey of Nebraska ran a lackadaisical campaign, was dubbed "Cosmic Bob" by the press, and was never taken seriously. Former governor Jerry Brown of California won several upset victories in the primaries, but his past record as a liberal reformer, a reputation for the offbeat that earned him the nickname "Governor Moonbeam" (just before the New York primary he announced that his running mate would be Jesse Jackson, thus eliminating any hope of winning that state's white, blue-collar vote),[26] and a lack of money doomed his campaign.

It is all too easy to explain away the victory of Arkansas governor William Jefferson Clinton by pointing to the rather weak field of candidates who opposed his drive for the nomination. Though this was a part of the story, it downplays the strengths of the Clinton juggernaut. Clinton had been working hard for the nomination since the mid-1980s, when he became chairman of the National Governor's Association. From this post, and through his tireless fund-raising and his speaking efforts on behalf of his fellow Democrats, Clinton earned a reputation as a tough campaigner. He was also known for his serious approach to domestic issues (Bush had appreciated his role at the 1989 education summit). Clinton's fund-raising team was the best in modern memory, and his simple message—"It's the economy, stupid"—struck home to a middle class that clearly perceived themselves to be worse off in 1992 than they had been four years earlier.

Besides offering a simple, easy-to-grasp slogan, Clinton and his handlers gave a new wrinkle to presidential politics, one that Bush and his campaign completely missed. This was best articulated in W. Lance Bennett's *The Governing Crisis: Media, Money and Marketing in American Elections.* In the new media of the 1980s and 1990s, there was a consistent need to reinvent oneself before the populace—to play to the public's short attention span and to give them something different on a daily basis. Clinton understood this, and because of his natural charisma and his comfort before the cameras was able to make it work. It was this constant reinvention of self, not his policy messages, that allowed Clinton to withstand revelations of marital infidelity, youthful indiscretions with marijuana, and draft dodging.[27]

The first negative challenge to Clinton's message on the economy was the Slick Willie motif: emphasizing the Clinton who had written to the director of the ROTC program at the University of Arkansas to thank him for "saving me from the draft," who had smoked marijuana as a youth but claimed he had never inhaled, and who had been charged in the press with having been a womanizer of mammoth proportions. Rather than avoiding the controversy, Clinton jumped to the offensive. With his wife at his side, he came tantalizingly close to admitting to an extramarital affair on CBS's *60 Minutes* on 26 January (Mrs. Clinton: "We've gone further than any one we know of, and that's all we're going to say").

By striking out at his accusers, Clinton turned his second-place finish in the New Hampshire primary into a triumph for an embittered candidate. Thus the "Comeback Kid" was born. But as Bennett pointed out, the "Comeback Kid" could win neither the nomination nor the election; for that, Clinton needed to adopt a statesmanlike approach. Enter "The Man from Hope," a particularly effective documentary on Clinton's life, played at the convention, which emphasized his rise from poverty and his message of hope (also conveniently the name of his hometown in Arkansas). If measured by the Gallup poll, the Democratic convention was a triumph. At its end, Clinton was the recipient of the highest postconvention bounce in the poll's history; his base of support grew from 40 percent just before the convention to 56 percent just after it. This surge turned Clinton's eight-point deficit against Bush into a twenty-two-point lead—a spectacular thirty-point swing in the race.

By presenting the nation with a new Clinton whenever adversity hit, the Democratic candidate had shown that he could weather an attack. In another election year, it might have been seen as crass opportunism. But in 1992 Clinton's makeovers played well with disenchanted voters who believed him to be under attack from the very institutions that they had come to hate. Perhaps it was as simple as former Reagan political adviser Ed Rollins claimed: "The country "[wasn't] as mad at [Clinton] like they were at the president, and he was three times the campaigner Bush was."[28]

It was the first time in American history that three southerners had vied for the presidency in the fall election. But at virtually every opportunity, Clinton beat both Bush and Perot to the punch. One of the most telling examples was in their response to Hurricane Andrew, which in September tore through South Florida, wreaking unbelievable devastation. The administration, having learned its lesson from its delay with the Los Angeles riots, took less than three days to send 35,000 troops and a task force, including Secretary of Transportation Andrew Card, to the stricken area. They stayed some seven weeks—time that several members of the task force could have been contributing to the campaign. But Clinton, not yet hamstrung by the demands of being president, could move faster. In the three-day window following the disaster, he had traveled to Florida to criticize the government's relief efforts.[29]

Among the alumni of the Bush administration, there is no shortage of culprits for the 1992 defeat. The vast majority of them blame the press. Granted, the press was not only virulently anti-Bush, but it openly flaunted that fact. One of the most oft-quoted statistics in my interviews with the Bush people was that following the election, 89 percent of the correspondents on the election trail said that they had voted for Clinton. Despite its hatred of the press, the Bush campaign nevertheless hoped that the journalists would eventually wise up to Clinton and report his trysts. David Bates remembers that Bush's people had heard reports that Clinton was sleeping with a reporter on his campaign plane, but instead of pushing the issue, the Bush campaign "kept waiting for the story to break." Bates observed that there were people in the campaign "thinking it was the media's job . . . we'd get hammered in the press if we were seen as peddling it too much."[30] Marlin Fitzwater remembered that Bush "had a curious code of media discipline that said: 'If I am doing the right thing, I can take any punishment.'"[31]

Other observers blame Bush's health, seeing him as more listless and disengaged during the campaign than ever before.[32] In January 1992, while on a state visit to Japan, Bush contracted a severe case of intestinal influenza and vomited on Prime Minister Kiichi Miyazawa, a scene that was inadvertently taped by Japanese television and soon replayed all over the world. In his memoirs, Marlin Fitzwater observed: "The old competitive juices that might have gotten the president into the 1992 campaign in the spring and summer seemed to have lost their edge. He desperately wanted to wait until after Labor Day to start the campaign. I think his body was a reluctant warrior."[33]

In a 1998 interview, Bush offered a response to those who blamed his health for the fate of the campaign; it deserves to be quoted at length:

> You know, Marlin Fitzwater wrote that, and of course I take violent exception to it, because I don't think that's true. I campaigned my heart out. . . . We just couldn't have done any more. . . . But the fact that Marlin felt that way makes me question my own view that it's all wrong, because he was right there by my side. I think that it's used *ex post facto* as an explanation.[34]

The fall campaign was clearly a grueling affair for Bush. He was exhausted, and his health often seemed on the verge of giving out. In the last weekend of the campaign, Bush made an appearance on *Larry King*

Live, despite a serious case of the flu. He campaigned hard, to the detriment of his health, right down to election day. There is absolutely no evidence of his giving up.

Yet neither of these frequently cited reasons explains why Bush lost in 1992. The problem was with the campaign itself. From the start, it lacked any focus, discipline, or conceptual strategy. John Sununu's condemnation—"It was the worst run presidential campaign in history"[35]—is undoubtedly part sour-grapes from a fired aide, but there is still more than a grain of truth to the assessment. There were several reasons for these shortcomings, not the least of which was that Atwater was dead and a disgusted Ailes sat out the campaign. In their stead was a troika of political operatives: Secretary of Commerce and chief fund-raiser Robert Mosbacher, pollster Robert Teeter, and Marriott executive Fred Malek, who had managed the 1988 Republican National Convention. None of them had any experience with running a national campaign, and the internecine fighting among them was bitter. Marlin Fitzwater recalls in his memoirs that when he was called upon to announce the campaign team to the press, the three men were arguing over whose name should go first in the press release; Mosbacher demanded that the phrase "standing at the president's side in campaigns for the last twenty years" be included. According to Fitzwater, Bush simply remarked, "Gee, if it's this bad on the first day, what are we in for?"[36] For his part, Fitzwater took an unannounced vacation in the middle of the primary season; press reports concluded that he was disgusted with the campaign.[37] One operative spoke for many: "No one ran 1992. No one was running the campaign in 1992. [It was] a campaign adrift."[38]

Quite aside from the backbiting, there was never any real strategy for victory. On 12 June, Teeter was asked to meet with David Demarest's speechwriters and explain the message of the campaign. As was his wont, Teeter brought along complicated flow charts. The first box was entitled "The Bush Record," which flowed to a box marked "Theme"; from that box flowed several policy boxes—domestic, foreign, social, but all the boxes were as yet unfilled. Demarest remembered Teeter looking at the speechwriters, pointing to the "Theme" box, and proclaiming, "Now, *that's* where we need your help." Thus, in Demarest's view, "The campaign manager had just admitted to us that the campaign had no theme or vision." For his part, Teeter reportedly told a colleague that "that was a bunch of dead weight I met with on Friday," and he hired a former public relations man for Kentucky Fried Chicken with no experience in a national campaign as the new campaign speechwriter.[39]

Without Atwater and Ailes to guide it, the Bush campaign seemed to want to ignore an offensive push altogether. Fearing that negative advertisements that criticized Clinton's character and focused on Perot's instability would boomerang, the Bush campaign delayed the airing of those ads until it was too late. Even then, they ran considerably watered-down versions of the ads, rewritten, in the words of one analyst, with a "touch of humor to soften their effect."[40]

In April, George W. Bush moved into his father's campaign in an attempt to right the rudder. It was not enough. All concerned knew that if the president was to have any chance of catching Clinton, Jim Baker had to leave the State Department and take over the campaign. But consumed by the Middle East peace process, Baker did not want to come on board. By the time Bush prevailed upon him to come back to the White House (on 13 August, ostensibly as chief of staff, replacing Skinner, but in reality to run the sagging campaign), it was too late (Clayton Yeutter caustically remembered, "It was too late when *I* came over").[41] Indeed, many close to the campaign remember with some bitterness that a disappointed Baker sat on his hands and did little to help the campaign, rather than be tied to a sinking ship.[42]

Further, Bush missed an opportunity to articulate his vision in the televised debates; one reason was that he was overprepared on the issue of the tax-cut pledge by Richard Darman, who was in charge of debate preparation (indeed, Bush did better in the last debate, when, in the words of one White House staffer, he said "nuts to everybody" and went to Camp David rather than practice.)[43] For many observers the defining media moment of the campaign came during the second presidential debate held in Richmond, Virginia, when an obviously preoccupied Bush, quite unaware that he was on camera, took a look at his watch, as if he were bored with the entire proceedings. Toward the end of the campaign, when he finally began to attack his opponent, Bush gave the appearance of a fighter who was flailing to get in a punch. His attacks against Clinton were shrill (at one point, he publicly castigated Clinton and his running mate, Tennessee senator Al Gore, by observing that "my dog Millie knows more about foreign policy than those two bozos");[44] thus they were easily deflected by the opposition, who ignored them as "cheap shots."

For Bush, the 1992 election was the complete inverse of the 1988 election. In his postelection analysis in 1988, Michael Dukakis had noted that one of the lessons he learned was to "respond quickly" to attack; in 1992, it was the Bush campaign's turn to forget that lesson of modern, media-driven elections. For most of the campaign, Bush waited for Perot and Clinton to self-destruct; Perot did so, Clinton did not. Those few times when Bush went on the attack, he faced a Clinton campaign that was masterful at in-

Ross Perot, Bill Clinton, and Bush, first presidential debate, Washington University, St. Louis, 11 October 1992. (Courtesy of the Bush Presidential Library)

stant reaction and spin. Clinton stuck to one issue—the economy—throughout the campaign, and Bush had no effective answer to his criticisms. Unlike 1988, when Atwater and Ailes were able to focus their advertisements on several effective symbols, the Bush media campaign in 1992 offered only a litany of accomplishments to offset Clinton's symbol of an economy gone awry and Perot's symbol of government gridlock. The Bush campaign never served its candidate by offering a cogent plan for how to beat either Pat Buchanan or Bill Clinton. Indeed, if there was a part of the Bush administration that showed no vision, it was the presidential campaign of 1992. Perhaps Fitzwater had the answer: "The president should have fired us all."[45]

That November Bill Clinton won 43 percent of the popular vote to George Bush's 38 percent and Ross Perot's astonishing 19 percent. The popular vote was indicative of the three-way race, where analyses showed that Perot drew voters away from both candidates. In every significant area of support, Clinton outpolled Bush—except for the Christian right (a group that had supported Bush throughout his presidency, a fact that surprised him).[46]

But in the electoral college, Clinton's victory was complete; he won 370 electoral votes to Bush's 168. Clinton made inroads in every area of the country; of the states that Bush had won in 1988, Clinton recaptured California, Pennsylvania, Ohio, and Illinois—four states with a combined total of 122 electoral votes. Perot's impact was largely on voter turnout; 1992 was the first time in thirty years that there had not been a decline. Clinton's victory was a personal one, with very short coattails. The Democrats lost nine seats in the House but retained their majority, and the party composition in the Senate did not change. Nevertheless, Bush's loss was complete; 27 percent of Republicans and 68 percent of Independents voted for Bill Clinton.

13

★ ★ ★ ★ ★

PATIENCE AND PRUDENCE

During his last plane ride on Air Force One in December 1992, traveling to his beloved Kennebunkport for the holidays, George Bush wrote a brief note to himself: "I hope history will show I did some things right."[1] Six years later, on 29 May 1998, George Bush did a favor for an old friend. On his way to his fifty-year reunion at Yale, Bush stopped to deliver a talk at Harvard University, where former senator Alan Simpson was a visiting professor at the John F. Kennedy School of Government. It was a singular experience; here was a comfortable, animated George Bush whom most of the country had never seen. His humor, delivered in a practiced deadpan, delighted the audience. Bush quipped that he refused to lecture them, taking his cue from Socrates, who had gone around giving advice, "and then they poisoned him." He remarked that he had been criticizing the national press all around the country, until a friend told him that such trash-talk was beneath him. Now he claimed that he had "joined Press Bashers Anonymous. It's been ten days since I joined, and I'm going through withdrawal symptoms." Bush then observed that he had invited Prime Minister Kiichi Miyazawa ("He was the guy I threw up on in Tokyo. Remember him?") to speak at the Bush Library. "He came, and I told him this time, the dinner's on me."

In a more serious mode, Bush took the opportunity to highlight what he believed were the major accomplishments of his presidency. On the world scene, he listed the fall of communism, the dismantling of the Berlin Wall, and a victory in the Persian Gulf War that "raised respect for America around the world [and] mysteriously and wondrously healed the wounds inflicted upon many who served in Vietnam." On the domestic front, Bush observed,

> We cleaned up the S&L crisis . . . [a] huge expenditure, but looking back, it was the right thing to do. . . . [We] cleaned up the environment with the Clean Air Act . . . [and] expanded opportunities for 37 million people with disabilities in a very bipartisan way [when] Congress passed the ADA and I was privileged to be the president who signed it. . . . We forewent the "reading of lips" by passing a budget agreement that put firm controls really for the first time on discretionary spending.[2]

George Bush did some things right, particularly when it came to foreign policy. Fundamental to his diplomacy was an improved relationship with the Soviet Union that led to the New World Order that he later claimed as his chief legacy. This new association with the Soviets was also the essence of the successful prosecution of the Persian Gulf War, the event that virtually every observer points to as the most important event of the Bush presidency. Unquestionably, there were far fewer successes in domestic policy. Nevertheless, the Americans with Disabilities Act and the Clean Air Amendments made a positive difference in the quality of life for millions of Americans.

Former President and Mrs. Bush leaving Washington, 20 January 1993. (Courtesy of the Bush Presidential Library)

Many recent observers have explained this mixed record by arguing that Bush was not a "leader" in the truest sense of the word. This argument is best articulated in Richard Rose's *The Postmodern Presidency: George Bush Meets the World*. Rose defines a leader as "active in promoting domestic politics, increasing federal spending, and introducing new legislation in Congress." He then finds Bush wanting in these areas and proclaims him instead to be a "guardian . . . [doing] a limited number of things that are obligations of the Oval Office and refraining from actions that expand the role of government." Rose concedes that "internationally, a guardian will be active," but he concludes that overall, a guardian president—Bush—is "a player, but not in charge."[3]

The "guardian president" hypothesis examines the ability of the president to lead despite facing obstacles such as a divided government. Put another way, it refers to the president's ability to play the hand that he is dealt. Rose and his many supporters see Bush as leading better in foreign policy than in domestic policy, certainly a defensible premise. Bush was undeniably proactive in foreign affairs, and he just as clearly did a "limited number of things" in domestic affairs. According to political scientist Byron E. Shafer, this pattern was quite predictable from the course of the development of modern American political culture. Shafer argues that since 1968, the nation had built up "cross-pressures" in its political system—conservative majorities on foreign affairs issues and liberal majorities on social welfare and economic issues. This development led to the rather consistent election of Republican presidents (with the exception of Jimmy Carter), who tend to control the foreign policy agenda, and of Democratic Congresses, who control the purse strings of domestic programming. Thus, faced with the resulting divided government, as well as with an opposition Supreme Court and a gaping budget deficit, Bush understandably succeeded in foreign policy and struggled with domestic policy.[4]

It can be argued, therefore, that Bush did the best he could with a weak hand. One must explore, then, why the vast majority of students of the Bush presidency have judged it a failure. Scholars and journalists alike seemingly fault Bush for not taking a more activist role in attempting to transcend the obstacles of the divided government he faced. In short, they label him a "do-nothing president." Rose's assessment of Bush as "not in charge" hints at this view; journalists Michael Duffy and Dan Goodgame are more blunt: "When faced with a decision, Bush often concluded that the best course was to do as little as possible."[5]

These critics most often cite two facets of Bush's style of governing to support their assessment. The first is his often overcautious approach to decision making. For this, they reprimand him with vigor, but they are hardly the first to do so. Dana Carvey, a gifted impersonator featured on *Saturday Night Live,* one of the most popular television shows of the 1980s, had Bush's voice and mannerisms down pat. His rendition of Bush's nasal twang—a cross between frigid Maine and deep-South Texas—and his stiff, pointing gestures was dead-on. But key to his caricature was his repetition of the phrases that Bush used to explain why he would not be rushed into making a quick decision: "Not gonna do it. Wouldn't be prudent." (Bush later joked to his Harvard audience, "Let me tell you something about that little guy—he must miss me—he made a *killing* off of me!") But Carvey was not the only humorist who poked fun at Bush's go-slow attitude. A 1989 cartoon in the *Washington Post* showed Bush in between two elderly women labeled as his "closest advisers: Patience and Prudence."[6]

The parodies closely aped reality. If there was any feature that the Bush administration did not represent, it was precipitous change. Indeed, change for change's sake was abhorrent to Bush's upbringing, political values, and personality. When he told the *Washington Post* that "we don't need to re-make society . . . we don't need radical new directions," he was not speaking figuratively.[7] More moderate by nature than either his predecessor or successor, Bush resisted the temptation to make hasty decisions. Instead, he chose to strive slowly and cautiously toward narrowly focused goals. There was thus a measured cadence to his administration that was often missing from more activist presidencies.

Despite the protests of many Bush critics, such caution does not translate to inactivity. Indeed, in Bush's case, his prudence was responsible for the most noted successes of his tenure. It is absolutely clear that Bush's judicious approach to the U.S.–USSR relationship, the *pauza,* was deliberately designed to take the post–cold war world to the next level of cooperation. It did so, and that collaboration worked in Bush's favor in both the Persian Gulf crisis and in the subsequent steps taken by the administration to bring the traditional enemies of the Middle East to the peace table in Madrid.

Perhaps Bush's prudent approach to decision making would have been more acceptable to the public had he been able to tell the nation what it had to gain by waiting for him. As they hold Bush responsible for being overcautious, so too do his critics chide him for having no vision. A vision is, at least in part, a dream for the future of the state. Political decision makers often make their vision known to their citizenry in the normal course of politicking or governing. The ability to articulate a political vision, however, has less to do with ideology than it does with rhetorical skill. David Demarest, Bush's director of communications, put it nicely: "[A] vision [is] a way of connecting the dots. . . . [It is] no good by itself, but it is a tool to motivate, to inspire."[8] The successful pronouncement of a vision calls for a leader gifted in the public aspect of politics. Articulating a vision is a highly emotional rhetorical task, one that calls for great eloquence, a great rapport with the governed, and the ability to make the governed believe in the dream.

This description does not fit George Bush. His public presidency was the weakest part of his tenure. He is the least introspective of men, never comfortable with articulating any abstract idea, much less with talking to the nation about what he stood for. As president, Bush consistently scorned the press' attempt to pin him down on what he derisively called "the vision thing." He never considered it a priority to place his actions as president in context for the American people, either during or after his tenure.

One must accept that Bush had no long-range vision for his presidency because he consistently said—both as president and in interviews following his presidency—that he had none. As he told two *New York Times* reporters in 1990, "Having vision does not necessarily mean having a fixed blueprint. It means having a general direction and an ability to redefine strategy as events require."[9] Bush bluntly told me in 1998, "[I] never tried to pigeonhole myself."[10]

It is true enough that in 1992 many Americans said they wished that Bush had articulated a vision for America. But it is arguable that neither Bill Clinton nor Ross Perot offered the public their vision of America's future. If they did, the polls make it clear that the electorate no more understood their vision than they did Bush's. The electoral verdict of 1992 notwithstanding, one is left to ponder whether articulating a vision is necessarily a good thing for a president. A grand vision undelivered often leads to a disappointing verdict by historians—so was the case with Ronald Reagan, whose administration clearly did not live up to the promise of its own rhetoric. Contemporaries can also rebel against dreams left unfulfilled. After Reagan, America eagerly welcomed a man who did not wax grandiloquent. Political pundit William Schneider summed up this feeling: "After eight years of Reagan, Americans may have had enough vision for a while."[11] It was more than enough to have stability, peace, and prudence. No less an observer of the Bush presidency than Hugh Sidey noted that while there were no great declarations, "I'm not sure the times called for that."[12]

Americans, particularly scholars of the American presidency, want their presidents to move fast. This, George Bush refused to do. He was both patient and prudent. Moreover, he refused to inflate his rhetoric to compensate for his caution by proclaiming a vast vision for the future. Thus, while facing a chaotic world and a weakened economy, Bush made few mistakes. Indeed, his foreign policy set the parameters for the post–cold war world that would define his successor's foreign policy agenda. Further, Bush's basic honesty and sense of government service brought no discredit to the office of the presidency, and his careful stewardship bequeathed to his successor a nation more stable than he had inherited from his predecessor. If that is not the stuff of presidential vision, it is, nevertheless, a more than adequate legacy.

NOTES

All public statements made by either Ronald Reagan or George Bush while president can be found in Ronald W. Reagan, *Public Papers of the Presidents: Ronald Reagan, 1981–1989,* 15 vols. (Washington, DC: U.S. Government Printing Office, 1982–1991), and George H. W. Bush, *Public Papers of the Presidents: George Bush, 1981–1989,* 8 vols. (Washington, DC: U.S. Government Printing Office, 1990–1993). Thus, speeches and proclamations by these two presidents are not cited in this book unless a videotape or script of a specific speech was consulted.

ACRONYMS AND SHORT TITLES

Bush PR	George Bush Presidential Records, GBL
Ford Library	Gerald R. Ford Presidential Library, Ann Arbor, Michigan
GBL	George Bush Presidential Library and Museum, College Station, Texas
Hofstra	Remarks to the Hofstra University Conference on the Bush Presidency, 17–19 April 1997
NJ	*National Journal*
NYT	*New York Times*
Bush *PP*	George H. W. Bush, *Public Papers of the Presidents: George Bush, 1981–1989,* 8 vols. (Washington, DC: Government Printing Office 1990–1993).
PBS	Public Broadcasting System
USN&WR	*U.S. News and World Report*
WP	*Washington Post*

WPNWE   *Washington Post National Weekly Edition*
WHORM   White House Office of Records Management
WHPO   White House Press Office

CHAPTER 1
THE LEGACIES OF RONALD REAGAN

1. "George Bush: A Sense of Duty," for Arts and Entertainment Network's *Biography* series (first broadcast November 1996).

2. Walter Dean Burnham, "The Reagan Heritage," in *The Election of 1988: Reports and Interpretations,* ed. Gerald M. Pomper (Chatham, NJ: Chatham House Publishers, 1989), p. 1.

3. Edward Derwinski, telephone interview with author, 6 October 1998.

4. Julie Kosterlitz and W. John Moore, "Saving the Welfare State," *National Journal (NJ)* (14 May 1988), p. 1278.

5. Michael Schaller, *Reckoning with Reagan: America and Its President in the 1980s* (New York: Oxford University Press, 1992), p. 47.

6. Turner Network Television (TNT) Special, "The Big 80s" (broadcast June 1998).

7. Kevin Phillips, *The Politics of Rich and Poor: Wealth and the American Electorate in the Reagan Aftermath* (New York: Random House, 1990), pp. 4, 10, 12, 15, 18; Michael Duffy and Dan Goodgame, *Marching in Place: The Status Quo Presidency of George Bush* (New York: Simon and Schuster, 1992), p. 17.

8. *NJ* (14 May 1988), p. 1284.

9. Schaller, *Reckoning with Reagan,* p. 69.

10. Phillips, *The Politics of Rich and Poor,* p. 28.

11. James A. Baker III, *The Politics of Diplomacy; Revolution, War, and Peace* (New York: G. P. Putnam's Sons, 1995) p. 79.

12. Duffy and Goodgame, *Marching in Place,* p. 19.

13. Jay McInerney, *Bright Lights, Big City* (New York: Vintage Books, 1984), p. 86.

14. "USA Statistics in Brief: 1986" (Washington, DC: U.S. Department of Commerce, Bureau of Census, 1986).

15. Schaller, *Reckoning with Reagan,* pp. 69, 75.

16. Ibid., pp. 85–86.

17. Quoted in ibid., p. 94.

18. Robert Shogan, *The Riddle of Power: Presidential Leadership from Truman to Bush* (New York: Dutton Books, 1991), p. 227.

CHAPTER 2
"ONE SHOULD SERVE HIS COUNTRY"

1. Fitzhugh Green, *George Bush: An Intimate Portrait* (New York: Hippocrene Books, 1989), p. 2.

2. Quoted in Herbert S. Parmet, *George Bush: The Life of a Lone Star Yankee* (New York: Scribner, 1997), p. 28.

3. "George Bush: A Sense of Duty," for Arts and Entertainment Network's *Biography* series (first broadcast November 1996).

4. Green, *Bush: An Intimate Portrait*, p. 19.

5. Ibid., p. 12.

6. "George Bush: A Sense of Duty."

7. Green, *Bush: An Intimate Portrait*, p. 23.

8. Parmet, *Lone Star Yankee*, p. 44.

9. "George Bush: A Sense of Duty."

10. Parmet, *Lone Star Yankee*, p. 42.

11. "George Bush: A Sense of Duty."

12. Parmet, *Lone Star Yankee*, p. 46.

13. Exhibit, George Bush Presidential Library and Museum, College Station, Texas (GBL); Joe Hyams, *Flight of the Avenger: George Bush at War* (New York: Harcourt Brace Jovanovich, 1991), p. 47.

14. Letter in exhibit, GBL.

15. Hyams, *Flight of the Avenger*, pp. 83–84.

16. "George Bush: A Sense of Duty."

17. Letter in exhibit, GBL.

18. Parmet, *Lone Star Yankee*, p. 59.

19. Bush comment in exhibit, GBL.

20. "George Bush: A Sense of Duty."

21. Parmet, *Lone Star Yankee*, p. 59.

22. Bush comment in exhibit, GBL.

23. Parmet, *Lone Star Yankee*, pp. 63–64.

24. Green, *Bush: An Intimate Portrait*, p. 47. Readers can judge Bush's baseball talent for themselves: in fifty-one college games, Bush hit .251 with two home runs and twenty-three runs batted in. Out of 451 fielding attempts at first base, Bush made only nine errors (exhibit, GBL).

25. Exhibit, GBL.

26. Ibid.; Green, *Bush: An Intimate Portrait*, p. 57.

27. Exhibit, GBL.

28. Parmet, *Lone Star Yankee*, p. 113.

29. Green, *Bush: An Intimate Portrait*, p. 106; exhibit, GBL.

30. Larry Temple, interview, Lyndon B. Johnson Library Oral History Project, 13 August 1970.

31. Chapin to Haldeman, 17 September 1969, in *From the President: Richard Nixon's Secret Files*, ed. Bruce Oudes, (New York, Harper and Row, 1988), p. 43.

32. Green, *Bush: An Intimate Portrait*, pp. 108–9; Walter Pincus and Bob Woodward, "Bush and the Politics of Who You Know," *Washington Post National Weekly Edition* (WPNWE), 22 August–28 August 1988, p. 14.

33. Pincus and Woodward, "Bush and the Politics of Who You Know," p. 15.

34. Colson to Pat O'Donnell, 24 July 1971, in Oudes, ed., *From the President*, p. 302.

35. Edward Derwinski, telephone interview with author, 6 October 1998; Green, *Bush: An Intimate Portrait*, pp. 120–22; John Robert Greene, *The Limits of Power: The Nixon and Ford Administrations* (Bloomington: Indiana University Press, 1992), pp. 110–12; Walter Isaacson, *Kissinger: A Biography* (New York: Simon and Schuster, 1992), p. 352.

36. In an interesting sidebar to this story, Nixon found himself quite unable to tell Dole the bad news. Instead, the president called Dole and asked him to prevail upon Bush to take over at the RNC—a job that Bush had already told the president he would take. Saying nothing to Dole about his commitment to Nixon, Bush allowed Dole to "talk him into" taking the position. When Dole later learned of Bush's and Nixon's duplicity, he grumbled that he had been "Bushwhacked."

37. Green, *Bush: An Intimate Portrait*, p. 135.

38. Greene, *Limits of Power*, p. 178; Parmet, *Lone Star Yankee*, p. 166.

39. Gerald R. Ford, *A Time to Heal: The Autobiography of Gerald R. Ford* (New York: Harper and Row, 1979), pp. 142–46; Green, *Bush: An Intimate Portrait*, pp. 139–40; John Robert Greene, *The Presidency of Gerald R. Ford* (Lawrence: University Press of Kansas, 1995), p. 30; Robert Hartmann, *Palace Politics: An Inside Account of the Ford Years* (New York: McGraw-Hill, 1980), pp. 222–39. In a 1990 interview, Ford aide Robert T. Hartmann showed me a slip of paper in Ford's handwriting. On it was a list of names, in this order—Bush, (Donald) Rumsfeld, (Elliot) Richardson, (Nelson) Rockefeller, and (Ronald) Reagan (Reagan's name had been badly misspelled by Ford). Ford wanted to have these men investigated prior to choosing a vice president. Before he passed the list on to his investigatory contact, Hartmann recopied the list, spelling Reagan's name correctly. The order was now Richardson, Rockefeller, Reagan, Bush, and Rumsfeld. Hartmann also asked Ford to tell him which ones he was really interested in. Hartmann checked three names—Rockefeller, Bush, and Rumsfeld (Robert T. Hartmann, interview with author, 22 March 1990).

40. Greene, *Ford*, p. 150.

41. Rourke to Marsh, 20 March 1975, John O. Marsh Files, Gerald R. Ford Presidential Library, Ann Arbor, Michigan, box 6, Bush: Possible New Situation folder.

42. Issacson, *Kissinger*, p. 670.

43. Rumsfeld to Ford, 10 July 1975, Richard B. Cheney Files, Ford Library, box 5, Intelligence: Appointment of CIA Director folder.

44. Kathryn S. Olmsted, *Inside the Secret Government: The Post-Watergate Investigations of the CIA and the FBI* (Chapel Hill: University of North Carolina Press, 1996), p. 222, n. 91.

45. Ford, *A Time to Heal*, p. 325.

46. Kissinger to Bush, 1 November 1975 (declassified cable); Bush to Kissinger, 2 November 1975 (declassified cable); Kissinger to Bush, 2 November 1975 (declassified cable); Henry Kissinger and Brent Scowcroft Files, Ford Library, box A1, Backchannel re: George Bush's CIA Appointment folder.

47. Connor to Friedersdorf, Memo, 22 November 1975, Gerald R. Ford Presidential Papers, Ford Library, Handwriting File, box 9, CIA folder no. 2.

48. *Christian Science Monitor* (2 June 1976), p. 26.

49. Bush to Ford (declassified), 3 August 1976, Gerald R. Ford Presidential Papers: Handwriting File, Ford Library, box 9, CIA folder no. 2.

50. Green, *Bush: An Intimate Portrait,* p. 166.

51. Parmet, *Lone Star Yankee,* p. 209.

52. Ibid., p. 224.

53. Robert Shogan, *The Riddle of Power: Presidential Leadership from Truman to Bush* (New York: Dutton Books, 1991), p. 257.

54. Green, *Bush: An Intimate Portrait,* p. 176.

55. Parmet, *Lone Star Yankee,* p. 226.

56. Ibid., pp. 227–29.

57. Green, *Bush: An Intimate Portrait,* pp. 176–77.

58. Chase Untermeyer, comments at Hoover Library Conference on the vice presidency, 27 October 1995.

59. Ed Rollins, *Bare Knuckles and Back Rooms: My Life in American Politics* (New York: Broadway Books, 1994), p. 170.

60. Chase Untermeyer, interview with author, 18 June 1996.

61. Parmet, *Lone Star Yankee,* p. 246.

62. See Chase Untermeyer, "Looking Forward: George Bush as Vice President," in *At the President's Side: The Vice Presidency in the Twentieth Century,* ed. Timothy Walch (Columbia: University of Missouri Press, 1997), p. 159.

63. David Valdez, *George Herbert Walker Bush: A Photographic Profile* (College Station: Texas A&M University Press, 1997), p. 30.

64. Hedrick Smith, *The Power Game: How Washington Works* (New York: Random House, 1988), p. 72.

65. Note in exhibit, GBL.

66. George Bush, *Looking Forward: An Autobiography* (New York: Bantam Books, 1987), p. 222; Chase Untermeyer, "Looking Forward," p. 161.

67. Untermeyer, "Looking Forward," p. 162.

68. C. Boyden Gray, interview with author, 18 April 1997.

69. Parmet, *Lone Star Yankee,* p. 292.

70. C. Boyden Gray, interview with author, 18 April 1997.

71. Untermeyer, "Looking Forward," p. 164.

72. Chase Untermeyer, interview with author, 18 June 1996.

73. C. Boyden Gray, interview with author, 18 April 1997; Lou Cannon, *President Reagan: The Role of a Lifetime* (New York: Simon and Schuster, 1991), pp. 127, 441, 821.

74. Geraldine Ferraro, interview with author, 29 July 1997.

75. Ferraro keeps an autographed picture of Bush in her Manhattan office. Dated 5 December 1984, it reads, "Let's debate. Better still, let's not debate. Let's Be Friends. George Bush" (Geraldine Ferraro, interview with author, 29 July 1997).

76. Jane Mayer and Doyle McManus, *Landslide: The Unmaking of a President, 1984–1988* (Boston: Houghton Mifflin, 1988), p. 218.

CHAPTER 3
"JUGULAR POLITICS"

1. *New York Times (NYT),* 18 May 1986, p. 50.

2. *WPNWE,* 9–15 June 1986, p. 12; NBC Nightly News, 4 May 1986.

3. *WPNWE,* 16–22 June 1986, pp. 12–13.

4. John Brady, *Bad Boy: The Life and Politics of Lee Atwater* (Reading, MA: Addison-Wesley, 1997), p. 36.

5. Ibid., p. 109.

6. Fitzhugh Green, *George Bush: An Intimate Portrait* (New York: Hippocrene Books, 1989), p. 82.

7. Bob Schieffer and Gary Paul Gates, *The Acting President* (New York: E. P. Dutton, 1989), pp. 343–44.

8. Ibid., p. 349.

9. Brady, *Bad Boy,* p. 162.

10. Herbert S. Parmet, *George Bush: The Life of a Lone Star Yankee* (New York: Scribner, 1997), p. 327.

11. John H. Sununu, interview with author, 8 July 1997.

12. Sig Rogich, telephone interview with author, 6 October 1998; *WPNWE,* 27 June–3 July 1988, p. 13.

13. Sig Rogich, telephone interview with author, 6 October 1998.

14. Michael Duffy and Dan Goodgame, *Marching in Place: The Status Quo Presidency of George Bush* (New York: Simon and Schuster, 1992), p. 23.

15. C. Boyden Gray, interview with author, 18 April 1997.

16. Sig Rogich, telephone interview with author, 6 October 1998.

17. *Washington Post (WP),* 15 November 1985. Kennedy announced that he would not be a candidate during a 19 December interview on the Cable News Network (CNN).

18. *WPNWE,* 2–8 February 1987, p. 4.

19. Andrew A. Card, interview with author, 18 April 1997.

20. *WPNWE,* 27 June–3 July 1988, p. 12; Andrew A. Card, interview with author, 18 April 1997.

21. Sig Rogich, telephone interview with author, 6 October 1998.

22. Bob Woodward, *The Commanders* (New York: Simon and Schuster, 1991), p. 57.

23. Jack Germond and Jules Witcover, *Whose Broad Stripes and Bright Stars? The Trivial Pursuit of the Presidency, 1988* (New York: Warner Books, 1989), pp. 379–83; Dan Quayle, *Standing Firm* (New York: Harper: 1994), p. 5; Schieffer and Gates, *Acting President,* p. 365.

24. David S. Broder and Bob Woodward, *The Man Who Would Be President: Dan Quayle* (New York: Simon and Schuster, 1992), pp. 35–38; Richard F. Fenno, *The Making of a Senator: Dan Quayle* (Washington, DC: Congressional Quarterly Books, 1989), p. 3.

25. Broder and Woodward, *The Man Who Would Be President,* pp. 15, 23.

26. Germond and Witcover, *Whose Broad Stripes and Bright Stars?* p. 378.

27. Daniel Heimbach, interview with author, 19 April 1997.

28. Fenno, *Making of a Senator,* p. 20.

29. Ibid., p. 8.

30. Broder and Woodward, *The Man Who Would Be President,* p. 27.

31. Parmet, *Lone Star Yankee,* p. 349.

32. Broder and Woodward, *The Man Who Would Be President,* p. 62; Parmet, *Lone Star Yankee,* p. 346.

33. Peggy Noonan, *What I Saw at the Revolution: A Political Life in the Reagan Era* (New York: Ivy Books, 1990), pp. 315–29; Bob Woodward, "The Anatomy of a Decision," *WPNWE*, 12–18 October 1992, p. 6.

34. Schieffer and Gates, *Acting President*, p. 367.

35. George Will, "The Rubber Ducky Campaign," (*Newsweek*, 26 September 1988), p. 84.

36. Brady, *Bad Boy*, p. 172.

37. Parmet, *Lone Star Yankee*, p. 336.

38. Andrew A. Card, interview with author, 18 April 1997.

39. Chase Untermeyer, interview with author, 18 June 1996.

40. Andrew A. Card, interview with author, 18 April 1997.

41. Michael Gilette, ed., *Snapshots of the 1988 Presidential Campaign*, Vol. 1: *The Bush Campaign* (Austin: LBJ School of Public Affairs, University of Texas, 1992), pp. 70–72.

42. Quoted in Brady, *Bad Boy*, p. 191.

43. *WP*, 3 September 1988, p. A8.

44. Quoted in Schieffer and Gates, *Acting President*, p. 372.

45. Germond and Witcover, *Whose Broad Stripes and Bright Stars?* p. 406.

46. Sig Rogich, telephone interview with author, 6 October 1998; C–SPAN video, "Presidential Campaign Commercials," broadcast on 2 October 1988 (ID no. 8705).

47. John G. Tower, *Consequences, A Personal and Political Memoir* (Boston: Little, Brown, 1991), p. 11.

48. When the electoral college finally met in January 1989, the final vote was 426 for Bush, 111 for Dukakis, with one vote cast for Lloyd Bentsen by Margarette Leach of West Virginia as a protest of the outdated electoral college system. As president of the Senate, George Bush proclaimed his own electoral victory (*NYT*, 4 January 1989, p. B6).

49. "Quest for the Presidency: The Candidates Debate," *Reader's Digest* (October 1988), p. 73.

50. *NYT*, 10 November 1988, p. B5.

51. William Boot, "Campaign '88: TV Overdoses on the Inside Dope," *Columbia Journalism Review* (January/February 1989): 27.

52. *NYT*, 12 November 1988, p. 8.

53. For end-of-election statistics, see *NYT*, 10 November 1988, pp. B6–B7, and *NJ*, 29 April 1989, pp. 1050–54.

54. Will, "Rubber Ducky," p. 84.

55. W. Lance Bennett, *The Governing Crisis: Media, Money, and Marketing in American Elections* (New York: St. Martin's Press, 1996), pp. 28–29.

56. Ibid., p. 29.

57. *NYT*, 9 November 1988, p. A25.

CHAPTER 4
"THE UNTOUCHABLES"

1. George Bush and Brent Scowcroft, *A World Transformed* (New York: Alfred A. Knopf, 1998), p. 18.

2. James A. Baker III, *The Politics of Diplomacy: Revolution, War, and Peace* (New York: G. P. Putnam's Sons, 1995), pp. 19–20.

3. Chase Untermeyer, interview with author, 18 June 1996; *WPNWE*, 6–11 December 1988, p. 12.

4. Andrew A. Card, interview with author, 18 April 1997.

5. Charles Peters, *How Washington* Really *Works* (Reading: MA: Addison-Wesley, 1992), p. 14.

6. Chase Untermeyer, interview with author, 18 June 1996.

7. *WPNWE*, 28 November–4 December, 1988, p. 13.

8. Michael Beschloss and Strobe Talbott, *At the Highest Levels; The Inside Story of the End of the Cold War* (Boston: Little, Brown, 1993), p. 8.

9. Shirley Anne Warshaw, *The Domestic Presidency: Policy Making in the White House* (Boston: Allyn and Bacon, 1997), p. 158.

10. *WPNWE*, 28 November–4 December 1988, p. 13.

11. Andrew A. Card, interview with author, 18 April 1997.

12. John H. Sununu, interview with author, 8 July 1997; *NYT*, 20 November 1988, p. 1.

13. Michael Duffy and Dan Goodgame, *Marching in Place: The Status Quo Presidency of George Bush* (New York: Simon and Schuster, 1991), p. 38.

14. *NYT*, 1 December 1988, p. B17.

15. *WPNWE*, 5–11 December 1988, p. 12.

16. Bob Woodward, *The Commanders* (New York: Simon and Schuster, 1991), p. 68.

17. Herbert S. Parmet, *George Bush: The Life of a Lone Star Yankee* (New York: Scribner, 1997), p. 360.

18. *NYT*, 25 November 1988, p. 1.

19. James P. Pfiffner, *The Bush Transition: A Friendly Takeover* (Richmond, VA: Institute of Public Policy, George Mason University, 1995). Indeed, James Baker was quoted as telling his staff, "Remember, this is *not* a friendly takeover" (quoted in Beschloss and Talbott, *At the Highest Levels*, p. 26).

20. See, for example, the observations in *NYT*, 17 January 1989, p. A1.

21. Philip D. Brady, interview with author, 17 April 1997; Edward Derwinski, telephone interview with author, 6 October 1998.

22. Richard Darman, *Who's in Control? Polar Politics and the Sensible Center* (New York: Simon and Schuster, 1996), p. 206.

23. *NYT*, 24 November 1988, p. B13, and 28 November 1988, p. 1; Bush and Scowcroft, *A World Transformed*, pp. 11–12; Woodward, *The Commanders*, p. 51.

24. Beschloss and Talbott, *At the Highest Levels*, p. 12.

25. *NJ*, 3 December 1988, p. 3087 (title of the article: "Scowcroft's Views Often at Odds with Those Held by Reagan's Team").

26. Bush and Scowcroft, *A World Transformed*, p. 19.

27. John Hart, *The Presidential Branch: The Executive Office of the President from Washington to Clinton* (Chatham, NJ: Chatham House, 1995), pp. 76–77.

28. Fitzhugh Green, *George Bush: An Intimate Portrait* (New York: Hippocrene Books, 1989), p. 112.

29. John G. Tower, *Consequences: A Personal and Political Memoir* (Boston: Little, Brown, 1991), p. 280.

30. *Atlanta Constitution*, undated (quoted in ibid., pp. 30–31).

31. Chase Untermeyer, interview with author, 18 June 1996.

32. Interview with author, not for attribution.

33. Quoted in Parmet, *Lone Star Yankee*, p. 373.

34. "Summary of Work Performed for Consulting Clients," undated, George Bush Presidential Records, GBL (Bush PR), Counsel's Office: Dean McGrath Files, Sherrie Marshall File—Working File for Hearing.

35. William Webster, interview with author, 8 July 1997.

36. Bush and Scowcroft, *A World Transformed*, p. 21.

37. *NYT*, 21 January 1989, p. 7.

38. *NYT*, 15 February 1989.

39. Duffy and Goodgame, *Marching in Place*, p. 37.

40. *NYT*, 5 February 1989, p. 1, 6 February 1989, p. A15, and 7 February 1989, p. A1.

41. Ibid., 15 February 1989, p. A1.

42. Ibid., 19 February 1989, p. E4.

43. Ibid., 26 January 1989, p. D23, and 29 January 1989, p. A1.

44. Ibid., 12 February 1989, p. 30.

45. Ibid., 2 February 1989, p. D20.

46. Woodward, *The Commanders*, pp. 58–59.

47. Press Pool Report, 8 February 1989, Bush PR, White House Press Office (WHPO), Lower Press Office Pool Reports, box 13, dated folder.

48. Bush to Charles L. Bartlett, 21 February 1989, Bush PR, White House Office of Records Management (WHORM) Subject Files: General, FG–37.

49. *NYT*, 10 February 1989, p. A1, and 11 February 1989, p. 10.

50. Ibid., 24 February 1989, pp. A1, D19.

51. "Report Together with Minority Views," 28 February 1989, copy in Bush PR, Counsel's Office, C. Dean McGrath Jr. Files, Tower Files: SASC—Report with Minority folder.

52. Schedule, 28 February 1989, Bush PR, White House Office of Legislative Affairs, Rebecca Anderson: Trip Files and Miscellaneous Files, Tower Nomination: 1989 folder.

53. *NYT*, 27 February 1989, p. A1.

54. Ibid., 24 February 1989, p. A1.

55. George Bush, interview with author, 9 November 1998.

56. On 5 April 1991, Tower, who had been named by Bush to the Presidential Intelligence Advisory Board, was killed along with twenty-two others, including one of his three daughters, in the crash of a commuter airplane off the Georgia coast.

57. Woodward, *The Commanders*, p. 71.

58. Colin Powell, *My American Journey* (New York: Random House, 1995), p. 405.

59. Richard B. Cheney, telephone interview with author, 7 March 1997.

60. Bush to Tower (xerox of photo with inscription), 15 March 1989, Bush PR, WHORM Subject File: General, PR005.

61. *NJ* (1 July 1989), pp. 1678–83.

62. Gloria Borger, "Dennis the Menace Comes in from the Cold," *U.S. News and World Report (USN&WR)* (27 March 1989), p. 27.

63. *WPNWE*, 13–19 March 1989, p. 12.

64. John M. Barry, *The Ambition and the Power: The Fall of Jim Wright—A True Story of Washington* (New York: Viking Press, 1989), p. 762.

65. John Brady, *Bad Boy: The Life and Politics of Lee Atwater* (Reading, MA: Addison-Wesley, 1997), pp. 241–47.

66. *NYT*, 26 August 1989, p. A1.

67. Ibid., 10 June 1990, p. 22, and 26 July 1990, p. A1.

68. *WPNWE*, 13–19 March 1989, pp. 6–7.

CHAPTER 5
"A LIMITED AGENDA"

1. Quoted in Kenneth T. Walsh, "Bush's First Quarter," *USN&WR*, 1 May 1989, p. 24.

2. *NYT*, 14 December 1988, p. 1.

3. "Veto Threats Outstanding as of July 25, 1991," Bush PR, WHPO, General Office Files, Press Office Subject File, box 90, Veto Threats folder no. 1.

4. Rob Portman, interview with author, 13 June 1997; Kenneth E. Collier, *Between the Branches: The White House Office of Legislative Affairs* (Pittsburgh: University of Pittsburgh Press, 1997), p. 242.

5. *NYT*, 9 March 1989, p. A20.

6. Interview transcript, Bush with *WP*, 23 March 1989, Bush PR, WHPO, Press Office Internal Transcripts, box 133, dated folder.

7. *NYT*, 24 March 1989, p. A13.

8. Ibid., 15 June 1989, p. A21.

9. Ibid., 9 November 1989, p. 2.

10. Exhibit, GBL.

11. *NYT*, 7 July 1989, p. B4.

12. Ibid., 25 July 1989, p. A17.

13. Ibid., 23 February 1990, p. 2.

14. Ibid., 26 January 1989, p. A23.

15. Bush to Lofton, 24 April 1986, Bush PR, Fitzwater Files, Subject File: Alpha File, box 1, Abortion folder.

16. Bush to Henry Hyde, 5 May 1989, Bush PR, WHORM Subject File: General, WE 003, box 34, no. 029331.

17. Ted Gest, "The Abortion Furor," *USN&WR*, 17 July 1989, p. 19.

18. Statement by the President, 3 July 1989, Bush PR, Fitzwater Files, OA 6784, Subject File: Alpha File, box 1, Abortion folder.

19. Morton Kondracke, "The New Abortion Wars," *New Republic* (28 August 1989), pp. 18–19.

20. Bush to Dole, 4 June 1991, Bush PR, WHPO, General Office Files, Press Office Subject File, box 83, Abortion folder. Bush used essentially this same boilerplate

when writing other members of Congress regarding his stance on abortion (see, for example, Bush to Robert Byrd, 17 October 1989, Bush PR, Fitzwater Files, box 1, Abortion folder).

21. Kenneth O'Reilly, *Nixon's Piano: Presidents and Racial Politics from Washington to Clinton* (New York: Free Press, 1995), pp. 392–93.

22. *NYT*, 13 April 1990, p. 2.

23. John Berlau, "The Quota Paradox," *Policy Review* (spring 1994): 7.

24. *WPNWE*, 13–19 March 1989, p. 4.

25. Brennan to Bush, 20 July 1990, Bush PR, Legislative Affairs, Rebecca Anderson Files, Souter Nomination folder.

26. C. Boyden Gray, interview with author, 18 April 1997. See also John H. Sununu, interview with author, 8 July 1997.

27. C. Boyden Gray, interview with author, 18 April 1997.

28. Rob Portman, interview with author, 13 June 1997.

29. Untermeyer to Souter, 3 February 1990, Bush PR, Personnel, Chase Untermeyer Files, Souter folder.

30. *Boston Globe*, 24 July 1990.

31. *Washington Times*, 24 July 1990, p. 10.

32. UPI story (Lexis Nexis Service), 19 March 1988.

33. *Chronicle of Higher Education* (6 September 1989), p. 5; Edith Rasell and Lawrence Mishel, "The Truth About Education Spending," *Roll Call* (21 May 1990), p. 23.

34. George Bush, interview with author, 9 November 1998.

35. *NYT*, 26 April 1989, p. B8.

37. Bush to Clinton, 29 September 1989, Bush PR, WHORM General File, Subject File, MC083600.

37. *NYT*, 19 December 1990, p. A1.

38. "America 2000: The President's Education Strategy, Fact Sheet," 18 April 1991, George Bush, *Public Papers of the Presidents*, 8 vols. (Washington, DC: Government Printing Office, 1990–1993) (Bush *PP*), 1991, 1: 389.

39. *Wall Street Journal*, 6 February 1991, p. A14.

40. *WP*, 28 April 1991, p. C7.

41. Susan Chira, "Lamar Alexander's Self-Help Course," *New York Times Magazine* (23 November 1991), p. 52.

42. Hugh Sidey, "Back in the Bully Pulpit," *Time* (23 January 1989), p. 19.

43. David Demarest, interview with author, 17 April 1997.

44. *WP*, 22 September 1989, p. A1; *NYT*, 23 September 1989, p. 1.

45. Fact Sheet, National Drug Control Strategy, 5 September 1989, Bush PR, WHPO, General Office Files, Press Office Subject File, box 84, Drug folder no. 3.

46. *NYT*, 31 March 1989, p. A11.

47. Ibid., 24 August 1989, p. B6.

48. Ibid., 21 January 1990, p. 2.

49. The bill, the Andean Trade Preference Act of 1990, was signed into law on 5 October 1990. See Bush PR, WHPO, General Office Files, Press Office Subject File, box 83, Andean—Caribbean Basin Initiative folder.

50. *NYT*, 5 April 1990, p. 2, and 14 April 1990, p. 2.

51. White House, "National Drug Control Strategy, February 1991," Bush PR, WHPO, General Office Files, Press Office Subject File, box 84, Drug folder no. 3. See also *NYT*, 1 February 1991, p. 2; *San Diego Union*, 16 June 1991, p. C2.

52. Rodman D. Griffen, *The Disabilities Act: Protecting the Rights of the Disabled Will Have Far-Reaching Effects*, No. 32 (Washington, DC: Congressional Quarterly, in conjunction with EBSCO Publishing, 1991), p. 999.

53. Major R. Owens, *Americans with Disabilities Act: Initial Accessibility Good but Important Barriers Remain* (Washington, DC: U.S. General Accounting Office, 1993), p. 1.

54. Bush *PP*, 1990, 2: p. 1068; Griffen, *Disabilities Act*, p. 996.

55. David Mervin, *George Bush and the Guardianship Presidency* (New York: St. Martin's Press, 1996), p. 98.

56. C. Boyden Gray, interview with author, 18 April 1997.

57. Letter in exhibit, GBL.

58. *NYT*, 1 December 1988, p. B15.

59. Ibid., 1 February 1989, p. 1.

60. Patrick Barry, "A Master Plan from Bush's Unlikely Star," *USN&WR* (24 July 1989), p. 24.

61. Skinner to Bush, 22 March 1990, Bush PR, WHORM Subject File: General, DI001.

62. Rogich to Bush, 30 March 1989, Bush PR, WHORM Subject File: General, DI001.

63. Richard E. Cohen, *Washington at Work: Back Rooms and Clean Air* (New York: Macmillan, 1992), p. 85.

64. Louis Jacobsen, "The Green Hornet," *NJ* (27 January 1996), p. 167; Margaret Kris, "Politics in the Air," *NJ* (6 May 1989), pp. 1098–1102.

65. Cohen, *Washington at Work*, p. 89.

66. "Fact Sheet: The Clean Air Act Amendments of 1990," 15 November 1990, Bush PR, Fitzwater Files, OA 6784, Subject File: Alpha File, box 6, Clean Air Act folder no. 3.

CHAPTER 6
PAYING FOR REAGANOMICS

1. Herbert S. Parmet, *George Bush: The Life of a Lone Star Yankee* (New York: Scribner, 1997), p. 367.

2. Press Pool Report, 13 February 1989, Bush PR, WHPO, Lower Press Office Pool Reports, box 13, dated folder.

3. *NYT*, 19 January 1989, p. B9.

4. Richard Darman, *Who's in Control? Polar Politics and the Sensible Center* (New York: Simon and Schuster, 1996), p. 200.

5. *NYT*, 9 January 1989, p. B6.

6. George Bush, interview with author, 9 November 1998.

7. Press Pool Report, 24 April 1989, Bush PR, WHPO, Lower Press Office Pool Reports, box 13, dated folder.

8. Darman, *Who's in Control?* pp. 205–9.

9. Interview transcript, Bush and Don Feder, 18 May 1989, Bush PR, WHPO, Press Office Internal Transcripts, box 133, folder OA6237.

10. Darman, *Who's in Control?* pp. 236–37.

11. L. William Seidman, *Full Faith and Credit: The Great S&L Debacle and Other Washington Sagas* (New York: Times Books, 1993), p. 178.

12. Ibid., p. 176; WPNWE, 26 June–2 July, 1989, pp. 6–8.

13. *NYT,* 11 January 1989, p. A1, and 31 January 1989, p. 1.

14. Ibid., 7 February 1989, p. D9; Catherine Yang, "Bush's S&L Plan: Full of Good Intentions—and Holes," *Business Week* (20 February 1989), p. 32.

15. Parmet, *Lone Star Yankee,* p. 395; Seidman, *Full Faith and Credit,* p. 209.

16. *WPNWE,* 15–21 May 1989, p. 14.

17. Karen Penmar, "Inflation Stages a Comeback," *Business Week* (3 April 1989), p. 32.

18. *NYT,* 13 October 1989, p. 2, 16 October 1989, p. 2, and 17 October 1989, p. 2.

19. Press Release, 29 January 1990, Bush PR, WHPO, General Office Files, Press Office Subject Files, box 83, Bush—1991 folder.

20. Darman, *Who's In Control?* p. 245.

21. George Bush, interview with author, 9 November 1998.

22. Darman, *Who's In Control?* p. 264.

23. See Charles Kolb, *White House Daze: The Unmaking of Domestic Politics in the Bush Years* (New York: Free Press, 1993), p. 56; David Mervin, *George Bush and the Guardianship Presidency* (New York: St. Martin's Press, 1996), p. 129.

24. Darman, *Who's in Control?* pp. 230–33.

25. Ibid., p. 255.

26. Ibid., p. 265.

27. Ibid., p. 269.

28. Parmet, *Lone Star Yankee,* p. 430.

29. Darman, *Who's in Control?* p. 251; Parmet, *Lone Star Yankee,* p. 433.

30. Michael Duffy and Dan Goodgame, *Marching in Place: The Status Quo Presidency of George Bush* (New York: Simon and Schuster, 1991), p. 119.

31. George Bush and Brent Scowcroft, *A World Transformed* (New York: Alfred A. Knopf, 1998), p. 363.

32. White House Press Release, 25 September 1990, Bush PR, WHPO, General Office Files, Press Office Subject Files, box 83, Bush—1991 folder.

33. Darman, *Who's in Control?* p. 272.

34. Ibid., p. 273.

35. Bush and Scowcroft, *A World Transformed,* p. 380.

36. Parmet, *Lone Star Yankee,* p. 470.

37. Ed Rollins, *Bare Knuckles and Back Rooms: My Life in American Politics* (New York: Broadway Books, 1996), pp. 199–208.

38. Parmet, *Lone Star Yankee,* p. 434.

39. Duffy and Goodgame, *Marching in Place,* p. 85.

CHAPTER 7
THE *PAUZA*, "PARTNERSHIP," AND PANAMA

1. See *NYT*, 8 December 1988, p. A17.
2. George Bush and Brent Scowcroft, *A World Transformed* (New York: Alfred A. Knopf, 1998), p. 7.
3. Michael Beschloss and Strobe Talbott, *At the Highest Levels: The Inside Story of the End of the Cold War* (Boston: Little, Brown, 1993), pp. 10–11.
4. Bush and Scowcroft, *A World Transformed*, p. 8.
5. Beschloss and Talbott, *At the Highest Levels*, p. 11.
6. Ibid., p. 34.
7. James Baker, interview with author, 17 April 1997.
8. James A. Baker III, *The Politics of Diplomacy: Revolution, War, and Peace* (New York: G. P. Putnam's Sons, 1997), p. xiii; David Mervin, *George Bush and the Guardianship Presidency* (New York: St. Martin's Press, 1996), p. 161.
9. Beschloss and Talbott, *At the Highest Levels*, p. 27.
10. Gen. Brent Scowcroft, interview with author, 11 June 1997.
11. Bush and Scowcroft, *A World Transformed*, p. 15.
12. *NYT*, 27 October 1989, p. 1.
13. James Baker, interview with author, 17 April 1997.
14. Mikhail Gorbachev, Remarks to the Hofstra University Conference on the Bush Presidency, 17–19 April 1997 (Hofstra), 19 April 1997.
15. Beschloss and Talbott, *At the Highest Levels*, p. 39.
16. Draft, Texas A&M Speech—Bush Markup, Bush PR, Office of Speechwriters, Speech File: Drafts, dated folder.
17. Bush and Scowcroft, *A World Transformed*, p. 54.
18. Press Release, 29 May 1989, Bush PR, Fitzwater Files, Subject Files: Alpha File, box 1, Arms Control folder; Bush and Scowcroft, *A World Transformed*, pp. 43–45, 79–85.
19. James A. Lilley, interview with author, 19 April 1997.
20. Ibid.; Bush and Scowcroft, *A World Transformed*, pp. 91–94.
21. See Dusko Doder, "Reinventing China," *New York Times Magazine* (17 May 1989), pp. 30–36.
22. Dusko Doder and Louise Branson, *Gorbachev* (New York: Penguin Books, 1990), pp. 363–64.
23. Baker, *Politics of Diplomacy*, p. 104.
24. James A. Lilley, interview with author, 19 April 1997.
25. Herbert S. Parmet, *George Bush: The Life of a Lone Star Yankee* (New York: Scribner, 1997), p. 392.
26. Bush and Scowcroft, *A World Transformed*, p. 89.
27. Gen. Brent Scowcroft, interview with author, 11 June 1997.
28. Undated Meeting Notes (Fitzwater's handwriting), Bush PR, Subject File: Alpha File, box 3, China folder.
29. Quoted in *USN&WR*, 5 June 1989, p. 27.
30. Bush and Scowcroft, *A World Transformed*, p. 98.
31. Baker, *Politics of Diplomacy*, p. 109.

32. Ibid., p. 110.

33. Gen. Brent Scowcroft, interview with author, 11 June 1997; Michael Duffy and Dan Goodgame, *Marching in Place: The Status Quo Presidency of George Bush* (New York: Simon and Schuster, 1991), p. 183; Parmet, *Lone Star Yankee,* p. 399.

34. Bush and Scowcroft, *A World Transformed,* p. 174.

35. James A. Lilley, interview with author, 19 April 1997.

36. Beschloss and Talbott, *At the Highest Levels,* p. 53.

37. Gen. Brent Scowcroft, Hofstra, 17 April 1997.

38. Bush and Scowcroft, *A World Transformed,* p. 117.

39. Beschloss and Talbott, *At the Highest Levels,* pp. 88–89.

40. Parmet, *Lone Star Yankee,* p. 407.

41. Beschloss and Talbott, *At the Highest Levels,* pp. 102–5; Bush and Scowcroft, *A World Transformed,* pp. 141–43; Duffy and Goodgame, *Marching in Place,* p. 188.

42. Mikhail Gorbachev, Hofstra, 19 April 1997.

43. Baker, *Politics of Diplomacy,* p. 161.

44. *NYT,* 26 October 1989, p. 2.

45. Ibid., 10 November 1989, p. 1.

46. Elizabeth Pond, *Beyond the Wall: Germany's Road to Unification* (Washington, DC: Brookings Institution, 1993), pp. 1–6.

47. Beschloss and Talbott, *At the Highest Levels,* p. 135; Bush and Scowcroft, *A World Transformed,* pp. 148–49; Duffy and Goodgame, *Marching in Place,* p. 135.

48. George Bush, interview with author, 9 November 1998.

49. Mikhail Gorbachev, Hofstra, 19 April 1997.

50. Baker, *Politics of Diplomacy,* pp. 168–71; Beschloss and Talbott, *At the Highest Levels,* p. 163; Bush and Scowcroft, *A World Transformed,* pp. 162–74.

51. Lance Morrow, "Gorbachev: The Unlikely Patron of Change," *Time* (1 January 1990), pp. 42–45.

52. Seymour Hersh, "Our Man in Panama: The Creation of a Thug," *Life* (March 1990), p. 90.

53. *NYT,* 19 January 1991, p. 2; Colin Powell, *My American Journey* (New York: Random House, 1995), p. 515; John Dinges, *Our Man in Panama: How General Noriega Used the U.S.—And Made Millions in Drugs and Arms* (New York: Random House, 1990); Frederick Kempe, *Divorcing the Dictator: America's Bungled Affair with Noriega* (New York: Putnam, 1990); Parmet, *Lone Star Yankee,* pp. 202–5.

54. Joseph L. Galloway, "Standoff in Panama," *USN&WR* (22 May 1989), pp. 28–29; *NYT,* 12 May 1989, pp. A1, 8.

55. Powell, *My American Journey,* pp. 420–21; Bob Woodward, *The Commanders* (New York: Simon and Schuster, 1991), pp. 85–93.

56. Interview transcript, Bush and Arnaud De Borchgrave, 15 May 1989, Bush PR, WHPO, Press Office Internal Transcripts, box 133, folder OA6237.

57. Richard B. Cheney, telephone interview with author, 7 March 1997.

58. *NYT,* 2 February 1989, p. A1.

59. Baker, *Politics of Diplomacy,* p. 22.

60. Powell, *An American Journey,* pp. 388–89.

61. Bush and Scowcroft, *A World Transformed,* p. 23.

62. *NYT,* 15 November 1988, p. B10.

63. William Webster, interview with author, 8 July 1997.

64. Ibid.

65. Woodward, *The Commanders*, p. 122.

66. Parmet, *Lone Star Yankee*, p. 413.

67. Ibid., p. 412.

68. William Webster, interview with author, 8 July 1997.

69. Baker, *Politics of Diplomacy*, pp. 185–86.

70. Gen. Brent Scowcroft, interview with author, 11 June 1997.

71. Woodward, *The Commanders*, p. 121.

72. Parmet, *Lone Star Yankee*, p. 414.

73. *NYT*, 15 October 1989, p. A1.

74. Woodward, *The Commanders*, p. 128.

75. Gen. Brent Scowcroft, interview with author, 11 June 1997.

76. Bush and Scowcroft, *A World Transformed*, p. 161.

77. Powell, *My American Journey*, pp. 440–45; Dan Quayle, *Standing Firm* (New York: Harper, 1994), chap. 16, passim.

78. Woodward, *The Commanders*, p. 149.

79. Release, Assistant Secretary for Defense (undated), Bush PR, Fitzwater Files, Alpha Files: Subject File, OA 6546, box 21, Panama folder no. 2.

80. Gen. Brent Scowcroft, interview with author, 11 June 1997; Baker, *Politics of Diplomacy*, p. 189.

81. Powell, *My American Journey*, pp. 423–25; Woodward, *The Commanders*, pp. 160–71.

82. Scott Slinger, "New Weapons, Old Problems," *Washington Monthly* (October 1990), p. 43.

83. Woodward, *The Commanders*, pp. 182–95.

84. *NYT*, 21 December 1989, p. 1.

85. Kennedy: 79 percent; Eisenhower and Johnson, 70 percent; Nixon, 61 percent; Carter, 51 percent; Reagan, 49 percent; and Ford, 45 percent (*NYT/CBS* News poll; see *NYT*, 19 January 1991, p. A20).

86. James Baker, interview with author, 17 April 1997.

87. *NYT*, 5 February 1990, p. 2.

88. Ibid., 17 January 1990, p. A8.

89. Ibid., 6 February 1990, p. A1.

90. Ibid., 18 April 1990, p. 2.

91. Beschloss and Talbott, *At the Highest Levels*, p. 223.

92. *NYT*, 13 June 1990, p. 2, and 17 July 1990, pp. A1, A8. Beschloss and Talbott, *At the Highest Levels*, p. 220; Bush and Scowcroft, *A World Restored*, pp. 279–89.

93. Parmet, *Lone Star Yankee*, p. 384.

CHAPTER 8
DESERT SHIELD

1. *Current Biography*, 1981. In a 1997 interview, William Webster revealed that the CIA had movies of Saddam sending twenty-three people out to be executed

because he knew that one of them was a traitor (William Webster, interview with author, 8 July 1997).

2. Lawrence Freedman and Efraim Karsh, *The Gulf Conflict, 1990–1991: Diplomacy and War in the New World Order* (Princeton: Princeton University Press, 1993), p. 39.

3. Ibid., p. 39.

4. Gen. Brent Scowcroft, interview with author, 11 June 1997.

5. George Bush and Brent Scowcroft, *A World Transformed* (New York: Alfred A. Knopf, 1998), p. 306; Freedman and Karsh, *The Gulf Conflict*, p. 25. See also Michael Klare, "Fueling the Fire: How We Armed the Middle East," *Bulletin of Atomic Scientists* (January/February 1990): 19–25, and Don Oberdorfer, "The War No One Saw Coming," *WPNWE*, 18–24 March 1991, pp. 6–10.

6. Rick Atkinson, *Crusade: The Untold Story of the Persian Gulf War* (Boston: Houghton Mifflin, 1993), p. 51.

7. Freedman and Karsh, *The Gulf Conflict*, p. 27; "The Ties That Bind," *WPNWE*, 24–30 September 1990, pp. 11–12.

8. Freedman and Karsh, *The Gulf Conflict*, p. 35.

9. *WPNWE*, 18–24 March 1991, p. 8.

10. Bob Woodward, *The Commanders* (New York: Simon and Schuster, 1991), p. 201.

11. Ibid., p. 201.

12. James A. Baker III, *The Politics of Diplomacy: Revolution, War, and Peace* (New York: G. P. Putnam's Sons, 1997), p. 268.

13. Woodward, *The Commanders*, pp. 199–204.

14. Freedman and Karsh, *The Gulf Conflict*, p. 44; Woodward, *The Commanders*, p. 206.

15. Atkinson, *Crusade*, p. 28.

16. Freedman and Karsh, *The Gulf Conflict*, p. 46.

17. Atkinson, *Crusade*, p. 1.

18. Ibid., p. 8.

19. Ibid., p. 3; Colin Powell, *My American Journey* (New York: Random House, 1995), p. 493.

20. Powell, *My American Journey*, p. 460.

21. Atkinson, *Crusade*, p. 107; Woodward, *The Commanders*, pp. 228, 247–55.

22. Powell, *My American Journey*, pp. 461–62; Woodward, *The Commanders*, pp. 205–10.

23. Michael Duffy and Dan Goodgame, *Marching in Place: The Status Quo Presidency of George Bush* (New York: Simon and Schuster, 1991), p. 132; Herbert S. Parmet, *George Bush: The Life of a Lone Star Yankee* (New York: Scribner, 1997), p. 446. A copy of the transcript of Glaspie's 25 July 1990 conversation with Saddam—the authenticity of which the State Department would neither confirm nor deny—is reprinted in Micha L. Sifry and Christopher Cerf, *The Gulf War Reader: History, Documents, and Opinions* (New York: Times Books, 1991), pp. 122–33. See also Bush and Scowcroft, *A World Transformed*, pp. 310–11.

24. William Webster, interview with author, 8 July 1997.

25. Bush and Scowcroft, *A World Transformed*, p. 309; Woodward, *The Commanders*, pp. 215–16.

26. Bush and Scowcroft, *A World Transformed*, p. 313.

27. Parmet, *Lone Star Yankee*, p. 443.

28. Bush and Scowcroft, *A World Transformed*, p. 416.

29. Baker, *Politics of Diplomacy*, pp. 1–16; Michael Beschloss and Strobe Talbott, *At the Highest Levels: The Inside Story of the End of the Cold War* (Boston: Little, Brown, 1993), p. 248; Bush and Scowcroft, *A World Transformed*, pp. 325–26.

30. Beschloss and Talbott, *At the Highest Levels*, pp. 261–62.

31. *NYT*, 11 September 1990, p. A1.

32. Bush and Scowcroft, *A World Restored*, pp. 325–26; Duffy and Goodgame, *Marching in Place*, p. 145; Powell, *My American Journey*, pp. 464–65; Woodward, *The Commanders*, pp. 239–42.

33. Bush and Scowcroft, *A World Transformed*, pp. 328–29.

34. Woodward, *The Commanders*, pp. 258–59.

35. Powell, *My American Journey*, p. 467.

36. Ibid., pp. 466–67.

37. Woodward, *The Commanders*, pp. 263–73.

38. Bush and Scowcroft, *A World Transformed*, p. 340.

39. *NYT*, 22 August 1990, p. A1 and 20 November 1990, p. A1.

40. *WPNWE*, 20–26 August 1990, p. 7.

41. Freedman and Karsh, *The Gulf Conflict*, p. 98.

42. Ibid., p. 216. One might ask how the nation, already deep in deficit, paid for the war. Douglas A. Brook, then the acting secretary of the army for Financial Management, was blunt: "We didn't." The Feed and Forage Act, an act that permitted the Northern cavalry to buy feed while they were marching through Georgia during the last days of the Civil War, allows for the deficit operation of the army in certain cases. This law was invoked in 1991 to allow the Congress to appropriate funds, despite a federal deficit and without congressional permission for it, in order to help a military mission. Brook remembered that most of the $19 billion ultimately spent by the army was appropriated in this fashion; in his words—"Spend it as if you have it" (Douglas A. Brook, interview with author, 17 April 1997).

43. Freedman and Karsh, *The Gulf Conflict*, pp. 110–27.

44. Fact Sheet, 13 February 1991, Bush PR, Fitzwater Files, OA 6784, Subject File: Alpha File, box 17, Iraq folder 1991 no. 2.

45. Press Release, 22 February 1991, Bush PR, Fitzwater Files, OA 6784, Subject File: Alpha File, box 17, Iraq folder 1991 no. 2.

46. Freedman and Karsh, *The Gulf Conflict*, p. 221.

47. James Baker, interview with author, 17 April 1997; Beschloss and Talbott, *At the Highest Levels*, p. 252; Bush and Scowcroft, *A World Transformed*, pp. 352–53.

48. Bush and Scowcroft, *A World Transformed*, p. 382.

49. Powell, *My American Journey*, pp. 470–71.

50. Bush and Scowcroft, *A World Transformed*, p. 353.

51. Ibid., pp. 321–24.

52. Atkinson, *Crusade*, p. 113.

53. *NYT*, 12 September 1990, p. 2.

54. Bush and Scowcroft, *A World Transformed*, p. 374.

55. *NYT*, 11 September 1990, p. A1.

56. Freedman and Karsh, *The Gulf Conflict*, p. 183.

57. William Webster, Hofstra, 18 April 1997.

58. Powell, *My American Journey*, pp. 478–80; Woodward, *The Commanders*, pp. 297–301. Baker later claimed that it was unfair to say, as did others at the time, that he acted as a "brake" on the administration as it moved toward the conflict: "What I wanted to do was to make sure we knew the consequences of force. . . . I never argued internally not to use force" (James A. Baker III, interview with author, 17 April 1997).

59. Atkinson, *Crusade*, pp. 58–61.

60. Ibid., pp. 483–85.

61. Atkinson, *Crusade*, p. 113; Powell, *My American Journey*, pp. 487–89.

62. It is possible that the honor of being the first American to compare Saddam to Hitler actually went to Sen. Claiborne Pell (D-RI), who, on the day of the invasion, called the Iraqi leader the "Hitler of the Middle East" (*NYT*, 2 August 1990, p. A1).

63. David Frost interview with George Bush, Public Broadcasting System (PBS) (first broadcast on 2 January 1991).

64. Baker, *Politics of Diplomacy*, p. 336.

65. Ibid.

66. Ibid.

67. *NYT*, 21 October 1990, p. 14.

68. "Out Now," advertisement in *Nation* (26 November 1990), p. 645.

69. Pat Buchanan, "How the Gulf Crisis Is Rupturing the Right," reprinted in Sifry and Cerf, *The Gulf War Reader*, pp. 213–15.

70. The papers from the Cato conference were published in *America Entangled: The Persian Gulf War and Its Consequences*, ed. Ted Galen Carpenter (San Francisco: Cato Institute Books, 1991).

71. Freedman and Karsh, *The Gulf Conflict*, p. 211.

72. Ibid., p. 218.

73. Ibid., p. 155.

74. *NYT*, 22 September 1990, p. 2.

75. James Baker, interview with author, 17 April 1997.

76. Letter on exhibit, GBL, and Bush and Scowcroft, *A World Transformed*, pp. 441–42.

77. *NYT*, 10 January 1991, p. A1; Baker, *Politics of Diplomacy*, p. 362; Bush and Scowcroft, *A World Transformed*, pp. 441–43.

78. Gen. Brent Scowcroft, interview with author, 11 June 1997.

79. George Bush, interview with author, 9 November 1998.

80. C. Boyden Gray, interview with author, 18 April 1997; interview with author, not for attribution.

81. *NYT*, 11 January 1991, p. A8.

82. George Bush, interview with author, 9 November 1998. See also Bush and Scowcroft, *A World Transformed*, p. 446.

83. Copy of NSD 54, on exhibit, GBL.

CHAPTER 9
DESERT STORM

1. Letter on exhibit, GBL.

2. Lawrence Freedman and Efraim Karsh, *The Gulf Conflict, 1990–1991: Diplomacy and War in the New World Order* (Princeton: Princeton University Press, 1993), p. 300; *WP*, 18 January 1991, p. A24.

3. *WPNWE*, 25–31 March 1991, p. 9.

4. Freedman and Karsh, *The Gulf Conflict*, p. 409.

5. Rick Atkinson, *Crusade: The Untold Story of the Persian Gulf War* (Boston: Houghton Mifflin, 1993), p. 264.

6. *WPNWE*, 25–31 March 1991, p. 8.

7. Fitzwater, Demarest, and Rogich to Sununu, 14 January 1991, Bush PR, Fitzwater Files, Subject File: Alpha File, box 17, Iraq folder 1991 no. 1.

8. Abe Dane, "Origins of the Scud Threat," *Popular Mechanics* (April 1991), p. 27; Colin Powell, *My American Journey* (New York: Random House, 1995), p. 511.

9. Atkinson, *Crusade*, p. 175.

10. Freedman and Karsh, *The Gulf Conflict*, pp. 307, 336.

11. Atkinson, *Crusade*, p. 130.

12. Ibid., p. 226.

13. Ibid., p. 160.

14. Ibid., p. 232.

15. Freedman and Karsh, *The Gulf Conflict*, p. 319. In a 1997 interview, William Webster argued that "it was my understanding that it had been identified back in [William] Casey's [Reagan's first director of the CIA] time . . . that it might've been used for chemical weapons storage," and that Arnett had been "sold a bill of goods" (William Webster, interview with author, 8 July 1997).

16. *NYT*, 15 May 1991, p. A6, and 6 June 1991, p. A9.

17. Atkinson, *Crusade*, p. 315; *WPNWE*, 18–24 November 1991, p. 32.

18. Atkinson, *Crusade*, pp. 272–88; George Bush and Brent Scowcroft, *A World Transformed* (New York: Alfred A. Knopf, 1998), pp. 469–70; Freedman and Karsh, *The Gulf Conflict*, pp. 327–29.

19. Human Rights Watch, *Needless Deaths in the Gulf War: Civilian Casualties During the Air Campaign and Violations of the Laws of War* (New York: Human Rights Watch, 1991), p. 4.

20. Atkinson, *Crusade*, p. 227.

21. Malcolm Browne, "The Military vs. the Press," *New York Times Magazine* (3 March 1991), pp. 27–30. See also Stanley Cloud, "Volleys on the Information Front," *Time* (2 February 1991), pp. 44–45; John Elson, "And on This Map We See . . .", *Time* (27 August 1990), p. 37; Andrew Sullivan, "The Big Schmooze," *Esquire* (October 1990), pp. 105–6; and *WP*, 9 August 1990, p. D1.

22. *NYT*, 21 January 1991, p. A1.

23. "Frontline: The Gulf War," PBS (Episode no. 2, first broadcast 10 January 1996).

24. Ibid.

25. Ibid.

26. Atkinson, *Crusade,* p. 474.

27. Powell, *My American Journey,* p. 524.

28. Bush and Scowcroft, *A World Transformed,* p. 486.

29. Powell, *My American Journey,* p. 525.

30. Powell, Memorandum for Correspondents, Bush PR, Fitzwater Files, Subject File: box 7, Desert Storm folder; Herbert S. Parmet, *George Bush: The Life of a Lone Star Yankee* (New York: Scribner, 1997), p. 484; Powell, *My American Journey,* p. 524.

31. Atkinson, *Crusade,* p. 9; Michael Gunter, "After the War: President Bush and the Kurdish Uprising," Hofstra, 18 April 1997; Scowcroft interview, "Frontline: The Gulf War," Episode no. 2.

32. Fred Barnes, "Hour of Power," *New Republic* (3 September 1990), p. 13.

33. *WPNWE,* 18–24 March 1991, p. 38.

34. Gen. Brent Scowcroft, interview with author, 11 June 1997.

35. Glen to Fitzwater, inserts dated 2 August 1990, Bush PR, Fitzwater Files, Subject File: Alpha File, box 17, Iraq folder 1990.

36. Gen. Brent Scowcroft, interview with author, 11 June 1997.

37. Michael Beschloss and Strobe Talbott, *At the Highest Levels: The Inside Story of the End of the Cold War* (Boston: Little Brown, 1993), p. 338.

38. "Frontline: The Gulf War," Episode no. 2.

39. Atkinson, *Crusade,* p. 488.

40. *WPNWE,* 22–28 April 1991, p. 6.

41. Powell, *My American Journey,* p. 531.

42. *Cleveland Plain Dealer,* 2 April 1991; *Los Angeles Times,* 2 April 1991; *San Francisco Examiner,* 15 March 1991; and *NYT,* 20 March 1991.

43. "Frontline: The Gulf War," Episode no. 2.

44. Parmet, *Lone Star Yankee,* p. 499.

45. James A. Baker III, *The Politics of Diplomacy: Revolution, War, and Peace* (New York: G. P. Putnam's Sons, 1995), p. 512.

46. James A. Baker III, interview with author, 17 April 1997; Bush and Scowcroft, *A World Transformed,* pp. 547–50.

CHAPTER 10
PRESIDENT BUSH

1. James A. Baker III, Hofstra, 17 April 1997.

2. Herbert S. Parmet, *George Bush: The Life of a Lone Star Yankee* (New York: Scribner, 1997), p. 366.

3. "George Bush: A Sense of Duty," for Arts and Entertainment Network's *Biography* series (first broadcast November 1996).

4. *NYT,* 4 July 1989, p. 34.

5. Interview with author, not for attribution.

6. David Mervin, *George Bush and the Guardianship Presidency* (New York: St. Martin's Press, 1996), p. 19.

7. Parmet, *Lone Star Yankee,* p. 486.

8. Hugh Sidey, interview with author, 17 April 1997.

9. Michael Duffy and Dan Goodgame, *Marching in Place: The Status Quo Presidency of George Bush* (New York: Simon and Schuster, 1991), p. 204.

10. *NYT*, 20 January 1989, p. 1.

11. Duffy and Goodgame, *Marching in Place*, p. 46.

12. Daniel Heimbach, interview with author, 19 April 1997.

13. George Bush, interview with author, 9 November 1998.

14. Ed Rollins, *Bare Knuckles and Back Rooms: My Life in American Politics* (New York: Broadway Books, 1996), p. 170.

15. George Bush and Brent Scowcroft, *A World Transformed* (New York: Alfred A. Knopf, 1998), p. 65.

16. Duffy and Goodgame, *Marching in Place*, p. 41.

17. James A. Baker III, *The Politics of Diplomacy: Revolution, War, and Peace* (New York: G. P. Putnam's Sons, 1995), p. 21.

18. *NYT*, 28 August 1989, p. A12.

19. Andrew A. Card, interview with author, 18 April 1997.

20. Michael Beschloss and Strobe Talbott, *At the Highest Levels: The Inside Story of the End of the Cold War* (Boston: Little, Brown, 1993), p. 18.

21. *WPNWE*, 5–11 February 1990, p. 16.

22. Bush and Scowcroft, *A World Restored*, p. 358.

23. Steven V. Roberts, "'Serving Your Country Is a Noble Cause,'" *USN&WR* (8 May 1989), p. 9.

24. *NYT*, 24 December 1989, p. 9.

25. Maureen Dowd, "In Bush's White House, the Press Secretary Is the One in the White Hat," *NYT*, 18 January 1990, p. A20; Marlin Fitzwater, *Call the Briefing! Bush and Reagan, Sam and Helen: A Decade with Presidents and the Press* (New York: Times Books, 1995), pp. 172–73; Bill McAllister and Lou Cannon, "Fitzwater: Another Face," *WPNWE*, 5–11 December 1988, p. 15.

26. Hugh Sidey, interview with author, 17 April 1997.

27. Fitzwater, *Call the Briefing!* p. 176.

28. George Bush, interview with author, 9 November 1998. See also Maureen Dowd, "Journalists Debate the Risks as President Woos the Press," *NYT*, 2 April 1989, p. A1.

29. Mark Rozell, *The Press and the Bush Presidency* (Westport, CT: Praeger Publishers, 1996), p. 149.

30. *NYT*, 31 December 1989, p. 1.

31. "President Is a Winner on Media Coverage," *Insight* (3 April 1989), p. 6.

32. *NYT*, 16 February 1990, p. A12.

33. Pool Report, 4 September 1990, Bush PR, WHPO, Press Office Pool Reports, box 14, dated folder.

34. *NYT*, 24 February 1989, p. A11.

35. Margaret Carlson, "The Silver Fox," *Time* (23 January 1989), pp. 22–26.

36. Barbara Bush, *Millie's Book: As Dictated to Barbara Bush* (New York: William Morrow, 1990). Her first book, *C. Fred's Story* (Garden City, NY: Doubleday, 1984), was a collection of anecdotes about Bush's late cocker spaniel. Proceeds of approximately $100,000 were donated to the Laubach Literacy Action and Literacy Volunteers of America.

37. *NYT*, 15 January 1989, p. 1.

38. Peggy Noonan, *What I Saw at the Revolution: A Political Life in the Reagan Era* (New York: Ivy Books, 1990), p. 314.

39. Interview with author, not for attribution.

40. Speechnotes on exhibit, GBL.

41. Mervin, *Guardianship Presidency*, p. 108.

42. "Reference Guide, Points of Light Movement," on display at Hofstra.

43. Mervin, *Guardianship Presidency*, p. 107.

44. Gregg Petersmeyer, Hofstra, 17 April 1997.

45. Noonan, *What I Saw at the Revolution*, p. 311.

CHAPTER 11
"THE SITUATION IS ABOUT AS BAD AS IT CAN BE"

1. Herbert S. Parmet, *George Bush: The Life of a Lone Star Yankee* (New York: Scribner, 1997), p. 470.

2. "Trend to Approval of President Bush's Overall Job Performance," Bush PR, Fitzwater Files, Subject Files, Alpha File, box 22, Political folder no. 1; Parmet, *Lone Star Yankee*, p. 497; *NYT*, 26 November 1991, p. A18.

3. Rich Bond, Hofstra, 19 April 1997.

4. David Bates, telephone interview with author, 24 August 1998.

5. Clayton Yeutter, interview with author, 8 July 1997.

6. For the story of Atwater's last days, see John Brady, *Bad Boy: The Life and Politics of Lee Atwater* (Reading, MA: Addison Wesley, 1997), pp. 267–69; chap. 11, passim.

7. Rich Bond, Hofstra, 19 April 1997.

8. *NYT*, 5 May 1991, p. 1. See also Marlin Fitzwater, *Call the Briefing! Bush and Reagan, Sam and Helen: A Decade with Presidents and the Press* (New York: Times Books, 1995), pp. 274–93.

9. *NYT*, 5 May 1991, p. 34.

10. *WP*, 21 April 1991, p. 1; Michael Duffy and Dan Goodgame, *Marching in Place: The Status Quo Presidency of George Bush* (New York: Simon and Schuster, 1991), pp. 124–30; Parmet, *Lone Star Yankee*, p. 492.

11. Fitzwater, *Call the Briefing!* p. 178.

12. Ibid., p. 177.

13. Ibid., p. 181.

14. Duffy and Goodgame, *Marching in Place*, pp. 126–27.

15. *WPNWE*, 9–15 December 1991, p. 12; Duffy and Goodgame, *Marching in Place*, p. 128.

16. Andrew A. Card, interview with author, 18 April 1997; Fitzwater, *Call the Briefing!* p. 188.

17. *WPNWE*, 15–21 June 1992.

18. Andrew A. Card, interview with author, 18 April 1997; several interviews with author, not for attribution; Fitzwater, *Call the Briefing!* p. 192.

19. Kenneth E. Thompson, ed., *Portraits of American Presidents*, vol. 10, *The Bush Presidency* (Lanham, MD: University Press of America, 1997), p. 23.

20. Andrew A. Card, interview with author, 18 April 1997.

21. Several interviews with author, not for attribution.

22. Shirley Anne Warshaw, *Powersharing: White House–Cabinet Relations in the Modern Presidency* (Albany: State University of New York Press, 1996), pp. 193–95.

23. Clayton Yeutter, interview with author, 8 July 1997.

24. Jane Mayer and Jill Abramson, *Strange Justice: The Selling of Clarence Thomas* (Boston: Houghton Mifflin, 1994), p. 13.

25. *NYT*, 2 July 1991, p. A1.

26. Copy of the phone logs in *The Complete Transcripts of the Clarence Thomas–Anita Hill Hearings, October 11, 12, 13, 1991*, ed. Anita Miller (Chicago: Academy Chicago Publishers, 1994), pp. 130–34.

27. Anita Hill, *Speaking Truth to Power* (New York: Doubleday, 1997), p. 138.

28. Miller, ed., *Thomas-Hill Hearings*, pp. 13–144.

29. Pool Report, dated (in error) 11 September 1991 (corrected to 11 October 1991), Bush PR, WHPO, Lower Press Office Pool Reports, box 14, dated folder.

30. *NYT*, 14 October 1991, p. A1.

31. Mayer and Abramson, *Strange Justice*, pp. 347–48.

32. John Berlau, "The Quota Paradox," *Policy Review* (spring 1994): 7.

33. *NYT*, 12 January 1991, p. 2, and 14 January 1991, p. 2; Douglas Stanglin, "Making His Move," *USN&WR* (21 January 1991), pp. 30–31; Michael Beschloss and Strobe Talbott, *At the Highest Levels: The Inside Story of the End of the Cold War* (Boston: Little, Brown, 1993), pp. 287–305.

34. Beschloss and Talbott, *At the Highest Levels*, p. 305.

35. Ibid., p. 47.

36. George Bush and Brent Scowcroft, *A World Transformed* (New York: Alfred A. Knopf, 1998), p. 500.

37. Ibid., pp. 510–17; Beschloss and Talbott, *At the Highest Levels*, p. 418.

38. *Wall Street Journal*, 29 August 1991, p. A1.

39. *NYT*, 21 August 1991, p. A1.

40. Ibid., 30 August 1991, p. A1.

41. Beschloss and Talbott, *At the Highest Levels*, p. 447.

42. Briefing Memo, 20 March 1991, Bush PR, WHPO, General Office Files, Press Office Subject Files, box 35, Justice folder.

43. *WPNWE*, 13–19 July 1992, p. 5.

44. *NYT*, 18 December 1991, p. A1.

45. Duffy and Goodgame, *Marching in Place*, p. 245.

46. *NYT*, 18 November 1991, p. A10.

47. James A. Barnes, "Where Are Those Gray Flannel Suits?" *NJ* (23 September 1995), p. 2370.

48. Douglas A. Brook, interview with author, 17 April 1997.

49. *NYT*, 12 April 1991, p. 2.

50. Interestingly, in a 1997 interview, Cheney echoed these thoughts, remembering that it was "very fortunate that we had the Reagan buildup" (Richard B. Cheney, telephone interview with author, 7 March 1997).

51. Sean O'Keefe, interview with author, 7 January 1999; David S. Sorenson, *Shutting Down the Cold War: The Politics of Military Base Closure* (New York: St. Martin's Press, 1998), pp. 31, 47, 95–97.

52. Many interviews with author. See also Clayton Yeutter in Thompson, ed., *Bush Presidency*, p. 48.

53. Fred Steeper to Bob Teeter, 16 March 1992, Bush PR, Fitzwater Files, Subject, box 21, Political File, folder no. 1.

CHAPTER 12
"THE PRESIDENT SHOULD HAVE FIRED US ALL"

1. Michael Beschloss and Strobe Talbott, *At the Highest Levels: The Inside Story of the End of the Cold War* (Boston: Little, Brown, 1993), p. 434.

2. Herbert S. Parmet, *George Bush: The Life of a Lone Star Yankee* (New York: Scribner, 1997), p. 504.

3. *NYT*, 7 February 1989, and 17 November 1989.

4. William Greider, *Who Will Tell the People? The Betrayal of American Democracy* (New York: Simon and Schuster, 1992), p. 15.

5. *NYT*, 2 June 1992, p. A10.

6. Doug Halbrecht, "Is Perot After the Presidency, or the President?" *Business Week* (6 April 1992), p. 41; *WPNWE*, 27 April–3 May 1992, p. 14; Gerald Posner, *Citizen Perot: His Life and Times* (New York: Random House, 1996), pp. 198–201.

7. *NYT*, 21 May 1992, p. A22.

8. Hugh Sidey, interview with author, 17 April 1997.

9. Parmet, *Lone Star Yankee*, p. 493.

10. James Carville and Mary Matalin, *All's Fair: Love, War and Running for President* (New York: Random House, 1994), p. 148.

11. Parmet, *Lone Star Yankee*, p. 493.

12. James Barnes, "Along the Campaign Trail," *NJ* (14 October 1992), p. 2540.

13. Michael Duffy, "How Bush Will Battle Buchanan," *Time* (2 March 1992), p. 21.

14. James J. Snyder, telephone interview with author, 14 October 1998.

15. David Demarest, interview with author, 18 April 1997.

16. Dan Quayle, *Standing Firm* (New York: Harper, 1994), chap. 32, passim.

17. Richard D. Land to Bush, 1 July 1992, Bush PR, Counsel's Office, Lee S. Lieberman Files, Subject Files, Gay Rights folder.

18. *NYT*, 10 March 1992, p. A1.

19. Quoted on NBC's "Super Tuesday" Television Coverage, 10 March 1992.

20. Hermann Von Bertrab, *Negotiating NAFTA: A Mexican Envoy's Account* (Westport, CT: Praeger Publishing, 1997), p. 8.

21. See James A. Baker III, *The Politics of Diplomacy: Revolution, War, and Peace* (New York: G. P. Putnam's Sons, 1995), pp. 606–9; David Mervin, *George Bush and the Guardianship Presidency* (New York: St. Martin's Press, 1996), p. 204; "InfoPacks': Mexico–U.S. Free Trade Agreement and Trade Issues: Background, Statistics, and Legislation." (IP 445M, Congressional Research Service, Library of Congress).

22. Rich Bond, Hofstra, 19 April 1997.

23. Molly Ivins, "A Feast of Hate and Fear," *Newsweek* (31 August 1992), p. 32.

24. Bill Whalen, "A Party's Time for Solving Riddles," *Insight* (27 March 1989), p. 8.

25. Paul Tsongas, *A Call to Economic Arms: Forging a New American Mandate* (Boston: Tsongas Committee, 1992), p. 5.

26. *NYT*, 13 April 1992, p. A17.

27. W. Lance Bennett, *The Governing Crisis: Media, Money and Marketing in American Elections* (New York: St. Martin's Press, 1996), p. 55.

28. Ed Rollins, *Bare Knuckles and Back Rooms: My Life in American Politics* (New York: Broadway Books, 1996), p. 217.

29. Andrew A. Card, interview with author, 18 April 1997; James Snyder, telephone interview with author, 8 October 1998.

30. David Bates, telephone interview with author, 24 August 1998.

31. Marlin Fitzwater, *Call the Briefing! Bush and Reagan, Sam and Helen: A Decade with Presidents and the Press* (New York: Times Books, 1995), p. 264.

32. Parmet, *Lone Star Yankee*, p. 502.

33. Fitzwater, *Call the Briefing!* p. 295.

34. George Bush, interview with author, 9 November 1998.

35. John H. Sununu, interview with author, 8 July 1997.

36. Fitzwater, *Call the Briefing!* p. 195.

37. *WP*, 4 April 1992.

38. Interview with author, not for attribution.

39. David Demarest, interview with author, 17 April 1997.

40. Stephen J. Wayne, *The Road to the White House, 1996: The Politics of Presidential Elections* (New York: St. Martin's Press, 1997), p. 219.

41. Notes for Press Secretary, n.d., Bush PR, Fitzwater Files, Subject File: Alpha File, box 1, Baker folder, Clayton Yeutter, interview with author, 8 July 1997.

42. Several interviews with author, not for attribution. See also Rollins, *Bare Knuckles and Back Rooms*, p. 87.

43. Interview with author, not for attribution.

44. *NYT*, 30 October 1992, p. A1.

45. Fitzwater, *Call the Briefing!* p. 322.

46. Chase Untermeyer, 18 June 1996, interview with author.

CHAPTER 13
PATIENCE AND PRUDENCE

1. Note on exhibit, GBL.

2. Speech at John F. Kennedy School of Government, Harvard University, 29 May 1998.

3. Richard Rose, *The Postmodern Presidency: George Bush Meets the World* (Chatham, NJ: Chatham House, 1991), pp. 48–49, 53, 307–8.

4. Byron E. Shafer, ed., *Present Discontents: American Politics in the Very Late Twentieth Century* (Chatham, NJ: Chatham House, 1997), pp. 153–57.

5. Michael Duffy and Dan Goodgame, *Marching in Place: The Status Quo Presidency of George Bush* (New York: Simon and Schuster, 1992), p. 12. Others who share this view of Bush are David Broder, "The Reactor President," *WPNWE,* 27 August–2 September, 1990, p. 4, and Charles Tiefer, *The Semi-Sovereign Presidency: The Bush Administration's Strategy for Governing Without Congress* (Boulder, CO: Westview Press, 1994).

6. *WPNWE,* 11–17 December 1989, p. 4.

7. Ibid., 14–20 November 1988, p. 6.

8. David Demarest, interview with author, 17 April 1997.

9. Maureen Dowd and Thomas Friedman, "The Bush and Baker Boys," *New York Times Magazine* (6 May 1990), p. 64.

10. George Bush, interview with author, 9 November 1998.

11. William Schneider, "The In-Box President," *Atlantic* (January 1990), p. 34.

12. Hugh Sidey, interview with author, 17 April 1997.

BIBLIOGRAPHICAL ESSAY

As historians begin to analyze presidential tenures after 1980, they will face a completely new set of archival rules. The archival record of those presidencies is governed by the Presidential Records Act of 1978 (PRA). Under that act, documents prepared by employees of the executive office in the performance of their daily duties are turned over to the National Archives for processing at a presidential library. However, in the processing of that material, the archivists are required under the PRA statutes to keep closed certain documents for a period of twelve years following the end of the administration. And even after that twelfth year, material no longer covered by the PRA may continue to be closed from public scrutiny under the terms of the Freedom of Information Act (FOIA), which closes material for the reasons listed under the PRA as well as for other reasons. The result is that much more material on the presidents since 1980 is closed to the researcher than was ever closed under any of the previous presidents, whose papers (with the exception of a large portion of Richard Nixon's) remain the personal property of that president. Particularly troublesome for the researcher is the closure of material in one area listed under the PRA: material that if released would disclose confidential advice between the president and his advisers, or among such advisers. The lack of access to such material severely limits any archival study of decision making in a presidential administration.

Thus it is with the material on deposit at the George Bush Presidential Library (GBL, College Station, Texas). The researcher is consistently frustrated at the amount of material that is closed under the statutes of the PRA or the FOIA; one cannot expect to make a serious dent in those restrictions until the year 2005, when the PRA restrictions are lifted. Yet at the time of this writing, the staff of the GBL has processed a surprisingly large amount of material. The Subject File of the White House Office of Records Management (WHORM), the filing successor to the old

White House Central File, is the system into which general correspondence is filed. Although the bulk of it is constituent correspondence, there are many letters from Bush included here. Thus, the WHORM file provides the best available archival evidence of Bush's decision making. This source should be followed by use of the files of the White House Press Office (WHPO). Of particular interest here is a small file of Internal Interview Transcripts— whenever Bush, Mrs. Bush, or a senior member of the administration was interviewed by a member of the press, the WHPO recorded that interview and provided all parties with a transcript. The frankness found in those transcripts, spanning the entire life of the administration, is quite useful. So are the Press Pool Reports, a small series of short reports on the president's daily activities written by a designated reporter (of the pool) to the entire White House Press Corps. The candor—and often raw humor—of these reports makes them not only insightful but quite quotable (my personal favorite of many was the one that began, "President Harrison . . . no, President Bush, walked into the press conference"). Also available in the WHPO files are 147 boxes of records from the files of Press Secretary Marlin Fitzwater. The researcher can also consult a file containing the President's Daily Diary and a detailed Speechwriting File, which often contains Bush's annotations on drafts submitted to him by his speechwriters.

There have also been several sets of material at the GBL processed under the terms of the FOIA. For this book, the most useful of these was the material pertaining to John Tower, AIDS/HIV policy, homosexuals, Somalia, and David Souter. It must be noted that even though all material is subject to document-level closures under the terms of the PRA and the FOIA, newly processed collections are appearing every day, particularly those released under the FOIA. For a complete update, consult the Bush Library website at http://www.csdl.tamu.edu/bushlib/.

There is also a wealth of Bush-related material in the papers of the presidents under whom he served. Sporadic entries are found in the files of the Lyndon B. Johnson Library (Austin, University of Texas), the Richard M. Nixon Presidential Materials Project (National Archives, College Park, MD), and the Gerald R. Ford Library (Ann Arbor, University of Michigan). Not surprisingly, the Ronald W. Reagan Library (Simi Valley, California) holds the most material, but the vast majority of it is presently closed under the terms of the PRA and the FOIA. The Reagan Library holds approximately 13,000 pages of Vice President Bush–related material. Though much of the Bush material in the Reagan WHORM was transferred to the Bush Library, there remains Bush-related material in twenty different WHORM Subject Files at the Reagan Library as well as a large amount of material in the files of other Reagan White House aides.

The vast majority of the papers of Bush's lieutenants is either in private possession or has been donated to an archives and is either restricted or not yet open to researchers. The exceptions at this writing are the Richard B. Cheney Files and Brent Scowcroft Files, Ford Library (consisting largely of material relating to Bush's tenure as DCI).

For the public record of the Bush presidency, consult George H. W. Bush, *Public Papers of the Presidents: George Bush, 1981–1989*, 8 vols. (Washington, DC: U.S.

Government Printing Office, 1990–1993), which includes all speeches, press releases, and public statements emanating from the White House or the 1992 presidential campaign. For background information, see also the *Public Papers of Richard M. Nixon* (6 vols., 1975), *Gerald R. Ford* (6 vols., 1975–1979), and *Ronald W. Reagan* (15 vols., 1982–1991). The Miller Center at the University of Virginia has made a key contribution to modern presidential historiography by publishing transcripts of presentations given by the alumni of the past ten presidencies. However, these volumes are marred by poor editing, proofreading, and lack of an index—Kenneth E. Thompson, ed., *Portraits of American Presidents*, vol. 10: *The Bush Presidency* (Lanham, MD: University Press of America, 1997), is no exception.

British journalist David Frost has done a series of interviews with Bush that is quite helpful. Frost's first set of interviews (including an interview with Mrs. Bush), first broadcast on the Public Broadcasting System (PBS) on 2 and 3 January 1991, was of particular interest because at the moment he interviewed Bush, Desert Storm was about to commence. The second, broadcast on the Arts and Entertainment Network in June 1998, shows a more contemplative Bush, thinking beyond the immediacy of his presidency and toward its legacy; of particular interest is a portion of the interview shot at the Berlin Wall.

It is impossible to research the modern presidency without using press reports—both in the popular newsmagazines of the period and in the more elite newspapers and political journals. Indeed, care must be give not to overrely on these sources, particularly when there is a dearth of available manuscript material. For a depth of political reporting available in no other source, scholars must begin their study of the modern presidency in the pages of the *National Journal (NJ)*. Despite the anti-Bush tone of its editorial page, the *New York Times (NYT)* continues to offer the best basis for a factual and chronological foundation for modern historical events. The *Washington Post (WP)* offers a greater depth of political reporting and analysis than does the *NYT;* it also offers an even deeper anti-Bush bias (for this book readers will find that I followed the reporting of the *WP* in its weekly version, the *Washington Post National Weekly Edition [WPNWE]*). Many popular newsmagazines were consulted in the course of my research; for depth of reporting, I found myself most often consulting the pages of *U.S. News and World Report (USN&WR)*.

Bush has written very little—indeed, with the exception of Harry Truman, he has published less than any other of the modern presidents. Nevertheless, both volumes of his memoirs succeed in conveying a voice unique to Bush as a writer. It is a literary voice that sets him apart from his post–World War II predecessors—he is chatty, anecdotal, informal, and only occasionally analytical. Bush's first memoir, *Looking Forward: An Autobiography* (New York: Bantam Books, 1987), written with his friend, journalist Vic Gold, is a classic campaign biography—little depth of analysis, coupled with a hasty storytelling by the authors. Bush's second memoir, written with Brent Scowcroft, is quite singular. *A World Transformed* (New York: Alfred A. Knopf, 1998) is a joint memoir by Bush and his director of national security, each of whom contributes to the volume in his own voice, with their contributions labeled by name. These recollections are fleshed out by lengthy inserts from Scowcroft's Memoranda of Conversations (Memcons), the vast majority of which are not yet available to scholars at the Bush Library. The result is a fascinating literary conversation between these two leaders about Bush's foreign policy (domestic policy is ignored). It is still overly long and prone to a moment-by-moment account; nevertheless, it is highly readable and offers a fresh approach to the genre of the presidential memoir. There has also been a strong photographic essay, David Valdez, *George Herbert Walker Bush: A Photographic Profile* (College Station: Texas A&M University Press, 1997). The author was Bush's official White House photographer, and the book's captions are written by Bush.

Bush has been the subject of two strong biographies and several lesser efforts. Herbert S. Parmet, *George Bush: The Life of a Lone Star Yankee* (New York: Scribner, 1997) is a strongly written and interesting read, one that makes good use of a wide number of interviews and of an exclusive access to many of Bush's restricted papers and diaries. Parmet is particularly strong in analyzing the interplay of Bush's northeastern and Texas roots, both on his personality and his politics. However, he chooses to spend most of his time on the prepresidential years, and the whole of 1992 is covered in less than twenty pages. Joe Hyams, *Flight of the Avenger: George Bush at War* (New York: Harcourt Brace Jovanovich, 1991), offers a generally positive view of Bush's World War II service, written with the assistance of the Bush White House. The style is graceful, and it remains the best treatment of its subject. Robert B. Stinnett, *George Bush: His World War II Years* (Washington: Brassey's, 1992), deals less with Bush than with World War II in general.

The most hagiographic Bush biography is Fitzhugh Green, *George Bush: An Intimate Portrait* (New York: Hippocrene Books, 1989). Completely uncritical of its subject and with little in the way of citation, the author irritates the reader by constantly dropping into the first person to tell the reader what *he* was doing at any point. Two biographies treat Bush as a common criminal. Webster Griffin Tarpley and Anton Chaitkin's *George Bush: The Unauthorized Biography* (Washington, DC: Executive Intelligence Review, 1992) is an anti-Bush screed written by two supporters of Lyndon LaRouche, who offer little substantive evidence for their message. Bill Weinberg, *George Bush: The Super-Spy Drug-Smuggling President* (New York: Shadow Press, 1992), labels Bush a "world-class drug trafficker. Sinister spymaster with tentacles spanning the planet—the most corrupt president in United States History" (1). It too has no real evidentiary support; both Tarpley and Chaitkin's and Weinberg's books can be safely ignored by the serious researcher. Instant historical analyses, shallow in their scope, include Mark Sufrin, *The Story of George Bush: The Forty-first President of the United States* (Milwaukee: Gareth Stevens Publishers, 1989), and Doug Wead, *Man of Integrity* (Eugene, OR: Harvest House Publishers, 1988).

Reference works with entries on Bush include Gaddis Smith, "George Bush," in *The Presidents: A Reference History*, ed. Henry F. Graff, 2d ed. (New York: Charles Scribner's Sons, 1996); Peter B. Levy, *Encyclopedia of the Reagan-Bush Years* (Westport, CT: Greenwood Press, 1996); and Gary Boyd Roberts, *Ancestors of American Presidents* (Boston: New England Historic Genealogical Society, 1989). "George Bush: A Sense of Duty," an hour-long production for the Arts and Entertainment

Network's *Biography* series (first broadcast November 1996), concentrates almost exclusively on Bush's prepresidential years. That background, based largely on interviews with Bush family members, is strong. However, the treatment of Bush's political career is perfunctory, and the fleeting treatment of his presidency is platitudinal.

The reporting of Walter Pincus and Bob Woodward is an excellent starting point for a study of Bush's prepresidential career. Their six-part investigative series, which ran in the *WP* on 10–16 August 1988, forms an excellent short biography of Bush in the years before he reached the White House. Richard Nixon, *Memoirs of Richard Nixon* (New York: Grosset and Dunlap, 1978), is surprisingly silent on Bush's role in the Nixon administration. A bit more useful is Walter Issacson, *Kissinger: A Biography* (New York: Simon and Schuster, 1992), which is good on the relationship between United Nations ambassador Bush and the Nixon White House—particularly on the issue of the expulsion of Taiwan. Both Gerald R. Ford, *A Time to Heal: The Autobiography of Gerald R. Ford* (New York: Harper and Row, 1979), and Robert T. Hartmann, *Palace Politics: An Inside Account of the Ford Years* (New York: McGraw-Hill, 1980), offer useful accounts on Ford's passing over of Bush for the vice presidency in both 1974 and 1976 as well as on Ford's choice of Bush as the American envoy to the People's Republic of China and as his director of Central Intelligence. See also Richard Ben Cramer, "How He Got Here," *Esquire* (June 1991), pp. 74–82+; John Robert Greene, *The Presidency of Gerald R. Ford* (Lawrence: University Press of Kansas, 1995); and Howard Kohn and Vicki Monks, "The Dirty Secrets of George Bush," *Rolling Stone* (3 November, 1988), pp. 41–44+.

Bush's vice presidency is examined by L. Edward Purcell, "George Herbert Walker Bush," in *The Vice Presidents: A Biographical Dictionary*, ed. L. Edward Purcell (New York: Facts on File, 1998), and in Chase Untermeyer, "Looking Forward: George Bush as Vice President," in *At the President's Side: The Vice Presidency in the Twentieth Century*, ed. Timothy Walch (Columbia: University of Missouri Press, 1997). It was also scrutinized in "Running Mate" (Public Broadcasting System, first aired October 1996). Despite the documented closeness of their relationship, in his *An American Life: The Autobiography* (New York: Simon and Schuster, 1990), Ronald Reagan all but ignores Bush. Not so Nancy Reagan. In *My Turn* (New York: Dell Publishing, 1989), she makes it clear that, at best, she tolerated her husband's vice president. However, a more balanced analysis on Bush's tenure as vice president can be found in the growing literature on the Reagan presidency. The most telling observations on Bush are in Lou Cannon, *President Reagan: The Role of a Lifetime* (New York: Simon and Schuster, 1991), which establishes the personal affinity between Reagan and his vice president. Herbert Abrams, *The President's Been Shot: Confusion, Disability and the 25th Amendment in the Aftermath of the Attempted Assassination of Ronald Reagan* (New York: W. W. Norton, 1992), concludes that Bush "took pains to keep his conduct loyal, dutiful and unassuming," but that during the crisis Edwin Meese, James Baker, and Michael Deaver "were the President of the United States" (187–88). On the most important moment of Bush's role in the 1984 election, see *The Bush-Ferraro Debate: October 11, 1984* (transcript from the Commission on Presidential Debates). Bush is mentioned in most of the works on the Iran-Contra scandal. But for reasons I have already mentioned, it has been difficult for observers to nail down the extent of his role in the scandal and the cover-up. Books that offer the most telling details are Jane Mayer and Doyle McManus, *Landslide: The Unmaking of the President, 1984–1988* (Boston: Houghton-Mifflin, 1988), and Theodore Draper, *A Very Thin Line: The Iran-Contra Affairs* (New York: Hill and Wang, 1991).

The best brief survey of the 1988 presidential election is found in the final three chapters of Bob Schieffer and Gary Paul Gates, *The Acting President* (New York: E. P. Dutton, 1989). Also useful for an overview of the election is Donald Morrison, ed., *The Winning of the White House, 1988* (New York: Time Incorporated Books, 1988). The best scholarly analysis of the election—indeed, one of the most thoughtful works on presidential politics written in recent years—is W. Lance Bennett, *The Governing Crisis: Media, Money, and Marketing in American Elections* (New York: St. Martin's Press, 1996). Using admirable detail and excellent anecdotal examples, Bennett argues that the 1988 election began a political age "in which electoral choices are of little consequence" (28). He suggests that successful presidential campaigns in the modern period are those that emphasize symbolism as opposed to issues—a fact that Bush's 1988 campaign understood and Michael Dukakis's did not. Much thinner in substance, but entertaining nonetheless, is Jack W. Germond and Jules Witcover, *Whose Broad Stripes and Bright Stars? The Trivial Pursuit of the Presidency, 1988* (New York: Warner Books, 1989). A great deal of press coverage resulted from the release of Richard Ben Cramer's *What It Takes: The Way to the White House* (New York: Random House, 1992). Most observers noted the informality of Cramer's "inside the campaign" writing style. However, that technique often becomes shrilly hyperbolic (particularly irritating is his use of capital letters and multiple exclamation points to get the reader's attention). Just as important to note is the fact that 125 of the 130 chapters of this massive work deal with the primaries as opposed to the general election.

The design of the Bush campaign is best explored in an excellent biography of its primary strategist, John Brady's *Bad Boy: The Life and Politics of Lee Atwater* (Reading, MA: Addison-Wesley Publishing Company, 1997). Peggy Noonan served as a speechwriter for both Reagan and Bush; her breezy *What I Saw at the Revolution: A Political Life in the Reagan Era* (New York: Ivy Books, 1990) is particularly interesting on the crafting of Bush's acceptance speech to the Republican convention ("a thousand points of light" and "read my lips"). For more information on the decision to include the "read my lips" sound bite, see Bob Woodward, "The Anatomy of a Decision," *WPNWE*, 12–18 October 1992, pp. 6–9.

The political background of Bush's vice president is well explored in Richard F. Fenno Jr., *The Making of a Senator: Dan Quayle* (Washington, DC: Congressional Quarterly Books, 1989). Best on the choice of Quayle as Bush's running mate—as well as offering one of the only detailed analyses of Quayle's contributions as vice president—is Bob Woodward and David S. Broder's *The Man Who Would Be President: Dan Quayle* (New York: Simon and Schuster, 1992). The penultimate conclusion of this brief book, taken from the author's reporting for the *WP*, shocked many Washington insiders: "It is clear that—all jokes aside—Dan Quayle has proved himself to be a skillful player of the political game, with a competitive drive that has been underestimated repeatedly by his rivals" (18). Quayle's autobiography,

Standing Firm (New York: Harper, 1994) is comparatively well written but serves primarily as a defense of its author from a myriad of political and press-related slights. See also "Running Mate" (above) for an interesting interview with Quayle and his wife, Marilyn; and Dan Quayle, "Standing Firm: Personal Reflections on Being Vice President," in Walch, ed., *At the President's Side* (above) for a not-altogether unbiased view of events.

An excellent series of interviews with the principals of the campaigns is Michael Gilette, *Snapshots of the 1988 Presidential Campaign: The Bush Campaign* (vol. 1), *The Dukakis Campaign* (vol. 2), and *The Jackson Campaign* (vol. 3) (Austin: Lyndon B. Johnson School of Public Affairs, University of Texas, 1992). There is no fully re-searched biography of Michael Dukakis. Richard Gaines and Michael Segal, *Dukakis: The Man Who Would Be President* (New York: Avon Books, 1987) is a syco-phantic campaign biography. See also William Boot, "Campaign '88: TV Over-doses on the Inside Dope," *Columbia Journalism Review* 2 (January/February, 1989): 23–29; Peter Davis and Martin Amis, "The Two Ring Circus and the White Man's Ball" (on the Republican and Democratic Conventions)," *Esquire* (November 1988): pp. 125–36; Gerald M. Pomper, ed. *The Election of 1988: Reports and Interpretations* (Chatham, NJ: Chatham House Publishers, 1989); "Quest for the Presidency: The Candidates Debate," *Reader's Digest* (October 1988), pp. 62–73; and Guido H. Stempel and John W. Windhauser, eds. *The Media in the 1984 and 1988 Presidential Campaigns* (Westport, CT: Greenwood Press, 1991).

An excellent analysis of the Reagan legacy to the Bush administration can be found in the 14 May 1988 *NJ*, which devoted its entire issue to "Reagan's Legacy: The Paradox of Power." See also Walter Dean Burnham, "The Reagan Heritage," in Pomper, ed. *The Election of 1988* (above). Michael Schaller, *Reckoning with Reagan: America and Its President in the 1980s* (New York: Oxford University Press, 1992), though based almost exclusively on secondary sources, nevertheless offers a par-ticularly balanced view of the Reagan legacy. James Pemberton, *Exit with Honor: The Life and Presidency of Ronald Reagan* (Armonk, NY: M. E. Sharpe, 1997), is a largely critical work that combines the first serious usage of the archival material at the Reagan Library with thoughtful, balanced prose.

All previous surveys of the Bush presidency flow from the ideas of English po-litical scientist Richard Rose. In his well-written, and significant, *The Postmodern Presidency: George Bush Meets the World* (Chatham, NJ: Chatham House, 1991), Rose advances the belief that Bush was a "guardian president [who] rejects the idea that leadership must be expansive" (308). Virtually every other survey of the Bush administration (most of which were written on the heels of the end of it; none of which uses manuscript sources) adopts Rose's hypothesis wholesale. In fact, sev-eral of them take his hypothesis beyond the available evidence. Michael Duffy and Dan Goodgame were two White House correspondents for *Time* magazine. Their rather long-winded *Marching in Place: The Status Quo Presidency of George Bush* (New York: Simon and Schuster, 1992) is highly critical of its subject and concludes that "Bush was popular, we finally realized, not despite his lip service approach to domestic policy but *because* of it" (12). David Mervin, *George Bush and the Guardianship Presidency* (New York: St. Martin's Press, 1996), the first true scholarly survey of the Bush presidency, uses several oral history interviews as he adopts Rose's hypothesis. The most balanced and value-free survey of the Bush years available is Leo E. Heagerty, ed., *Eyes on the President—George Bush: History in Essays and Cartoons* (Occidental, CA: Chronos Publishing, 1993). The basis of the book is a collection of the best political cartoons from the period, and the fifteen essays that accompany those cartoons—written by scholars and journalists—are both reflective and entertaining. Offering more limited assistance to the researcher are Ryan J. Barilleaux and Mary E. Stuckey, *Leadership and the Bush Presidency* (Westport, CT: Praeger, 1992); Colin Campbell and Bert Rockman, eds. *The Bush Presidency: First Appraisals* (Chatham, NJ: Chatham House, 1991); Dilys Hill and Phil Williams, eds., *The Bush Presidency: Triumphs and Adversities* (New York: St. Martin's Press, 1994); Kerry Mullins and Aaron Wildavsky, "The Procedural Presidency of George Bush," *Political Science Quarterly* (spring 1992): 31–62; and Charles Tiefer, *The Semi-Sovereign Presidency: The Bush Administration's Strategy for Governing Without Congress* (Boulder, CO: Westview Press, 1994). Of the several useful chapters on Bush in recent studies on the modern presidency, one should consult Paul Brace and Barbara Hinckley, *Follow the Leader: Opinion Polls and the Modern Presidents* (New York: Basic Books, 1992); Charles O. Jones, *Separate but Equal Branches: Congress and the Presidency* (Chatham, NJ: Chatham House, 1995); Robert Shogan, *The Riddle of Power: Presidential Leadership from Truman to Bush* (New York: Dutton Books, 1991); and Stephen Skowronek, *The Politics Presidents Make: Leadership from John Adams to George Bush* (Cambridge: Belknap Press of Harvard University Press, 1993).

Shirley Anne Warshaw is, at present, the preeminent authority on White House–cabinet relations. Her *Powersharing: White-House Cabinet Relations in the Modern Presidency* (Albany: State University of New York Press, 1996) surveys the effect of the cabinet upon policy from Nixon to Clinton. Regarding Bush, Warshaw argues that one of the reasons for what she believes to be his failed domestic policy was that the cabinet became "coopted and oriented toward departmental rather than presidential objectives," due to a lack of White House control (197). Warshaw's *The Domestic Presidency: Policy Making in the White House* (Boston: Allyn and Bacon, 1997), a study of the White House Office(s) of Domestic Policy since 1968, is a much more mature book than *Powersharing*. The Bush administration is still seen as having no coherent policy agenda, but the story is told more fully, particularly through a brief encapsulation of the White House role in the Clean Air Act Amendments. See also John Burke, *The Institutional Presidency* (Baltimore: Johns Hopkins University Press, 1992); Kenneth E. Collier, *Between the Branches: The White House Office of Legislative Affairs* (Pittsburgh: University of Pittsburgh Press, 1997); John Hart, *The Presidential Branch: The Executive Office of the President from Washington to Clinton* (Chatham, NJ: Chatham House, 1995); Judith E. Michaels, *The President's Call: Executive Leadership from FDR to George Bush* (Pittsburgh: University of Pittsburgh Press, 1997); and Judith E. Michaels, "A View from the Top: Reflections of the Bush Presidential Appointees," *Public Administration Review* 55 (May/June 1995): 273–83.

Although I take issue with the hypothesis stated in its subtitle, James P. Pfiffner's *The Bush Transition: A Friendly Takeover* (Richmond, VA: Institute of Public Policy,

George Mason University, 1995) is an important work. No detailed biography of John Tower yet exists, nor is there a balanced secondary study of his catastrophic appointment process. We are left only with Tower's *Consequences: A Personal and Political Memoir* (Boston: Little, Brown, and Company, 1991), an angry, and ultimately completely unconvincing book, which blames Sam Nunn for personally scuttling the nomination to advance his own presidential ambitions, hints at gossip about the private life of a reporter who covered his bid for cabinet confirmation, and attempts an explanation for all the charges against him (his explanation for the charges of drunkenness is particularly unconvincing). For the inevitable fallout from the Tower defeat, see John M. Barry, *The Ambition and the Power: The Fall of Jim Wright—A True Story of Washington* (New York: Viking Press, 1989).

Each of the memoirs written by Bush's domestic policy aides is defensive in tone and offers no balanced treatment of policy development. See, for example, Charles Kolb, *White House Daze: The Unmaking of Domestic Policy in the Bush Years* (New York: Free Press, 1993); James P. Pinkerton, *What Comes Next: The End of Big Government—and the New Paradigm Ahead* (New York: Hyperion, 1995); and John Podhoretz, *Hell of a Ride: Backstage at the White House Follies, 1989–1993* (New York: Simon and Schuster, 1993). But there are several interesting and often strong specific studies of domestic decision making under Bush. Two government publications, Rodman D. Griffen, *The Disabilities Act: Protecting the Rights of the Disabled Will Have Far-Reaching Effects* (No. 32, Washington, DC: Congressional Quarterly, in conjunction with EBSCO Publishing, 1991), and Major R. Owens, *Americans with Disabilities Act: Initial Accessibility Good but Important Barriers Remain* (Washington, DC: U.S. General Accounting Office, 1993), are indispensable to a study of the ADA. Kenneth O'Reilly, *Nixon's Piano: Presidents and Racial Politics from Washington to Clinton* (New York: Free Press, 1995), is quite critical of Bush's civil rights policies; in his chapter on Bush, "The Quota Kings," he concludes that Bush appealed to white nationalism in an effort to protect his electoral base. More balanced, although also critical of its subject, is John Berlau's "The Quota Paradox," *Policy Review* (spring 1994): 7, which analyzes Bush's high approval ratings among African Americans despite his opposition to racial quotas and his initial refusal to sign the Civil Rights bill of 1991. See also Stephen Schull, *A Kinder Gentler Racism? The Reagan-Bush Civil Rights Legacy* (New York: M. E. Sharpe, 1993).

The work of Robert J. Goldstein is critical to an understanding of the flag-burning controversy. See his *Burning the Flag: The Great 1989–1990 American Flag Desecration Controversy* (Kent, OH: Kent State University Press, 1996) and *Saving "Old Glory": The History of the American Flag Desecration Controversy* (Boulder, CO: Westview Press, 1995). Richard E. Cohen's well-written *Washington at Work: Back Rooms and Clean Air* (New York: Macmillan, 1992) takes the reader through the complexities of crafting and adopting the Clean Air Act Amendments of 1990, concluding that the lion's share of the credit for the bill goes not to Bush but to Senate Majority Leader George Mitchell. For studies of Bush's drug policies, see Charles M. Fuss Jr., *Sea of Grass: The Maritime Drug War, 1970–1990* (Annapolis, MD: Naval Institute Press, 1996); Al Giordano, "The War on Drugs: Who Drafted the Press?" *Washington Journalism Review* (January–February, 1990): 20–24; and Howard Kohn,

"Cowboy in the Capital: Drug Czar Bill Bennett," *Rolling Stone* (2 November 1989), pp. 41–43. On the abortion issue, see Ted Gest, "The Abortion Furor," *USN&WR* (17 July 1989), pp. 19–20; and Morton Kondracke, "The New Abortion Wars," *New Republic* (28 August 1989), pp. 18–19. Education policy is discussed in Susan Chira, "Lamar Alexander's Self-Help Course," *New York Times Magazine* (23 November 1991), pp. 52+; and Edith Rasell and Lawrence Mishel, "The Truth About Education Spending," *Roll Call* (21 May 1990), p. 23. Gregory Alan-Williams, *A Gathering of Heroes: Reflections of Rage and Responsibility—A Memoir of the Los Angeles Riots* (Chicago: Academy Chicago Publishers, 1994), is brutally direct, reading as a cathartic venture for the author.

Despite their political importance to the administration, very little of analytical substance has been written on Bush's economic policies. The student is left with two tremendously self-serving memoirs: L. William Seidman, *Full Faith and Credit: The Great S&L Debacle and Other Washington Sagas* (New York: Times Books, 1993), who blames his political demise on John Sununu; and Richard Darman, *Who's in Control? Polar Politics and the Sensible Center* (New York: Simon and Schuster, 1996), who blames the budget crisis of 1990 on Newt Gingrich. On the S&L crisis, see also Martin Mayer, *The Greatest Ever Bank Robbery: The Collapse of the Savings and Loan Industry* (New York: Scribner, 1990); Steven Pressman, "Behind the S&L Crisis," *Editorial Research Reports* (4 November 1988), p. 550; and Catherine Yang, "Bush's S&L Plan: Full of Good Intentions—and Holes," *Business Week* (February 1989), p. 32. Useful synopses of the major opinions of the Supreme Court during the Bush years (as well as a particularly useful chronology of events) are found in Arthur L. Galub and George J. Lankevich, *The United States Supreme Court*, vol. 10, *The Rehnquist Court: 1986–1994* (Danbury, CT: Grolier Educational Corporation, 1995).

Each of the major studies on the nomination of Clarence Thomas to the Supreme Court has been openly challenged as to both balance and accuracy. The book that makes the most obvious attempt at objectivity (despite the author's ultimate conclusion that Thomas was guilty of the charges levied against him) was written by *Wall Street Journal* reporters Jane Mayer and Jill Abramson, *Strange Justice: The Selling of Clarence Thomas* (Boston: Houghton Mifflin Company, 1994). Nevertheless, as a work of journo-history, one must be wary of their sources. More skewed in its analysis is Timothy M. Phelps and Helen Winternitz, *Capitol Games: The Inside Story of Clarence Thomas, Anita Hill, and a Supreme Court Nomination* (New York: Harper Perennial, 1992). One must obviously be cautious when using Anita Hill's *Speaking Truth to Power* (New York: Doubleday, 1997), although it is a necessary read on the subject and does serve to reconstruct the maze of depositions and testimony in a logical manner. Ultimately, then, there has been no satisfying statement of "who lied" in their testimonies; historians must at this point judge for themselves by reading Anita Miller, ed., *The Complete Transcripts of the Clarence Thomas/Anita Hill Hearings* (Chicago: Academy Chicago Publishers, 1994), which also includes samples of the submitted evidence.

Two excellent books analyze the sociocultural scene during the Bush years. William Greider's *Who Will Tell the People? The Betrayal of American Democracy* (New

York: Simon and Schuster, 1992), is superb and caustic in its criticism of the "politics as usual" mentality; his placing the blame squarely on the American people made it one of the most talked-about books of the election year. The second is Kevin Phillips, *The Politics of Rich and Poor: Wealth and the American Electorate in the Reagan Aftermath* (New York: Random House, 1990), who makes a clear case that the Reagan years despoiled the American economy.

As is the case with domestic policies, there is, as yet, no single monograph that surveys Bush's foreign and national security policies. George Bush and Brent Scowcroft, *A World Transformed* (above), James A. Baker III, *The Politics of Diplomacy: Revolution, War, and Peace* (New York: G. P. Putnam's Sons, 1995), and Colin Powell, *My American Journey* (New York: Random House, 1995), offer the memoirs of four of the five major players in the Bush administration's foreign and national security policies (Richard Cheney has yet to write his autobiography). For the unique closeness of the Bush-Baker relationship, see Maureen Dowd and Thomas L. Friedman, "The Fabulous Bush and Baker Boys," *New York Times Magazine* (6 May 1990), pp. 34–36+. Robert W. Tucker and David C. Hendrickson, *The Imperial Temptation: The New World Order and America's Purpose* (New York: Council on Foreign Relations Press, 1992), attempt to place Bush's foreign policies into a broader, international perspective.

The best book on the Soviet-American relationship during the Bush years is Michael Beschloss and Strobe Talbott, *At the Highest Levels: The Inside Story of the End of the Cold War* (Boston: Little, Brown, 1993), a fascinating read that establishes the success of Bush's cautious policies toward Mikhail Gorbachev. Also on the U.S.–Soviet relationship, see Archie Brown, *The Gorbachev Factor* (New York: Oxford University Press, 1997); Dusko Doder and Louise Branson, *Gorbachev: Heretic in the Kremlin* (New York: Viking, 1990); Raymond L. Garthoff, *The Great Transition: American-Soviet Relations and the End of the Cold War* (Washington, DC: The Brookings Institution, 1994); Mikhail Gorbachev, *Memoirs* (New York: Doubleday, 1996); and Jack F. Matlock, *Autopsy of an Empire: The American Ambassador's Account of the Collapse of the Soviet Union* (New York: Random House, 1995). Bob Woodward, *The Commanders* (New York: Simon and Schuster, 1991), studies military decision making in the Bush administration. It is also the best available study of the decision making associated with both Operation DESERT SHIELD and the Panamanian Operation (Operation JUST CAUSE). Additional works on the Panamanian episode are John Dinges, *Our Man in Panama: How General Noriega Used the U.S.—and Made Millions in Drugs and Arms* (New York: Random House, 1990); Eytan Gilboa, "The Panama Invasion Revisited: Lessons for the Use of Force in the Post–Cold War Era," *Political Science Quarterly* (1995–1996): 539–62; Seymour Hersh, "Our Man in Panama: The Creation of a Thug," *Life* (March 1990), pp. 81–85+; and Frederick Kempe, *Divorcing the Dictator: America's Bungled Affair with Noriega* (New York: Putnam, 1990). Elizabeth Pond, *Beyond the Wall: Germany's Road to Unification* (Washington, DC: Brookings Institution, 1993), is the standard work on the subject, as is David S. Sorenson, *Shutting Down the Cold War: The Politics of Military Base Closure* (New York: St. Martin's Press, 1998).

Not surprisingly, the richest part of the Bush literature deals with the Persian Gulf War. Three books serve in tandem as a superb survey of both the political and diplomatic decision making leading up to the war as well as the military aspects of the conflict. The student should begin with Lawrence Freedman and Efraim Karsh, *The Gulf Conflict, 1990–1991: Diplomacy and War in the New World Order* (Princeton: Princeton University Press, 1993). Theirs is a masterful study of the international origins of the war; as such, they offer a strong account of the genesis of what Bush called his "New World Order." Next consult Woodward, *The Commanders* (above) for a sage "insider's" treatment of the White House national security decision making process. Finally, for the military decision making during DESERT STORM (the buildup to war and DESERT SHIELD receive little attention here), see Rick Atkinson, *Crusade: The Untold Story of the Persian Gulf War* (Boston: Houghton Mifflin, 1993). His is an accessible survey that draws many interesting historical parallels in a first-rate analysis.

Bush and Scowcroft, *A World Transformed* (above), offer an interesting view of how Scowcroft won the battle for Bush's mind, helping to position the administration toward the offensive option that would become DESERT STORM. Powell, *An American Journey* (above), offers the other side of the policy debate, as he admits that he argued in favor of giving the economic sanctions more time to work (a revelation first released in Woodward, *The Commanders*). General Norman H. Schwartzkopf, *The Autobiography: It Doesn't Take a Hero* (New York: Bantam Books, 1992), is hagiographic and self-effacing.

Mark Grossman, ed., *Encyclopedia of the Persian Gulf War* (Santa Barbara, CA: ABC–Clio, 1995), is particularly useful, not only for its entries but also for its 144-page appendix of documents and its 162-page chronology. Micha L. Sifry and Christopher Cerf, *The Gulf War Reader: History, Documents, and Opinions* (New York: Times Books, 1991), is a particularly useful collection of primary sources. Other useful reference pieces on the war include Col. Arthur H. Blair, *At War in the Gulf: A Chronology* (College Station: Texas A&M University Press, 1992); and *The Gulf Crisis: A Chronology, July 1990–July 1991* (U.S. Information Service, U.S. Embassy, London, 1991).

"The Gulf War" (first broadcast on the PBS series *Frontline* on 9 and 10 January 1996) makes for fascinating viewing. With the notable exception of Bush, each of the major American decision makers and generals is interviewed for the program. It also features comments from Margaret Thatcher and Tariq Aziz as well as scholarly appraisals. The program's chronology is true to events, and it is quite gripping in its narration (complete transcripts of the interviews are also available on the internet at http://www.wgbh.org).

Theodore Draper's commentaries for the *New York Review of Books* ("The Gulf War Reconsidered," 16 January 1992, pp. 46–53, and "The True History of the Gulf War," 30 January 1992, pp. 38–45) are critical essays that offer an interesting overall view of the conflict. Alan Friedman, *Spider's Web: The Secret History of How the White House Illegally Armed Iraq* (New York: Bantam Books, 1994), explores the relationship between the United States and Iraq prior to the 1990–1991 crisis. For a strong look at the military strategies, see Michael R. Gordon and Gen. Bernard E. Trainor, *The General's War: The Inside Story of the Conflict in the Gulf* (Boston: Little, Brown,

1995). Malcolm Browne, "The Military vs. the Press," *New York Times Magazine* (3 March 1991), p. 27–30+, is the best view of its subject. See also W. Lance Bennett and David L. Paletz, eds., *Taken by Storm: The Media, Public Opinion, and U.S. Foreign Policy in the Gulf War* (Chicago: University of Chicago Press, 1994); Andrew Sullivan, "The Big Schmooze," *Esquire* (October 1990), pp. 105–6; and Stanley Cloud, "Volleys on the Information Front," *Time* (2 February 1991), pp. 44–45. For insights into the opposition to the war in the United States, see Pat Buchanan, "How the Gulf Crisis Is Rupturing the Right," reprinted in Sifry and Cerf, eds., *The Gulf War Reader* (above); and Ted Galen Carpenter, ed., *America Entangled: The Persian Gulf War and Its Consequences* (San Francisco: Cato Institute Books, 1991). On the question of Bush's authority to commit troops within the purview of the War Powers Act, Michael Glennon, "The Gulf War and the Constitution," *Foreign Affairs* (spring 1991): 84–101, offers a full analysis. The question of international law is explored in two articles by Christopher Greenwood, "Iraq's Invasion of Kuwait: Some Legal Issues," *World Today* (March 1991), pp. 39–43, and "New World Order or Old? The Invasion of Kuwait and the Rule of Law," *Modern Law Review* 55 (March 1992): 153–78. Human Rights Watch, *Needless Deaths in the Gulf War: Civilian Casualties During the Air Campaign and Violations of the Laws of War* (New York: Human Rights Watch, 1991), is the most thorough study on the war's fatalities.

A truly balanced study of the often acerbic relationship between Bush and the press has yet to be written. The student must consult sections in virtually all the secondary sources on the administration—the richest information is found in the literature on the press and the Persian Gulf war (above)—and the newsmagazines and newspapers of the period. Mark J. Rozell's, *The Press and the Bush Presidency* (Westport, CT: Praeger Publishers, 1996) suffers by completely ignoring the broadcast media; however, the author includes a rather interesting chapter based on seven interviews with Bush's press advisers. Marlin Fitzwater, *Call the Briefing! Bush and Reagan, Sam and Helen: A Decade with Presidents and the Press* (New York: Times Books, 1995), offers wonderful anecdotes and insight.

Bush as a public speaker has been the subject of several excellent graduate-level essays in rhetoric, but again, there is no scholarly monograph. See Heidi Erica Hamilton, "A Call to Arms: A Rhetorical Analysis of Two Speeches by President George Bush" (Master's thesis, University of North Carolina, 1993), and Michael J. Maguire, "The Ritual of Rebirth: Images of Savagery in George Bush's Persian Gulf Rhetoric" (Master's thesis, Mankato State University, 1992). For a comic look at Bush's penchant for the malapropism, see *New Republic, Bushisms: President George Herbert Walker Bush, In His Own Words* (New York: Workman Publishing, 1992). My personal favorite: a Bush quip at the 1991 Country Music Awards ceremony in Nashville, when he referred to the Nitty Gritty Dirt Band as the "Nitty Ditty Nitty Gritty Great Bird" (24).

Not surprisingly, Barbara Bush's *A Memoir* (New York: St. Martin's Press, 1994) is a defense of her husband's actions and policies. But the book is an important read, if for no other reason than that Bush has yet to write a complete memoir of his own life and because much of his personal life is glazed over in *Looking For-*

ward (above). Mrs. Bush's fleshing out of the scenes of their life together is singular in its contribution to the literature—particularly interesting are her treatment of the death of their daughter from leukemia, the diagnosis of their son with dyslexia, and the pain of the campaign of 1992. An engaging writing style also separates this book from others of the species; like her husband, the author has a keen eye for the telling anecdote. Mrs. Bush's other two books, "coauthored" with her dogs, *C. Fred's Story* (Garden City, NY: Doubleday, 1984) and *Millie's Book: As Dictated to Barbara Bush* (New York: William Morrow and Company, 1990), are delightful reading, occasionally offering an interesting insight into life in the White House. The royalties from these two books raised a sizable sum for literacy groups. Donnie Ratcliffe, *Simply Barbara Bush: A Portrait of America's Candid First Lady* (New York: Warner Books, 1989), is a hastily written work, done during the 1988 campaign. Pamela Kilian, *Barbara Bush: A Biography* (New York: St. Martin's Press, 1992), is the same, only written during the 1992 campaign (although Kilian does include five pages of Mrs. Bush's favorite recipes). For a less superficial study of Mrs. Bush's role in the 1988 campaign, see Ann Grimes, *Running Mates: The Making of a First Lady* (New York: William Morrow and Company, 1990).

The best analytical treatment of the presidential election of 1992 is Bennett, *The Governing Crisis* (above). His thesis of the "constant campaign," discussed in chapter 12 of this book, is an important premise that sheds new light on modern presidential campaigning. Stephen J. Wayne, *The Road to the White House, 1996: The Politics of Presidential Elections* (New York: St. Martin's Press, 1997), is a strong survey, interspersing thoughtful scholarly analysis with insider anecdotes that are often found nowhere else in the literature on the campaign. Jack Germond and Jules Witcover's *Mad as Hell: Revolt at the Ballot Box, 1992* (New York: Warner Books, 1993), offers more coverage on the general election campaign than did their *Whose Broad Stripes and Bright Stars?* (above). Also, their 1992 entry does a better analytical job; their dissection of voter anger is useful. Gil Troy, "Stumping in the Bookstores: A Literary History of the 1992 Presidential Campaign," *Presidential Studies Quarterly* (fall 1995): 697–710, is a useful bibliographical essay, although it tends to overemphasize books that critique the political system of the time instead of reviewing the available survey treatments of the campaign.

Full bibliographical analyses of Bill Clinton and Ross Perot are available in other volumes. The two established starting points for their first presidential campaigns are Stephen A. Smith, ed., *Bill Clinton on Stump, State, and Stage: The Rhetorical Road to the White House* (Fayetteville: University of Arkansas Press, 1994), and Gerald Posner, *Citizen Perot: His Life and Times* (New York: Random House, 1996). Memoirs of the campaign are few—perhaps because the Clinton people have yet to write theirs, there were too few Perot insiders, and the Bush people are still having trouble assigning blame for the debacle. What little exists in the way of reminiscences of the campaign can be safely dismissed; for examples of sycophantic self-promotion in book form, see Mary Matalin and James Carville, *All's Fair: Love, War, and Running for President* (New York: Random House, 1994), and Ed Rollins, *Bare Knuckles and Back Rooms: My Life in American Politics* (New York: Broadway Books, 1996).

The presidential primary process is critically analyzed in Robert D. Loevy, *The Flawed Path to the Presidency, 1992: Unfairness and Inequality in the Presidential Selection Process* (Albany: State University of New York Press, 1995). The impact of the new media on the campaign is best seen in Larry King, *On the Line: The New Road to the White House* (New York: Harcourt-Brace Company, 1993). See also *1-800-President: The Report of the Twentieth Century Fund Task Force on Television and the Campaign of 1992* (New York: Twentieth Century Fund Press, 1993), and Tom Rosensteil, *Strange Bedfellows: How Television and the Presidential Candidates Changed American Politics, 1992* (New York: Hyperion Press, 1992). On campaign rhetoric, see Robert E. Denton, ed., *The 1992 Presidential Campaign: A Communication Perspective* (Westport, CT: Praeger, 1994), and Smith, *Bill Clinton on Stump* (above). Of the many available postmortems, the most thought-provoking are Seymour Martin Lipset, "The Significance of the 1992 Election," *Political Science and Politics* (March 1993): 7–16, and Grover G. Norquist, "The Unmaking of the President: Why Bush Lost," *Policy Review* (winter 1993): 10–17.

On Bush's activities since his presidential tenure, see Robert N. Butler, "George Bush Did It Right with Parachute Jump," *Geriatrics* (May 1997), p. 14; Stephen Glass, "Peddling Poppy," *New Republic* (9 June 1997), pp. 20–24; Victor Gold, "George Bush Speaks Out," *Washingtonian* (February 1994), pp. 38–41; Amy Kover, "George Bush, Corporate Shill," *Fortune* (17 March 1997), p. 46; and Hugh Sidey, "Bush's Final Salute," *Time* (7 April 1997), p. 56.

On the recent development and the available resources of the George Bush Presidential Library, see Leslie Busler, "Sorting Through the President's Mail: Person to Person with David Alsobrook" (library director), *Insite* (November 1997), pp. 28–31; Candace Leslie, "What About Us? The Community's Relationship with the George Bush Presidential Library and Museum," *Insite* (November 1997), pp. 20–23+; and Richard Stewart, "A Stroll Through the Century," *Texas Magazine (Houston Chronicle)* (2 November 1977), pp. 8–12.

INDEX